Score	For	Against	Venue	Date
100*	WORCESTERSHIRE	NOTTINGHAMSHIRE	WORCESTER	
214*	WORCESTERSHIRE	OXFORD UNIVERSITY	WORCESTER	
154*	WORCESTERSHIRE	GLAMORGAN		
177*	OTAGO	WELLINGTON		
104	OTAGO	AUCKLAND		
115	OTAGO	NORTHERN DIST.		
121*	OTAGO	INDIA		
117	NEW ZEALAND	INDIA		
169	WORCESTERSHIRE	NOTTINGHAMSHIRE		
135*	WORCESTERSHIRE	SOMERSET		1976
150	WORCESTERSHIRE	SUSSEX	OVE	1976
120	WORCESTERSHIRE	NORTHAMPTONSHIRE	NORTHAMPTON	1976
113	NEW ZEALAND	INDIA	KANPUR, INDIA	1976
177*	NORTHERN DIST.	CENTRAL DIST.	NAPIER, N.Z.	1976-7
153	WORCESTERSHIRE	HAMPSHIRE	WORCESTER	1977
141*	WORCESTERSHIRE	GLAMORGAN	SWANSEA	1977
131	WORCESTERSHIRE	SOMERSET	WORCESTER	1977
127	WORCESTERSHIRE	NORTHAMPTONSHIRE	NORTHAMPTON	1978
155*	WORCESTERSHIRE	HAMPSHIRE	PORTSMOUTH	1978
150	WORCESTERSHIRE	SURREY	WORCESTER	1978
101	WORCESTERSHIRE	ESSEX	CHELMSFORD	1978
202*	WORCESTERSHIRE	WARWICKSHIRE	EDGBASTON	1978
115	WORCESTERSHIRE	GLOUCESTERSHIRE	WORCESTER	1978
148*	WORCESTERSHIRE	YORKSHIRE	WORCESTER	1979
109	WORCESTERSHIRE	LANCASHIRE	SOUTHPORT	1979
118	WORCESTERSHIRE	SUSSEX	WORCESTER	1979
131	WORCESTERSHIRE	SURREY	GUILDFORD	1979
120	WORCESTERSHIRE	LEICESTERSHIRE	LEICESTER	1979
150*	WORCESTERSHIRE	NOTTINGHAMSHIRE	WORCESTER	1979
108	WORCESTERSHIRE	WARWICKSHIRE	WORCESTER	1979
135	WORCESTERSHIRE	GLAMORGAN	WORCESTER	1979
136	OTAGO	AUCKLAND	ALEXANDRA N.Z.	1979-80
228*	WORCESTERSHIRE	GLOUCESTERSHIRE	WORCESTER	1980
100	WORCESTERSHIRE	MIDDLESEX	WORCESTER	1980
115	WORCESTERSHIRE	YORKSHIRE	BRADFORD	1980
101	WORCESTERSHIRE	WARWICKSHIRE	EDGBASTON	1980
182*	WORCESTERSHIRE	DERBYSHIRE	WORCESTER	1980
168	WORCESTERSHIRE	ESSEX	COLCHESTER	1980
103*	WORCESTERSHIRE	KENT	WORCESTER	1980
104*	WORCESTERSHIRE	SUSSEX	WORCESTER	1981
101	WORCESTERSHIRE	ESSEX	WORCESTER	1981
168	WORCESTERSHIRE	YORKSHIRE	WORCESTER	1981
161	WORCESTERSHIRE	NORTHAMPTONSHIRE	STOURBRIDGE	1981
101	WORCESTERSHIRE	NORTHAMPTONSHIRE	STOURBRIDGE	1981
111	WORCESTERSHIRE	GLOUCESTERSHIRE	WORCESTER	1981
130*	WORCESTERSHIRE	GLAMORGAN	SWANSEA	1981
147*	WORCESTERSHIRE	WARWICKSHIRE	WORCESTER	1981
139	WORCESTERSHIRE	WARWICKSHIRE	WORCESTER	1981
239*	WORCESTERSHIRE	OXFORD UNIVERSITY	THE PARKS	1982
311*	WORCESTERSHIRE	WARWICKSHIRE	WORCESTER	29 May 1982

GLENN TURNER'S
CENTURY OF CENTURIES

By Glenn Turner
My Way

GLENN TURNER'S CENTURY OF CENTURIES

Ray Cairns Glenn Turner

HODDER AND STOUGHTON
AUCKLAND LONDON SYDNEY TORONTO

Typeset by Rennies Illustrations Ltd, Auckland.
Printed and bound in Hong Kong for Hodder and Stoughton Ltd, 44-46 View Road, Glenfield, Auckand, New Zealand.

Acknowledgements

We could never have produced this record of *Glenn Turner's Century of Centuries* without the writings of many journalists, all round the world but particularly those in England and New Zealand. Assuredly, no-one has witnessed more, and written more of, Glenn Turner's centuries than Jack Godfrey, the recently retired cricket writer of the Worcester *Evening News*. In recent years, it has been his successor, Chris Oldnall, whose writings have produced so much valuable background. In New Zealand cricket, tests and tours, Dick Brittenden and Don Cameron have chronicled much of the Turner career. Similarly, in his native Dunedin, Dudley Manning, Brent Edwards and Alan McDonald proved of inestimable value. There are many, many others, most of them unidentified whose writings helped us in the compilation of this record. Foremost among these are the Yearbooks: the New Zealand Cricket Almanack, Wisden and the Worcestershire C.C.C. Yearbook. Some of their details did not agree, but we feel we made the appropriate amendments.

There are also the photographers, who have captured Glenn Turner — and the others in the portraits in this book — for perpetuity. Special mention must be made of Ken Kelly and Des Woods.

Then there are the men who also 'scored' Glenn Turner's centuries. One of the authors scored all 100; I 'scored' a few. We were helped by many others, led by the lovable old 'R-S', the late Arthur Ross-Slater; and other Worcestershire scorers, Jim Sewter and Arthur Potter; and the other county scorers in England; the provincial scorers in New Zealand; the test scorers; the touring scorers, one of whom, Ian Walter, has recorded here one famous innings, in run chart form. Without these people, none of the centuries would have been 'scored'. This book, and the figures it contains, is a tribute to all scorers.

Finally, we pay our greatest acknowledgements to our wives, Kerry (Cairns), and Sukhi (Turner). Without their patience, understanding and encouragement, and despite the querulous curiosity of our children, this book might not have been possible.

Standard cricket style of abbreviations have been used throughout the book, the customary dismissal symbols, and with an asterisk indicating a not out score. Initials are used in all scoreboards at first mention, and deleted subsequently.

Glenn Turner: Friend and Cricketer

I cannot claim a lifetime friendship with Glenn Turner, but half a lifetime, anyway. I was 18 years old, a cadet reporter with *The Press* in Christchurch; Glenn, 17, a sixth-former of Otago Boys' High School or, perhaps more to the point, the key player in his school's cricket and hockey first elevens. The occasion was the Annual Match — the capitals are deliberate, for I do not place much store in these occasions of fading snobbery — between OBHS and Christ's College at cricket. The day, 2 December 1964, was scorching hot and, in those days when Annual Matches were covered religiously and with discrimination by newspapers, it was a daunting assignment. Otago's No. 3 and captain, who had bowled his off-spinners for long enough to take six Christ's College wickets the previous day, batted virtually all this day, getting slower the longer and hotter the day wore on. He was hung over, as related much later, because his billeter was his elder brother, Brian, rather than a Christ's College pupil and they 'had had a few', as we say in New Zealand. His coach on the occasion was Frank Cameron, who was not unduly per-turbed at Turner's rate of scoring because a first innings win is better than no win at all in an Annual Match. He probably saw it as useful batting practice for his young captain, too, because Turner was scheduled to bat about five places higher than Cameron in his first Plunket Shield match, against Canterbury, a little over three weeks later.

Much contact after that was limited, save when, as the Canterbury scorer of the day, I would drop into the Otago dressing room whatever figures were wanted at the end of a session.

Our friendship firmed, during my two years in England; in 1969 when I toured with the New Zealand touring team, of which Turner was a young member, and then, in 1970 I became a fairly regular visitor to Worcestershire games, when other sporting and reporting assignments allowed.

The 1969 tour was a difficult time for Turner. He faced the conflicting pulls of county and country; his ambition was such that he had an almost desperate desire to play for his

The family man: Glenn and Sukhi with 11-week-old Natasha in 1977.

Glenn and Natasha leave Christchurch in April 1982 for a final season with Worcestershire.

country as often and as well as he could. But, capped only the year before by Worcestershire, I think there was a lurking worry that country before county would cost him a great deal in financial terms and even more in terms of security, future and competitive opportunity.

That resolved, Turner, not an insensitive person, then found an underlying hostility towards him within the team. Not from all sides, it should be hastily added; how could one consider that of the kindly Barry Milburn, probably the most loyal of cricketers and team-mates, and I feel sure that the rough-tough bulldog heart of Bob Cunis harboured an admiration of the Turner single-mindedness. Things boiled up, in a minor sort of way, at Westcliff-on-sea, when it was decided that the major cricket practice of the next morning would be an early-morning run. That did not fit Turner's pattern of preparation for first-class cricket; he was halfway through his 1969 year of work; and his programme did not include what he saw as a meaningless run. He said so. He was told he would take part, because everyone was. He repeated he would not. He was accused of a lack of team-spirit. The run went ahead. Turner did not.

The next year, 1970, solely in the professional atmosphere,

Turner blossomed and flowered. That was the year that Tom Graveney finished in first-class cricket and predicted Turner would be the batsman of the seventies; Turner saw out the last day of 1979 with another century and a tally for the decade matched by no-one round the world. I was privileged to watch many of the Turner innings of that season, some of the 10 centuries, a Worcestershire record. I became probably as great an habituee of New Road, and 'Mrs B's', where Glenn and Vanny Holder had their digs, and of the Shakespeare pub in Worcester, as anyone from outside the county borders. I returned to New Zealand, a few weeks ahead of Glenn, eager to tell anyone who was interested just what a 'different' batsman he was.

Sad to say, not many really wanted to know. Dick Brittenden did, but Dick always welcomed cheering news about New Zealand cricket because he, probably more than anyone, had seen so many dark days. He was genuinely pleased, even if he had irked and offended Glenn with an observation in India a year earlier that Glenn should consider himself fortunate that sport was taking him round the world. 'Don't they realise,' said Glenn in a letter, 'that I'm not lucky or fortunate?' meaning that he had created his own fortune, good or otherwise, with his own hard work. I think we felt an affinity in those days because I, in a far, far more modest way, had also taken off in pursuit of development of my job; and that job, like Glenn's, was about sport.

The 1970-71 southern summer was an intensely difficult time for Glenn. He has written about the mediocre jobs organised for him; he has barely mentioned the continuing hostility, this time at Otago level. He might, on the right occasion, tell with a chuckle that his opening partner of that year, Lance Pearson, always took strike, an opener's idiosyncrasy that has never bothered Glenn. Pearson considered himself better — which, gently, is and was nonsense — and being No. 1 in the scorebook reinforced that view.

There was another side to Glenn's nature that I saw in Dunedin, the patient, tolerant, young man, bailed up in a bar by a bore. The sharp eyes, not then wrinkled as they are with the crow's feet created by staring, thousands of times, down the pitch, pleaded silently for saviour. The saviour was one Keith Murdoch, now remembered only in connection with an Angel, a punch and a sacking, but a knight on that occasion. Yeah, he'd go in and rescue Glenn. And the strongest shoulders in world rugby elbowed into the conversation, and the bore seemed to shrug off the interruption with the view that an All Black would do just as well as an All White. Some time later, the big black eyes of the admirable Murdoch were pleading the same message for help. But who'd fall for that twice?

The story and stories of the Century of Centuries tell much of the developing and maturing of Glenn, always a mature person, anyway.

But there are some other stories. Take nicknames, and those of All Blacks are legend. Take cricketers and, 'Paddles' (Richard Hadlee) and perhaps 'Words' (Ken Wadsworth) apart, all are related to a name. In New Zealand, there were Tails and Haster or Hasto, and Polly, and Congo, and Milly, and Warders. 'Bogo' was John Reid and 'Snippet' was Noel McGregor, but they weren't on everyone's lips or regularly in print.

The public knows little of the Turner nicknames, though I know of three. There was the predictable 'Turns', which was in line with the diminutives of the 'Dowls' period. There was also 'Crunchy', which somehow or other I used pretty frequently in the early days. A batsman who whacked the ball was often said to 'crunch' it — it was the same principle as bestowing on a tall man the nickname of 'Tiny'.

Then, at Worcester, when I was calling him 'Crunchy', Basil D'Oliveira, Vanny Holder and Brian Brain — particularly those three, a fading memory tells me — were calling Glenn 'Budge' or 'Budgie'. Not because he wouldn't budge at the crease, but because those little birds of the same name were said 'to cheap'. The misspelling is deliberate, but the men of Worcester did not mean to imply that their emerging young Kiwi was mean or tight with his money. They saw him as 'careful' — careful in his cricket, careful with the management of his life, his cricket, and his money, as befitting a young fellow born and bred in Dunedin, the southern

The cricketer: Turner in the cathedral calm of the Worcestershire dressing room, 1982; and acknowledging applause on reaching his double-century against Warwickshire, May 1982.

The friend (and rival): Turner and Zaheer Abbas at Bristol, May 1982, when both had six times scored two centuries in a match. Turner was the first to 100 centuries, but the Pakistani was first to equal, and in November 1982 to surpass, Wally Hammond's record of seven times scoring a pair of tons. Zaheer, presently approaching 100 first-class centuries, is the only player to score double and single centuries in the same match four times.

hemisphere Edinburgh. The Worcester people admired him, too, utterly, unhesitatingly, and that could not always be said of his countrymen. Because whatever Glenn did, he did it 'My Way', and the record certainly shows he took the blows and did it his way.

He can be a most stubborn person, yet often so flexible too. A contradiction? Take fruit. When he could barely walk, he wouldn't eat fruit; he still won't, and even a well-loved gin and tonic would be rejected — has been rejected — because a slice of lemon had tainted, poisoned, it. Dare tell him that his favourite food, ice cream — often with custard, and that's another story, for another time — is flavoured with fruit and he will discourse at length, but vaguely about additives, and 'not real fruit' and similar self-justification.

All geniuses, or genii, are allowed their little foibles, and Glenn Turner became a genius of the art of cricket. To command such a place in cricket does not demand any special physical qualities, not even necessarily for a fast bowler. It is strength of personality and character which distinguishes the greatest players, and more than anything, a strength of concentration. Glenn Turner had, and has, these qualities in considerable measure; that is why he is a great player.

His elder brother, Brian, had very similar qualitities —and the younger, Greg, whom I have known since a lad of seven, shows every sign already of the same, in his sport, golf — but Brian did not have the tolerance, nor the preparedness to compromise, that Glenn showed. Glenn accepted indignities unbecoming to his profession; he compromised, and bowed the knee, because he felt for so long that he owed New Zealand cricket something, even if New Zealand never really gave him very much. He worked at time-and-a-half at his job, and with the overtime pay, in all those years he kept returning to New Zealand from tiring English county seasons. But when he turned down the overtime — the God-given right to any staunch New Zealand union man — the union man turned on him, and accused him of disloyalty. So did his fellow-player, and there were few of them fit to take the field with him.

Glenn Turner, as I write, has returned to New Zealand cricket for the 1982-83 season. Maybe the day of Glenn's full retirement is not too far distant, even if he is never likely to actually *announce* it. His style has always been to make a decision or a commitment for the coming season only. Already Worcestershire has lost him, and the 'Fostershire' county of old is mourning the loss of the finest batsman of all its history. He could play in England again, in the final Prudential Cup competition, but his homeland has little more to see of the finest batsman, the finest cricketing technician, it has produced.

I will regret that passing into memory of a rich talent, just as I have regretted his absences in recent seasons while appreciating and understanding his reasoning. It rankled then, and it rankles still, to hear the ill-informed comments that 'he was after the money', when Glenn, in fact, earned less by not playing, and has so often given his services for nothing. I remember the addressing of my East Christchurch-Shirley club's jubilee dinner, the patient chats to enraptured teenagers, the speeches to school assemblies, and money was never mentioned. That deserves to strike a painful chord with some.

That Glenn Turner will endure, even if there is a limited life for the Glenn Turner, Century-Maker. But many, many of those centuries, those 100 we have reviewed in this book and the others besides, must have given much pleasure at the time. Maybe even to the knockers?

Ray Cairns
Christchurch, 1982

A Philosophy of Batsmanship

Scoring hundreds didn't really come into my mind when I first started playing first-class cricket, though I had had them in school first eleven and trial matches. For me, then, it was just a matter of application at the crease, staying out there and doing as well as I could. I didn't think in terms of tons, just of establishing myself in the side, and that meant staying out in the middle. That meant a slow rate of scoring then, and what I couldn't understand in those early days was that other people used to get so upset and even angry at my rate. I felt the opposition was meant to be better than me, anyway — to a certain extent, I suppose one had a certain inferiority complex then, especially as in my first game, I came up against a fellow like Dick Motz, an established New Zealand bowler, and throughout the Plunket Shield series, I kept coming up against other New Zealander bowlers, and they were meant to be good enough to get me out. If they couldn't get me out, I thought I'd done all right.

The other thing is that in a way, I wasn't playing for myself, as the Otago team I played for in those early days wasn't a particularly good one. In three days, there was always going to be a result, so occupation of the crease, from a team point of view, was doing a good job, especially as we had enough 'strikers' to give it a whack at the other end. Perhaps if I hadn't been in that particular predicament, it would have come to me at an earlier stage that I needed to put bat to ball. But it never really arose.

I had three seasons of that type of cricket for Otago, and when I started for Worcestershire — and by that I mean after qualifying — I was batting at No. 6 or even 7 in the order, and it was much of the same thing, except that we had rather better batting. And centuries, obviously, weren't really going to be possible that low in the order. Then, as it happened, I had the opportunity to open and the runs started to come; I talk about that in Century No. 1, but I was still largely, at that stage and for the next year or two, a grafter.

It wasn't until 1970, the 10-centuries-for-Worcestershire-season, that I would describe myself or my innings as con-

Turner's colleagues at Worcestershire had a profound influence on his early batmanship development.

Tom Graveney leads Worcestershire for the final time, against Warwickshire at New Road, September 1970.

Don Kenyon (left) and Martin Horton in the pre-Turner days at Worcester. But Turner had important links with both, Kenyon as his first captain, Horton in his capacity as national director of cricket coaching in New Zealand.

Ron Headley and Turner scored 4049 runs between them for Worcestershire in 1970, but strangely, they seldom prospered together.

Rodney Cass, wicket-keeper in the early 1970s, and Vanburn Holder, the West Indian and a worthy servant of his county, were close companions of Turner in his young days with Worcestershire.

trolled strokeplay. I was opening with Ronnie Headley in those days, and he'd be out after an hour or so for 40-odd. I'd still be there at lunch with about the same — only scored in twice the time. That didn't make much sense to me, but then I obviously started to grow in confidence as the runs came, and I suppose that when one grows a little bit older, one's personality changes. Your demands on yourself, your expectations of yourself, increase; you start to be prepared to take more chances. I don't know when specifically this change took place, though Tom Graveney has his views on that: a limited-over game against Essex mentioned later. Certainly, limited overs forced my progress. I was forced into a corner: I had to play shots from the outset or I didn't play. Then I found I had a lot more ability than I had given myself credit for. Not that it was all sparkling strokeplay then, this controlled strokeplay, but my run-rate was quite good and I was not too dour. I scored the runs all round the wicket, generally speaking, but I didn't dong them over the top and the cut and hook didn't feature much at that stage. Basically, I wasn't prepared to throw caution to the winds, but I had enough shots to be able to work it around, and keep the score ticking over between the boundary shots. I think it is important to emphasise that I was then a *line* player and not a *length* player; and that if a guy bowled well at me, I'd let him bowl at me, and I'd *collect*. That is a term I use a lot, I'm told, and generally refers to the good balls. A lot of established players, even, will play just a dead-bat shot, getting it nowhere, getting nothing for it, waiting for the bad ball and hitting it to the boundary. But those marginal balls, those that perhaps demand defence — instead of 100 per cent defending them, all you do is just angle the bat a little, push at it a little more firmly so it goes somewhere and you can get a single. It keeps the run-rate ticking over. You don't go absolutely dead.

One reason I could collect, even back then, was that I was very conscious of the location of my off-stump. I trained very, very hard on that to the extent of letting go in the nets a lot of balls, even those which would shave or sometimes even hit, the off-stump. I reckoned that after a while, by standing

16

still, I could even nominate which stump it had hit, without even looking around. It got to the stage — and early in the season, I was letting go balls whenever I could, not playing the ball if I didn't have to — that I knew where my off-stump was to such an extent that guys wouldn't believe that I was letting go balls when I did! But my whole approach was survival. The first thing I thought of when the bowler was coming up was survival, not to get out. But as I've progressed, of course, my opinion has reversed completely: I look to score off each ball bowled to me, and if I can't, I defend it.

I won't take credit for planning my career, or my approach to batting. It just came natural to me to play like that. I was miserable; I didn't like failure; I didn't want to get out. Therefore, it just so happened that I developed a very sound defensive technique, and it was only with confidence and more exposure to the game, and the developing of my personality that I branched out from there. Maybe, on reflection, that is the way to develop one's career, to do it that way

The 1974 county champions. Back row (from left): *Arthur Ross-Slater (scorer), Gordon Wilcock, Ravi Senghera, Jim Yardley, Paul Pridgeon, John Inchmore, Rodney Cass, Keith Wilkinson.* Front row: *Glenn Turner, Alan Ormrod, Norman Gifford (captain), Basil D'Oliveira, Brian Brain.*

17

round. So many youngsters these days are doing it the other way round. They're under so much pressure to hit the ball from the outset that they have to do a complete circle: back to the drawing board to work out a decent defensive technique, bat for a while defensively, then back on attack. So very few come into the game and start off aggressively and develop enough success to stay that way. They have to tighten up one way and another. I simply started off that way.

Now, I know, I've loosened my game up, so I'm more vulnerable to getting out. But on the other hand, it's not too much of a risky thing, as my success rate indicates, and that is due in fair part to my becoming a *length* player, as well as a *line* player; you need to be both to be complete at the highest level.

When I was just a *line* player, that meant that no matter what the length of the ball, if I didn't have to play it, I wouldn't. If someone wanted to bowl outside off-stump, I just let them bowl there to their heart's content. The ball could be a rank half-volley, which another player would crash through the covers — I would just let it go. I'd concentrate on the line entirely. But also, a guy could bowl one short of a length, a bouncer, and I'd just go under it, or stand up and defend it. I was so stereotyped then that I believed any shots entailing playing across the line just weren't on. I couldn't believe some batsmen would cut: it was taking a chance. I used to say to myself: Wait and let the ball come — more, perhaps, than I do now. That used to be virtually all I would say to myself — let it come, let it come. I was largely known then as a front-foot player and I guess I was particularly strong on the off-side, a driver of the ball. That would have changed in the mid-1970's: guys started dragging it down, bowling short to me a lot. So I had to change and then I became more of a back-foot player than a front-foot player. I was still able to drive, but the ball had to be that little bit further up to me. But I became very strong off the back foot, and that was part of becoming a line *and* length batsman. That develops the ability to play successfully the ball on the awkward length, the pushing-forward length that no-one wants to play unless he has to. In some ways, you should be letting those go as they have the potential to get you out, and you can't really score off them. So while I am still (and need to be) conscious of line, I am now far more the length batsman and I can get into position to play a full range of shots — even to those pushing-forward-length balls. Part of this getting into position is improvising. Improvisation has come into a lot of the art of batting — getting outside leg-stump to hit through the off, or the other way round. It is freeing your arms, irrespective of the line of the ball, so you are taking the game to the bowler, rather than he taking it to you. But to do that, you must keep your head still and keep your body-weight well adjusted. There is a tendency, when you've gone outside leg, for you to have moved your body-weight that way.

You have to make sure when the ball reaches you that you've got yourself back on balance and able to play the ball to the off-side with your momentum going that way. You have to come back at the ball. Failure to do so is a common fault and a common cause of dismissal in a player otherwise, and commendably, trying to improvise.

This *manner* of batting is only one of many facets important to my batting. Take stance. I've never really been a croucher, but now I would say that I stand taller at the crease than I did before. I think I almost accentuate the standing-up-straight bit, because I believe you get a better view of things from higher up. You've got more control over the ball if it bounces that little bit on you. It gives you more options.

Then you must remember natural strengths. Early in the season, because I am a natural right-hander, my right hand is so much stronger than my left that it tends to take over until I've played a few innings. That is a major problem as I am so reliant on my left hand. So I have to consciously tell myself to grip tightly with my top hand, and slacken off with my bottom (right) hand. Further on that, and to ensure that I don't close the face of the bat, I deliberately start with it 'opened', more so than I would later in the innings. In short, working out the shortcomings, realising them, and doing something about them.

Part of doing something about them is the weight of my bat, which has become the subject of some attention. The

Alan Ormrod was Turner's partner in many thousands of runs for Worcestershire, both among only six players to pass 20,000 runs for the county.

Norman Gifford, Worcestershire's captain for the majority of Turner's county career.

latest one, the one I was using at the end of my last English season, is 3lb 5oz, which I think is the biggest Duncan Fearnley has made. Now, even though I don't have any wrists or forearms to speak of, I still find no major problems in wielding a bat of this size. Sure, there is not quite the same flexibility of a really light bat and I am not that strong in the wrists — though I suppose I must be strong enough for my size — but I find the advantages quite outweigh that disadvantage, too. The edges are very thick edges, and if I only get half the bat to the ball, it tends to fly over the inner ring; it seems to clear the field better, I feel. Also, once you get the bat up, if you get it up straight, gravity brings it down the same way. It is harder to put it off line. And it helps to balance that strong right hand thing I mentioned.

The only regular means of trying to eliminate the problems before they confront one is the matter of 'checks' and preparation for an innings, every innings. It is not always possible to have a knock before a first-class innings. Away from Worcester, for example, unless you're on a county's No. 1 ground, the nets just aren't available. It's even worse in

New Zealand. In fact, only at Eden Park is it possible to have a knock before a day's play. The others just don't have nets, and I like to have anything between five minutes and 15 minutes — if they are available.

Fitness is another matter, and I think too few do enough repetition training. After all, running between the wickets or in the field is all speed work; a certain level of stamina is demanded simply so the recovery rate is good. But if I feel at the start of the season that I am reasonably fit, my momentum carries me through, particularly if I get in a good trot — a batting trot! In the mornings, in those cases, I run maybe only a kilometre — it depends on the day, if it is hot or cold — just to loosen up. Then I have a few stretching excercises; the net; then half an hour in the pavilion. I sit down with a cup of tea, and I always have my pads on a quarter-hour before I go out. I sit down and compose myself, go through my checks, start thinking; getting myself into a higher pitch, especially nowadays, as I'm prepared to hit the first ball out of the ground if it's in the right place. Therefore I get myself to a pitch whereby I think I can achieve this. There is a difference batting second, of course, and I start working it out when the declaration is obviously coming — as it has usually been the case at Worcester in recent seasons! — and with the compulsory 100 overs declaration that was always obvious.

I have been asked, at different times, if one stroke gives me more satisfaction than the others and I suppose, on the off-side at least, it has to be my 'flat-bat' shot, the square slash. It just goes so well; it really does whistle to the boundary, and I guess that's a reasonably good shot. It's always nice to hit the ball through the covers, especially when it's hit well; and picking the ball up over the top is a good one because you have to be very careful judging the line. I guess the drop-kick, the pick-up shot, is one of the easiest to play, because you're using the momentum of the ball as well as the bat, but the main problem there is picking up the line.

Against the spinners, I think I would enjoy as much as anything what I've picked up in the last few seasons: the chipping of the ball into space. I do it off the seamers as well, though generally they don't have a man in the outfield, around mid-wicket, not when they start bowling, anyway. Sometimes the really negative ones do, and it means collecting — picking up the ones and twos — a little bit irksome but it does place you on top, if not exactly off to a flier, because of this negative approach.

But back to the off-spinners, and they generally have a long-on or a deep mid-wicket, and a man on the sweep, backward of square. What I do to an off-spinner is to chip him short of the boundary fielder, clear of the inner ring in there for the single, and that requires a bit of precision. It gives you a bit of a kick, not just the timing of the shot, but the weight, if you like. Sometimes you even get the guy, there to stop the single, going back and not quite getting to it, and the outer guy sprinting desperately in and not quite making it. It can be that touch and go. So you really need to watch the length of the boundaries, too, and a longish boundary, to be preferred, has the deep guy fairly well back. Even then your touch has to be pretty fine, as I've actually got out a couple of times through hitting one *better* than I wanted to. On the other side of the card, I've sometimes had the shot going that well that they've had the field set in such a way that they've had a man halfway as well as a man all the way and the man saving the single. So you've virtually got three in a line, and that, of course, opens up other areas in which you can play.

There are other shots that aren't necessarily the best one plays, but which must be played in a particular fashion. For example, back in my more restrained days, my rule of thumb with an in-swing bowler would be to make sure I was not playing it too far from myself. With an off-spinner on a turning wicket, and knowing with some confidence that an lbw would not be given on the front foot, I knew I would be playing the bat-behind-pad technique. You wouldn't want to be playing ahead of your pads, in case you exposed the edge of the bat and were caught round the corner. These general principles, of course, hold good today, except that I would be approaching those bowlers in a more positive frame of mind. Perhaps the approach to an out-swinger underlines that. In my *line* days, he might have been left

Basil D'Oliveira, South African-born, is now the Worcestershire coach.

alone, but because I've become much more of a *length* player, I'll go for the half-volley, I have to *really* go for it. What happens otherwise is that you tend to only go half at it; you don't quite get there; you try to check your shot; and then you nick it. I just say: Right; *all* everything or nothing. And if you're good enough, you will succeed. Against real pace, too, I think I've modified my methods. I mentioned the improvisation thing, and really that means that I tackle them more now. Previously, I just used to play and place, deflect, them. But in limited-over cricket, especially, you have to take the game, the attack, to them, and now if anyone has a go at me from the fast bowling group, I'll have a go back at them.

The old belief that one should always get in line for each and every delivery is false when trying to score freely from a quick bowler. If a quickie continually bowls short, it is far wiser to get *out* of line — as I said earlier, freeing one's arms so as to be able to propel the ball with a great deal more force than would otherwise be the case.

But — and this applies to any bowling — you must not be too premeditated. You can't elect to play a particular shot in advance; what you must be is razor-sharp to get into the position for **that** shot, if that is the shot demanded. You've got to keep yourself on edge for your nomination or selection of shots, the sort of shots I play now. In fact, I now find that if I don't start to go at the ball, and back myself to play it effectively, my feet stop moving. I don't get into position to play the ball, and I'm worse off as a consequence — worse off blocking than if I was actually playing positively. This has brought me a bit of stick over the last couple of years at Worcester, because it's been felt that I've played badly when I've hit the ball straight up in the air, and made what looks like a bad mistake.

But they've forgotten that quite often I've had three figures beside my name, or I've got a 60 in an hour. The traditional English pro, however, has been brought up in such a stereotyped manner that he can't cope with that — to allow flair to come through, and that's what it is. It's allowing your natural game to come through. Maybe the reference to the traditional pro is a generalisation, but it really refers to those with a very strict background of coaching and conformity. A lot of them, I'm afraid and I feel, don't get the most out of themselves because they're actually frightened of breaking with the implanted, imprinted ideas.

Perhaps I can best illustrate that with the change of my own attitude. Once, the way I played, I would play to the end of a session. When I got to the last couple of overs before lunch, before tea, before stumps, I'd make sure I didn't make a mistake. Now, my feeling is that I'm in at that stage; I'm better equipped to deal with the bowling in the last over before a break than in the first after it. If I get anything loose at that stage, I'll take advantage of it.

Another illustration, and if it is a criticism of my last county captain, Phillip Neale, I mean it very gently. Every time in my last season at Worcestershire, before I went out to bat, he'd sit down with me at some stage before I went out, and he'd tell me: 'I'd like you to see these opening bowlers off in the first 10 overs, and then go about playing your shots. But we really need to see them off first, because our strength of batting isn't really that great further down.' I noticed he never said anything to Alan Ormrod, because Alan Ormrod was and is a very orthodox player, although he's also a very successful player. Phillip Neale's come down the wicket even

The county ground at New Road, Worcester, through the eye of the cathedral.

after I've got a hundred — he did it after I got what was very nearly the fastest 100 of last season, against Lancashire, 83 minutes or something. He said: 'Come on, we don't want you getting out now' — amazing!

Having said that, I think it is appropriate to comment now that I've only just come to realise that the old diehard attitudes and feelings of other people are so imprinted on one that if you are not careful, you start thinking as you are 'supposed' to think, or as someone else feels you should think. In so many cases, they're wrong and now I work out what I believe is right. Firstly, of course, you must work out a method: everyone must find a method they can repeat and which is successful for them and that takes a lot of discussion, a lot of practice, and a lot of self-analysis to get to that point. Having got to that point some time ago, I find now that the challenge, the hardest part to work on, is trying to ignore the outside influences. By that, I mean the people trying to inflict their concerns, or their fears, or their wills — on you to do well. They inflict them on you half the time if you're not careful; things like: 'Ooh, don't forget you're playing for your country'; or 'don't worry if you fail — just do your best.' They put negative thoughts into your mind.

They talk to you at the wrong time, just when you're about to go out to bat, instead of just letting you sort yourself out. In other words, the pressures imparted by outside influences are the biggest problems that any established player — any player, in fact — can have.

Glenn Turner

1

106* for Worcestershire v Middlesex, New Road, Worcester, 17, 18 August 1968

Worcestershire 242/3 decl (G. M. Turner 106*, T. W. Graveney 62, B. L. D'Oliveira 40*) drew with **Middlesex** 108/3 (M. J. Smith 52; L. J. Coldwell 3/38).

First innings: not out 106

This otherwise unmemorable match — rain delayed the start on the Saturday by three hours and washed out the Monday's (third day) play altogether — was made distinctive on hindsight because it was the first run, if you like, towards a century. Under any circumstances, however, this would have been seen as a critical point in a young batsman's development. Turner was then three months past his 21st birthday and, before the season started, he had scored 694 runs in his 20 matches since starting for Otago as a slip of a lad of 17. His average was a respectable near-25 but, in his first full season for Worcestershire since qualifying, he had been far from a success.

Batting at number seven, sometimes number six, he scored only 418 runs at the mediocre average of 17. Then, without warning, Turner was promoted to open the innings with Ron Headley, and at the expense of Duncan Fearnley. The results were immediate: 764 runs in the final 10 games of the season, an average in those games of 42, and the respectable first season's tally of 1182 runs at 29.

I'd been too cautious about my game, too aware or too concerned that I had to succeed. I'd been into bed by 9 o'clock, living a life to which I was unsuited and unused. Then with opening and the first century, I started living more normally, not hitting the grog, but going out at night. That meant I relaxed more, and of course, I could relax a great deal more after this innings: it was trebly significant being my first ton, it brought up my 1000 for the season, and

I got my county cap.

Certainly, Turner's century and all that went with it was virtually the only highlight of this rain-ruined match. Peter Parfitt, the Middlesex captain, misread the pitch when he put Worcestershire in to bat. Dry at one end, drying at the other in sun and wind, it ironed out to a pleasant batting strip. Turner took four and three-quarter hours over his century, slow progress in hindsight, but swift enough compared with his early innings in New Zealand. Unusually, for Headley enjoyed a very successful career with Worcestershire, it was the first century by an opener for the county for a year, and the opening partnership with Headley was worth 56.

Better were to come. After Alan Ormrod, another with whom Turner was to enjoy productive partnerships, was out at 61, Turner and his captain, Tom Graveney, added 119, the first coming in 45 minutes, Turner went to his own 50 in 142 minutes, and at stumps — 148 for two after 63 overs — he was 84. The century partnership arrived in 143 minutes, then there was 62, unbeaten, with Basil D'Oliveira, and in that, the 50 took only 39 minutes. Turner's century contained 10 fours and all told, he batted a neat 300 minutes.

2

167 for Otago v Wellington, Carisbrook, Dunedin, 31 December 1968, 1 January 1969

Wellington 392/5 decl (B. A. G. Murray 213, J. F. M. Morrison 75, G. P. Bilby 56; R. S. Dunne 3/47) and 51/2 drew with **Otago** 421 (G. M. Turner 167, R. W. Hutchison 66, G. D. Alabaster 47*, W. J. Mitchell 47; P. B. McGregor 5/85, H. A. Morgan 3/108).

First innings: c and b McGregor 167

This was Turner's first season back in Dunedin since becoming a professional. He had missed the previous season because of the need to stay in England to qualify, and his three previous seasons in the Otago team had realised 680 runs in 18 games. So to the second match of the season, a season of much importance with the West Indies due after — as it happened — a rather disastrous tour of Australia, and with the team to tour England to be named near the end of the season. Not that that really occupied Turner's mind; his priority was to win a place in the test team for the home series. Unwittingly, Wellington and that fine performer, Bruce (or 'Bags') Murray, provided the occasion. Their first innings provided Otago with only a first innings win or an outright loss for which to play.

*This was an example of the criticism I often receive for scoring slowly — batting for myself — being unfounded, or if you like, of my slow batting **not** being to the detriment of the team. It was an example of us having only a first innings win to play for, and getting it. It was a grafting innings, a typical requirement of the 'Brook in those days — slow track, slow outfield. The deflections, the nicks through slips, never went through to the fence. Off the likes of Dick Motz — or Tails in this innings — you'd only ever get two. I had the shots then, but I was not prepared to play them. I recall that the Wellington players were irritated and frustrated, but in* *those early days, I couldn't understand people getting upset at my slow scoring: I thought they were good players and should be able to get me out. A few of them used to throw the ball at me in frustration. But remember, I wasn't established anywhere by then.*

Slow progress, indeed it was, as Turner and Wayne Blair scored 31 in the first hour. Nor was the going easy, for at lunch, Blair and Noel McGregor were both out — Turner had scored 31 in the morning session — and when Murray Parker was out after 53 minutes' batting, having helped Turner add 39, Otago was 87 for three. But the first real moves towards that first innings win came when John Mitchell joined Turner, then on 35. By tea, they had virtually doubled the score, Turner had scored another 60, and he reached his century in 301 minutes. But after they had added 117 in 165 minutes, Mitchell was out at 204 for four, and another long partnership was demanded.

So entered Ray Hutchinson, and the pair were still together at stumps (284 for four), Turner 150 after 410 minutes. His century had included just nine fours, but he batted with increasing confidence, with the Wellington total that much closer, into his third 50, and unleashed many booming on-and cover-drives from a tiring attack. But Turner tired as well, and the next day he showed the results of his full day's labour, by struggling for a further 115 minutes for only 17 runs more on this pitch which was playing extremely truly. But, almost as ever, the Carisbrook outfield was not the fastest in the land, and while there were 14 fours in Turner's innings, there was also a heavy preponderance of threes — the first of his double-centuries could well have come in this innings.

The one careless stroke of this momumental innings had Turner caught and bowled by Peter McGregor, in truth a batsman but a handy medium-pacer — and sometime leg-spinner — as well. He had then batted a quarter-hour short of nine hours, easily the longest innings of his career to that point, and he and Hutchinson had added 119 in 212 minutes for the fifth wicket. When Turner was out, at 313 for five, Otago still needed 70 for the first innings lead, but Gren

Alabaster, the captain, saw it there. There was a very handy look to the Wellington attack: Mike Coles, often on the borderline of test selection, opening with Gary Snowden; McGregor and the persevering Harry Morgan with their medium-pace; and the varied leg-spin of three test batsmen, Bruce Murray, John Morrison and Bruce Bolton. Against this attack, Otago reached its highest total since Bert Sutcliffe's team of nine years previously scored 435 for nine declared against Central Districts, also at Carisbrook.

3

123 for South Island v West Indies, Carisbrook, 22, 24 February 1969

West Indies 307/8 decl (M. C. Carew 76, B. F. H. Butcher 58, C. H. Lloyd 57, R. C. Fredericks 37) and 306/4 (Lloyd 205*, C. A. Davis 69) drew with **South Island** 413/8 decl (G. M. Turner 123, K. J. Wadsworth 103, B. F. Hastings 85, G. D. Alabaster 31).

First innings: c R. B. Kanhai b L. A. King 123

The West Indians declared an hour before stumps on the first day, having scored freely from a South Island XI which was clearly chosen as a team of prospective test players: none of the established men were called up. Nor was there an auspicious start to the South innings, Bevan Congdon being out for 12 (and Turner three not out) in the 35 minutes of play possible before dull light had its way. But Turner and Wayne Burtt (16) scored 60 together in 100 minutes on the Monday morning, before Turner and Brian Hastings settled into a profitable partnership, one which helped them both towards their test debuts. The pitch offered little to the bowlers, and Turner, on the front foot for the most part, advanced to the highest score at that stage by any New Zealander against the West Indies. Hastings, who had a bad middle patch to his innings, outscored his younger partner — his 50 took 124 minutes, Turner's 167 — but in the two hours between lunch and tea, they scored 112. Turner was then 101, his century taking 262 minutes, and their third wicket 173-run partnership came in 222 minutes. Turner's 123, finished when he was caught at slip by Rohan Kanhai from the opening bowler, Lester King, took a minute over six hours, included eight fours, and 11 threes: that slow Carisbrook outfield again!

This was my first international century, and although I'd scored only one century in England, I felt I'd become estab-

lished because I had been capped and had averaged 42 in the second half of the previous English season. I felt I was ready for test cricket, especially as I was a New Zealander, because guys had got in our test team on far less. Way back, early in 1966, I'd been given my so-called 'chance', for the President's XI against the touring MCC side: they'd batted me at number seven. This game was another sort of trial and after it, and because I was then 21½ and had played about 50 first-class matches, I felt I had asserted my right to play test cricket. So this match was doubly significant, and the opposition doubly fearsome. Three of their quicks in this game were King, Charlie Griffith and Richard Edwards, the man they rather foolishly left out of their team to tour England on our twin tour a few months later. David Holford, Sobers's cousin and a leg-spinner, plus 'Joey' Carew and Charlie Davis were the other bowlers.

It was off Davis that Turner reached his 50, with a straight drive early in the lunch-to-tea session which was so profitable. Indeed, Turner scored 57 to the 54 of Hastings in that two-hour period, helped immeasurably by an over from Carew in which Turner three times thrashed fours through the heavily patrolled leg-side field to move into the nineties. That burst of aggression done, Turner passed his century, was dropped from Griffith — who was mainly content to pitch wide of the off-stump — then, an over after Hastings had fallen to Davis, to be caught at slip from a defensive stroke.

4

124 for New Zealand v Middlesex, Lord's, 17 July 1969

Middlesex 325 (C. T. Radley 82, W. E. Russell 65, P. H. Parfitt 53, F. J. Titmus 52; H. J. Howarth 6/99) and 162/5 decl (J. M. Brearley 41, Radley 37; Howarth 3/43) drew with **New Zealand** 289/6 decl (G. M. Turner 124, M. G. Burgess 65, V. Pollard 56; J. S. E. Price 3/62) and 182/9 (B. A. G. Murray 50, Burgess 36, B. R. Taylor 34, G. T. Dowling 31; H. C. Latchman 3/39).

First innings: c J. T. Murray b Price 124
Second innings: c Latchman b Price 1

Turner's fourth century, and each one of them of its own special importance: his first, his first in New Zealand, his first in 'international' cricket, and now his first at Lord's in his first appearance at 'Headquarters'. It could be said, too, that this was made against the best attack from which Turner had scored a century. There were two internationals, John Price of England and Alan Connolly of Australia; there was another handy medium-pacer, Keith Jones, who had been round the counties a bit; Harry Latchman, the West Indian Cockney to bowl his leg-breaks; Peter Parfitt, the captain, and Norman Featherstone, from southern Africa originally, with off-spin.

And there was that combination of Fred Titmus and John Murray, that more than anything, which made it a difficult debut at Lord's. I suppose someone has a count of just how many wickets they got between them for Middlesex, and just the knowledge that Murray was behind the stumps made Titmus so difficult, the psychological pressure that Freddy wasn't alone. But for all that, I feel I was able to relax a shade because they were prepared to use the looser spinners. That happened then in touring team games, as the counties generally had to make all the play; it was certainly the case against our team.

One of the 'looser' spinners indeed provided Turner with his one opportunity for batting devilment in what was otherwise a circumspect innings, occupying 322 minutes. He struck Latchman for five fours in the space of two overs; he hit 16 all told. But Turner had precious few opportunities to bat like a spendthrift, for this was a critical time in the New Zealand tour. Partly because of rain, the first match, against Yorkshire, was a one-innings-each affair; the unlikely opposition of Scotland was well beaten; rain took over again with Derbyshire reeling; a draw with Surrey; a loss to Essex and the sea fret at Westcliff. A worthy performance was required at Lord's, but Middlesex's first innings, even after more magnificent bowling from Hedley Howarth, was the springboard for a New Zealand defeat.

In retrospect, then, Turner played perhaps the most critical innings of the tour, his team in dire straits after its first hour of batting and 21 for two. Perhaps little wonder that Turner was so intent on survival, particularly against 'Sport' Price, whose run started wide of mid-off, and that he should take 35 minutes to score his first run. He and Mark Burgess, whose 25th birthday it was, scored 49 together in the hour before lunch, when Turner was 30.

But he lifted the brake pedal after lunch: 20 in 31 minutes, and the half-century thus 149 minutes. The fluent Burgess, when out for 65, had helped Turner produce 125 runs for the third wicket, in 131 minutes, but this was still not a time for batting recklessness. Turner was then 64, and he was joined by a gritty partner in Vic Pollard, certainly in better form than he was to be later in the tour. Together they added 117 in 126 minutes, including Turner's lambasting of Latchman, and Turner had passed his century in 285 minutes.

5

110 for New Zealand v Pakistan, the Stadium, Dacca, 8, 9 November 1969

New Zealand 273 (G. M. Turner 110, M. G. Burgess 59; Intikhab Alam 5/91 and 200 (Burgess 119*; Intikhab 5/91, Pervez Sajjad 4/60) drew with **Pakistan** 290/7 decl (Asif Iqbal 92, Shafqat Rana 65, Aftab Gul 30; H. J. Howarth 4/85) and 51/4 (R. S. Cunis 4/21).

First innings: c Shafqat b Pervez 110
Second innings: c Intikhab b Pervez 26

The background to the test and, indeed, to the test selections for the twin series tour of the Indian sub-continent, is as curious as it is illogical, particularly as it relates to Turner. Before arriving in India, he had played five test matches, all as an opener. His scores were 0 and 40, 74 and 1, 30 and 38 against the West Indies. In England, 5 and 43* in the first test, that not out both the lowest score for one batting through the innings, and Turner the youngest to do so. He missed the second test with a broken knuckle in his hand; 53 and 25 at The Oval in the third test. But in India, captain Graham Dowling started messing about with Turner's batting position.

I opened at Bombay, batting a very long time for very few: 24 and 5. And we lost. We won at Nagpur, and that was when I started going down the order. I scored 2 batting at number five in the first innings, 57 at number three in the second. Then to Hyderabad: 2 (still at number three) and 15* batting at number seven. It was ridiculous to me; I was an opener, and if I wasn't worth opening with, why have me in the team? The theory was that we should try and score as many runs as possible off the quicks before the spinners came on — but they were often on after four overs! And this idea of my batting low so we could whack the new ball: Dowling got 14 in a morning at Hyderabad. Anyway, I was left out of the first *test at Karachi, and I was left out at Lahore, but we won that, and that was something. The Pakistanis went overboard after that loss: they dropped Younis and Mushtaq, two they brought back from England, and we felt we had been done a marvellous favour. Younis, in fact, never played for Pakistan again. They did us another favour, too, with the pitch, just old mud baked hard, with a lot of cracks in it. There was not a blade of grass to be seen anywhere, not a good result wicket. Certainly not the sort they should have prepared wanting to draw the series. And I came back into the test team for Bryan Yuile, who had strained a neck muscle taking off Peter Cook and Dudley Moore. I don't really think I came in, as one local newspaper commented, because the test was over six days and with us one up, we would be obviously looking at drawing rather than winning!*

Strange to relate, then, that Turner outscored his partners on this amazing pitch, which had the ball alternately sitting up and staring at the batsman, then scurrying through without a backward look. At stumps, New Zealand was 172 for four in six hours, Turner 99*.

Murray was quickly out for seven, the score 13. Then Dowling — he was now at number three — helped Turner add 54 in two hours, Dowling just 15 of them. In 68 minutes, Turner and Congdon added 32: Congdon 6. There were 48 in 99 minutes for the fourth wicket with Hastings: Hastings 22. Not that Turner himself was the Galloping Major; it was two hours — at 11.30 am! — before he hit his first boundary. And the next morning, it took Turner 15 minutes — or 376 minutes all told — to reach his century, and he went on wearily for an hour and a half on that second day, scraping together another 11 runs, and the end result was a partnership of 79 in two and a half hours with Burgess. He batted 445 minutes, surprisingly well short of his longest innings, and hit a mere seven fours. But when the great second innings rearguard action of Burgess and Bob Cunis is taken into account, it played its major part in New Zealand's first series victory.

It was a success achieved against a mightily proficient spin attack, too. After Saleem Altaf and Asif Iqbal had done their duty with the new ball, the latter's bowling star then on the wane, there was a three-pronged spin attack to face: Pervez Sajjad, arguably then the best left-armer in the business, Intikhab Alam, certainly the best leg-spinner, and Mohammad Nazir, the little off-spinner who had commenced his test career at Karachi with seven for 99. Together, they bowled 134 overs and it was Pervez who had Turner, caught by Shafqat Rana.

6

122 for Worcestershire v Essex, New Road, 17, 18 June 1970

Essex 237 (G. Barker 124; V. A. Holder 5/55) and 181/3 decl (B. E. A. Edmeades 66, G. A. Saville 65*) lost to **Worcestershire** 226/4 decl (G. M. Turner 122, J. A. Ormrod 46) and 193/4 (Turner 72, T. W. Graveney 53*, R. G. A. Headley 39).

First innings: c S. Turner b D. L. Acfield 122
Second innings: c E. R. Presland b Turner 72

Though it paved the way for an outstanding Worcestershire victory, and it was the starting point of Turner's record 10 centuries for the county in the season, it is not an innings which he remembers of any great importance. But the opposition was one of some significance, for six weeks earlier, in a John Player League match at Chelmsford, Turner had played an innings regarded by Tom Graveney as the turning point of his batting, and batting attitude. It was an innings in which he first displayed the confidence to hit 'over the top', and this later first-class innings contained much of his new freedom.

From 23 for none overnight, Turner 12 and Ron Headley 7, Worcestershire lost Headley at 33, and its innings really revolved round Turner and Alan Ormrod. Strange how when either Headley or Turner prospered, the other failed. The 50 partnership with Ormrod took 72 minutes, and soon afterwards, Turner reached his own 50 in 139 minutes. The 100 partnership — the stand was eventually worth 123 — came in 138 minutes, Turner's own 100 in 237 minutes, with 12 fours, and he batted 260 minutes before being fourth out at 198. The second innings, though not a century, represented the fifth innings, of the seven in which Turner had batted in county games at New Road that season, in which he passed 50. And it was a fine example of Turner's new-found pace judgement: Worcestershire needed five an over, but from the first 19 overs, scored only 65. Then Turner and Graveney were mainly responsible for 128 off the final 20 overs, the winning runs coming as five leg-byes from the fourth-last ball, with Turner out shortly before, at 186.

The Essex attack was its long-standing and very proficient mixture of Keith Boyce's considerable pace, with John Lever to share the new ball, and three spinners, Ray East (left-arm), David Acfield (off-break) and Robin Hobbs (leg-spin).

7

137 for Worcestershire v Hampshire, Southampton, 29, 30 June 1970

Worcestershire 200 (T. W. Graveney 59, B. L. D'Oliveira 35; P. J. Sainsbury 5/40) and 325/6 decl (G. M. Turner 137, J. A. Ormrod 49, G. R. Cass 46*, E. J. O. Hemsley 36; T. E. Jesty 3/101) drew with **Hampshire** 303/5 decl (B. A. Richards 94, B. L. Reed 89, D. A. Livingstone 70) and 116/2 (Richards 66).

First innings: c G. R. Stephenson b A. T. Castell 18
Second innings: st Stephenson b Castell 137

A fluent Tom Graveney had provided the only batting stability of the first innings and after being lambasted by Barry Richards, Worcestershire faced a difficult situation. But it was one righted by Turner, especially, and the faithful Alan Ormrod. In 115 minutes to stumps on the second day, Worcestershire reached 87 for the loss of Ron Headley, Turner 46 of them and Ormrod 32. With the first ball of the overcast third day, Turner on-drove the ninth of the 20 fours he was to strike in this innings, to reach his 50. He followed that with an on-driven three, and another boundary to Ormrod through the covers had the first over of the day realising 11 runs.

But Worcestershire had trouble in maintaining that progress in the face of the nagging length of Peter Sainsbury, and they scored only 32 from the 18 overs of the first hour — 21 from 17 overs after that slightly hysterical start. But Sainsbury's long occupation of the bowling crease brought increased scoring opportunities, and Turner was not slow to use his feet to the slow left-armer. Just after losing Ormrod, when they had put on 97 for the second wicket, Turner skipped down the pitch and lofted Sainsbury straight for a long, long six. Turner's century came in 233 minutes, he was 123 at lunch, and in 10 flamboyant minutes after the interval, he added 14 of the 21 scored in that time by him and Ted Hemsley. Until beaten by a leg-break and stumped, Turner

41

had batted 275 minutes, his 50 partnership with Hemsley taking 43 minutes; all told, they added 87 for the fourth wicket, which fell at 238.

We hadn't batted all that well in the first innings, and it was an awkward situation. But we had to keep things moving along to have a winning chance and the track was good enough — Richards and the others had shown that — to be able to drive with some confidence and freedom. There was quite a high proportion of boundaries in this innings, but I found that when things got a little bogged down, I was in good enough nick to keep the singles coming with pushes — even if against the line, from Sainsbury — off my pads.

8

154* for Worcestershire v Gloucestershire, Bristol, 1 July 1970

Worcestershire 313/2 decl (G. M. Turner 154*, J. A. Ormrod 118) and 210/4 decl (Ormrod 83, Turner 56, G. R. Cass 31*) drew with **Gloucestershire** 213 (R. W. Phillips 41, D. A. Allen 41; N. Gifford 4/44, V. A. Holder 3/48) and 263/7 (R. B. Nicholls 69, M. Bissex 66, D. R. Shepherd 49; Holder 5/73).

First innings: not out 154
Second innings: c J. Davey b A. S. Brown 56

In conditions so cool that the players welcomed the hot nourishment brought out as drinks, and on this slow pitch, Turner eventually required 330 minutes to score his second successive century and then his highest score in England. But it was an innings of increasing mastery over the bowlers as he and Alan Ormrod developed on the opening partnership of 28 between Turner and Headley, 27 of them having come in the first seven overs. The pair who were to go on to each score more than 20,000 runs for Worcestershire, scored their 50 partnership in 52 minutes, the 100 in a minute over two hours, and the 200 took 205 minutes. All told, they scored 239 in 242 minutes, Ormrod hitting 13 fours in that time, and for a change, he outscored Turner. The latter's 50 took 133 minutes, his 100 in 238 minutes, and after hitting nine fours, he went to his 150 with a sweetly struck six off David Smith, that sturdy medium-pacer who had bowled so well in New Zealand with Dennis Silk's MCC team when Turner was a 13-year-old!

Turner, and Worcestershire, batted into the third session, too. At lunch, Turner (44) and Ormrod (34) had taken their county to 92 for one; tea showed a score of 225 for one (Turner 111, Ormrod 98). They had to contend with a variety of bowlers — or was it that the Gloucestershire bowlers were never allowed to settle down? — for five were used before lunch: Jack Davey, the big left-armer was one to get some life from this slow pitch, Smith, Tony Brown, the captain, John Mortimore and Mike Bissex. And Gloucestershire's third spinner, David Allen, was on straight after lunch!

The pitch did nothing towards bringing about a result, although a well-placed Worcestershire team got 210 in only 160 minutes in the second innings, and set Gloucestershire 311 in four hours. The home team made a brave attempt on this pitch in which stroke-making was always difficult. Turner's century, for example, included 42 singles.

9

112 for Worcestershire v Leicestershire, New Road, 18, 20 July 1970

Leicestershire 328 (C. C. Inman 82, P. T. Marner 51, B. J. Booth 46, G. D. McKenzie 37, B. Duddleston 32; N. Gifford 4/53, R. G. M. Carter 3/92) and 233/7 decl (Dudleston 112, Booth 50; J. A. Standen 3/62) drew with **Worcestershire** 296/3 decl (G. M. Turner 112, J. A. Ormrod 67, T. W. Graveney 44*, T. J. Yardley 36*) and 101/1 (Ormrod 33*).

First innings: c and b Marner 112
Second innings: not out 29

On another placid New Road pitch, the Worcestershire batsmen compared badly with the men of Leicestershire. It could be said, not too unkindly, that after the Lord Mayor's Show provided by Peter Marner — three sixes and seven fours in his hurricane half-century — and Clive Inman, who struck 14 fours, mostly cover-driven, in his 82, the Worcestershire innings was a comparative dung-cart. The half-hour to stumps were bright enough: 19 to Ron Headley, 17 to Turner and an extra. But they could add only 25 in 45 minutes next morning, before Headley was out, 13 short of his 1000 runs for the season, and the first hour produced a mere 30 runs. Turner had his moments, particularly against the left-arm spin of David Steele and the fast-medium of John Pember. But he had his lucky moments, too, playing Pember on to his leg-stump without dislodging a bail, and surviving a difficult chance at leg-slip. Ormrod had an even worse time of it. He struggled for 75 minutes to reach seven and it seemed a blessed relief — not least to Ormrod — when he lifted Steele to Graham McKenzie at mid-on. Astonishingly, he dropped it, and Ormrod in the next 10 minutes to lunch, scored another five runs! Turner was then 74 of the 122, after 52 overs, his 50 having taken 124 minutes. His second 50 took a further 110 minutes, and when he was out at 207 for two, having struck 15 fours, he and Ormrod — but mostly Turner

45

— had scored 145 together. Their 100 partnership had taken a laborious 142 minutes.

Turner batted just under four hours for his century; Brian Dudleston scored at a similar pace in Leicestershire's second innings; and Marner killed off the game when he batted too long to provide a chance of a result. He eventually set Worcestershire 266 to win in 70 minutes and the final 20 overs, a target never conceivable against an attack consisting of McKenzie, Marner, Jack Birkenshaw, Steele and Pember. Indeed, Marner did not even bowl in the second innings.

10

106 for Worcestershire v Warwickshire, Edgbaston, Birmingham, 25, 27 July 1970

Warwickshire 150 (R. N. Abberley 52; V. A. Holder 4/41) and 217/4 (J. A. Jameson 94, R. B. Kanhai 40, Abberley 36) drew with **Worcestershire** 368 (R. G. A. Headley 108, G. M. Turner 106, T. J. Yardley 61, T. W. Graveney 34; W. Blenkiron 5/89).

First innings: lbw b W. N. Tidy 106

There is no questioning the significance of this innings: Turner's first of 11 centuries against Warwickshire bowlers, and the halfway step towards his 10 centuries in the season. As was often the case in these early days, and even allowing for the 'new' Turner who could hit 'over the top', he played second fiddle for some time to the aggression of Ron Headley. But for both, it was a comfortable position in which they found themselves, for Warwickshire gave a mediocre batting performance on the Saturday, on a fine pitch, and Headley (75) and Turner (38) had taken their side to 114 in 100 minutes by stumps.

Between then and the resumption, Worcestershire suffered a crushing John Player League defeat (the county scored only 90, to lose by 119 runs, Headley getting a duck and Turner 24). But the three-day game was a different kettle of fish, even if Headley appeared to be suffering post-duck blues. His 75 on the Saturday had come in 34 overs, a healthy scoring rate indeed, but he laboured for 50 minutes for another five runs on the cold, windy, showery Monday morning, while Turner took the initiative. Even so, Headley's head-start had him first to his fifth century of the season, in 172 minutes, but after he had hit his eighteenth boundary in 62 overs, the 185-run stand came to an end.

But Turner continued his quiet, accomplished way, and he too reached his fifth century of the season 23 minutes after lunch — when he had scored 87 in 210 minutes — but with only seven fours. Turner, who had reached his 50 in 128 minutes, also had a 51 partnership in 44 minutes with Alan Ormrod, but a leg-spinner, Warwick Tidy, had both in six balls, Turner being dismissed at 239 for three, in 243 minutes. The other bowlers used by Warwickshire were the test men, David Brown, Billy Ibadulla and Lance Gibbs, with Bill Blenkiron the other opener.

11
118* for Worcestershire v Somerset, New Road, 31 July 1970

Somerset 184 (M. Kitchen 47, A. Clarkson 32; V. A. Holder 5/39) and 270/7 decl (Clarkson 63, P. J. Robinson 36, T. W. Cartwright 36, R. T. Virgin 33; Holder 3/66) lost to **Worcestershire** 154 (N. Gifford 38*, R. G. A. Headley 30; G. I. Burgess 5/45, Cartwright 4/44) and 301/3 (G. M. Turner 118*, T. J. Yardley 60*, T. W. Graveney 46, Headley 31).

First innings: c Virgin b Cartwright 10
Second innings: not out 118

This was the middle of a purple patch for Turner: his sixth century of the season and the record now truly in sight, his fourth in the month of July (and another was completed on the last day of June), the third successive match in which he scored a ton. There was not an auspicious start to the match, however, a drying wicket contributing to two of the lowest scores of the season at New Road. But as the pitch dried, so it rolled out slow and easy, but Worcestershire still faced the daunting task of scoring 301 in three and three-quarter hours, or a little over four an over. But Turner paced the innings to perfection, again, with more than a little help from his friends. There was 51 with Headley (31), 71 with Ormrod (31), 62 with Graveney, the old master getting 46 of them, and an unbeaten 117 in 67 minutes with Jim Yardley, whose 60 not out included 10 fours.

When Tom was out at 184, we'd scored at only about three and a half an over and Arthur Jepson, one of the umpires, suggested we might as well flag it away. We needed to get up close to six an over, 117 off the final 20 overs, and that was not regarded then as being on. But I said we'd go on, as we had nothing to lose, and in point of fact, we got the runs with nine balls to spare. Tom Cartwright got most upset in that dig, because he'd had a ball in the first innings: four for 44 off

*37 overs on that pitch which suited his particular talents. I
started hitting him over the top, and even charged him once
or twice. His only answer was to call me a Kiwi c..., but I
guess I finished ahead, because he took two for 69 and I got
an En Oh. And that helped give me my most satisfaction to
that point, not only because it was a century, but because I
saw it through to the end. It's always more satisfying in a
run-chase to see it through yourself. Of course, the guys in
the dressing room were particularly elated, as they didn't
really think it was possible, either. In many ways, that century and the win it brought typified what cricket was all
about — a great individualistic team game. You play a
substantial part, a personal success being largely responsible
to contributing to a team victory. It is always doubly satisfying that you are personally able to do well.*

There are some revealing statistics in the Turner innings,
and in those partnerships mentioned earlier. The first 50
with Ormrod took 41 minutes, that with Graveney 34 (and in
their 45-minute 62 including 46 to Graveney alone!), and the
first two 50s of the Yardley partnership took 36 and 26
minutes respectively. The innings really needed that boost,
for it was a formidable target facing Worcestershire, even if
the openers got 32 from the first nine overs from the seamers,
and at lunch (Headley 30, Turner 11), they had 41 from 12
overs, Yardley provided just that hurry-along, whacking 10
fours, many of them in the air, while Turner hit a total of 15
fours in becoming the first batsman of the season to pass 1400
runs. The two 23-year-olds were mightily well received by
their home crowd, and an interesting sidelight is that Yardley was the only player in the home team who was born
within the county's boundaries. The other participating in
the match was the Somerset all-rounder, Peter Robinson, not
called on to bowl in this match with Brian Langford settling
for himself, Roy Palmer, Cartwright, John Roberts and
Graham Burgess. From them, Turner reached his 50 in 109
minutes, his century 103 minutes later, and his total innings
lasted 234 minutes.

12
110* for Worcestershire v Northamptonshire, Wellingborough, 11 August 1970

Northamptonshire 234 (Mushtaq Mohammed 73, D. S. Steele 53, P. J. Watts 35; N. Gifford 5/42) and 146 (H. M. Ackerman 82; Gifford 4/30, V. A. Holder 3/18) lost to **Worcestershire** 157 (R. G. A. Headley 31; J. Swinburne 4/71, Mushtaq 3/29) and 229/3 (G. M. Turner 110*, J. A. Ormrod 37, B. L. D'Oliveira 32).

First innings: c and b D. Breakwell 18
Second innings: not out 110

In the only match of Northamptonshire's season at the Wellingborough School Ground, Turner scored one of his finest centuries and, yet again, it was one of those 'paced' innings which took Worcestershire to a slightly unexpected victory. As is often the case with a ground rarely used for county cricket, the pitch was not at all easy at any time, as Turner relates, and despite the suggestion in Wisden that it improved on the final day.

It was rain-affected and turned square: it did NOT improve on the last day at all. Hence, Northants did not declare, they couldn't really on the ratio of runs and time remaining — we needed 224 in five hours — but they certainly thought they had enough anyway. In 1970, you know, I was very conscious of judging the line to a very fine degree and I was always prepared to let the ball go, even when it was very close to my off-stump, particularly if it was on that awkward length you didn't want to play at. This innings perhaps best typified it: Dennis Breakwell was the left-arm slowy for Northants, a very handy performer, even if he bowled the odd loose one, who had become his team's front-line spinner after being only fourth choice the previous season. He was pitching on the off-stump, and I was letting them go! The art is not to play at one on an awkward length if you don't have to. I feel that was the best innings I played relating to judgement of line in difficult conditions, and when that judgement was crucial to one's success. So far as defensive technique and all those other factors are concerned, I still consider that innings was my best.

Until Turner's final innings mastery, spinners held sway, Gifford taking his five for 42 from 45.3 overs (and four for 30 from 18 second innings overs), while the Northants bowling in the first innings was led by John Swinburne, an off-spinner, and Mushtaq, with his leg-breaks. Those two, Breakwell and Brian Crump, an opening bowler, did the bulk of Northant's second innings bowling: 74 of the 90 overs.

While Turner feels this was probably his best technical innings, that is not to say he had no problems on this difficult pitch. Before lunch, he survived two lbw appeals from Breakwell, and had some problems with Swinburne. But he steadily gained an ascendancy, without running riot in the speed of run-scoring. The first 50, in fact, took 99 minutes, the second in 114 (completed just after tea, when Turner was 99), and the 110 took 250 minutes. With Headley, Turner had an opening partnership of 34; then there were 80 with Alan Ormrod, the first 50 taking only 37 minutes. Next came 86 in rather more sober fashion with Basil D'Oliveira, and a final 29 unbeaten with Tom Graveney, who scored 23 of them.

13

142* for Worcestershire v Derbyshire, Chesterfield, 12, 13 August 1970

Derbyshire 268 (J. F. Harvey 80, I. R. Buxton 57, P. J. K. Gibbs 45, R. W. Taylor 30; R. G. M. Carter 4/64, V. A. Holder 3/45) and 349/3 decl (C. P. Wilkins 102*, Gibbs 83, M. H. Page 80, D. H. K. Smith 49) drew with **Worcestershire** 305/3 decl (G. M. Turner 142*, T. W. Graveney 64*, R. G. A. Headley 40, T. J. Yardley 40) and 100/4 (Graveney 46*).

First innings: not out 142
Second innings: lbw b Buxton 0

The most lasting features of this match were not the centuries of Turner and Chris Wilkins, the other high innings, the characteristically graceful final innings of Tom Graveney in the shadow of the crooked spire. It was the unhappy ending to a match in which Ian Buxton unquestionably placed individual above team and match. He extended the Derbyshire second innings purely to allow Wilkins to reach a century in 74 deliveries, placing him among the contenders for a Ford Capri; Graveney missed his own royal chance of winning the car by declaring. It left Worcestershire needing 313 in less than three hours, a task not feasible, even on the kindly Queen's Park pitch.

This was, Turner recalls, not one of his most testing innings, and on that placid pitch, success came readily to his following sound principles. So while it was not a lightning pace, it was a sound one, and at lunch, Turner was 43 in a score of 97 for two. Ron Headley had gone at 62, bowled by Phil Russell, Ormrod 13 runs later, caught at the wicket by Bob Taylor from the off-spinners of Edwin Smith. But there was a rollicking partnership with Jim Yardley to follow, the 50 coming in 42 minutes, the 100 in 111 minutes. Then Graveney took over in this glittering display from an old master. The 50 partnership with Turner arrived in a mere 29 minutes; they had 125 together in 26 overs. Turner's own 50 took 135 minutes, the 100 a further 94 minutes and he batted 278 minutes all told, hitting 23 fours. There are two diverting side-issues to this innings. One was that the crowd rose to Yardley when he came out to bat at No 4; then sat down when they saw it was not Graveney! And the other is the typically delightful description by Alan Gibson, in *The Times* of this innings: 'His innings, as usual, followed the pattern of the silk-moth fighting its way out of the cocoon — the struggles are painful, but the end-product pretty, and the by-product valuable.'

14
140 for Worcestershire v Yorkshire, New Road, 15, 17 August 1970

Yorkshire 213 (D. E. V. Padgett 36, R. A. Hutton 34, P. J. Sharpe 30; N. Gifford 3/39, R. G. M. Carter 3/67, B. M. Brain 3/74) and 164/8 (J. D. Woodford 48; Gifford 6/43) drew with **Worcestershire** 432/8 decl (G. M. Turner 140, T. W. Graveney 100*, R. G. A. Headley 91).

First innings: st D. L. Bairstow b G. A. Cope 140

This was the equalling of the great Cyril Walters' record of 1933, but not Turner's most flowing or most authoratitive innings, and all told, it took him 375 minutes. But it was the last confirmation of judgement and faith that Worcestershire needed for its decision to sign on the Warwickshire unwanted of three years earlier. All else that Turner did just topped off this match, when he equalled the performance of a man who captained his county and his country, and another opening batsman.

Yet another Worcestershire opener deserves a mention here, too, for Ron Headley was out a mere nine runs short of what would have been his sixth century of the season. It was Headley who led the way early in the innings, and who had a shade more good fortune; Turner who had the greater patience and feeling for later in the innings. Headley, however, was the pace-setter, and at stumps after 25 overs, he had scored 34 of the 53, Turner just 15. By lunch, which came at 67 overs, Headley had gone, swishing at Geoff Cope and being caught at the wicket by David Bairstow, but Turner was 70 and with the air of a man who knew and insisted he should reach this century. There had been some flowing cover-drives, particularly, and one of the brightest features of the innings was the smart running between the wickets; a more doubtful feature was surviving a very confident lbw appeal when swinging at Cope. And after bringing up the innings 100 in the 42nd over, Turner went into a strangely passive phase against Brian Close's Yorkshire seam attack. In a period of more than half an hour, Turner scored from only one run-productive shot, a four which the square-leg fieldsman should really have stopped. But as often happened in Turner's century-making career, he would emerge from such inertia as he did in this, hitting Tony Nicholson, of brief England interest as an opening bowler, for three fours in an over, to go from 43 to 55, and to raise the 150 in the 57th over.

The 169-run partnership, the third of three figures for the first wicket between Turner and Headley, eventually took 208 minutes, and this was surely the springboard for a run assault. But the Yorkshire bowlers stuck very doggedly to their task; they must have, for Turner neglected few scoring opportunities — they were just rather intermittent, and in the first 10 overs after lunch, Turner and Alan Ormrod scored only 13 runs. When Worcestershire reached 200, in 255 minutes, Turner was then 82 from 80 overs; when it passed 300 — and he was out at 308 for four — in six hours and one minute, 108 overs had been bowled. But he still struck 18 fours, and if that first 50 had taken 192 minutes, the second, completed with a cut backward of square, came in only 80 minutes, with the comforting assurance of Tom Graveney at the other end, encouraging a releasing from the strictures of earlier.

After the criticism from the previous match of a delayed declaration, it was interesting to note that Graveney chose to take the Worcestershire innings into the third day and, spread over all three days of the game, it lasted a total of eight and three-quarter hours, easily the longest and also the biggest Worcestershire innings of the season. But bat too long or not, Yorkshire only just saved the match, the ninth wicket pair having to survive the final 12 overs, or half an hour.

15

133* for Worcestershire v Warwickshire, New Road, 2, 3 September 1970

Warwickshire 163 (D. L. Amiss 47; R. G. M. Carter 4/60) and 322/4 decl (R. B. Kanhai 132*, J. A. Jameson 59, R. N. Abberley 56, M. J. K. Smith 42) drew with **Worcestershire** 253/2 decl (G. M. Turner 133*, J. A. Ormrod 60, T. W. Graveney 43*) and 179/5 (R. G. A. Headley 70, Turner 36; L. R. Gibbs 3/58).

First innings: not out 133
Second innings: c D. J. Brown b K. Ibadulla 36

The winning of the toss was critical to Turner's receiving a final chance to claim C. F. Walters's record as his own, a record that should really have been tucked safely under his belt by then. After going to nine centuries against Yorkshire, Turner still had four matches left in the season, and in the first of them, against Lancashire, he scored 73 and 99 — more on that later. Then there was a double failure (9 and 18) against Essex; success (31 and 64) against Surrey but no century still.

New Road provided a rain-freshened pitch for Tom Graveney's final championship match, and Warwickshire capitulated in three hours, Turner playing his part by bowling one of his rare and brief spells (two overs, one maiden, six runs) and having Billy Ibadulla lbw. Ron Headley was out early, but Turner and Alan Ormrod survived the day and as the pitch dried out to what some would call a typical Worcester featherbed, so they prospered. They scored 126 together, before Ormrod was out for 60, then Graveney gave his adopted home crowd a fine farewell, though as the junior partner, in his unbeaten 43 towards a third wicket stand of 124. Turner reached his century in 236 minutes and in the second innings chimed in with 36, and an opening partnership of 85 with Headley, before being caught by David Brown. Off whom? Off Ibadulla.

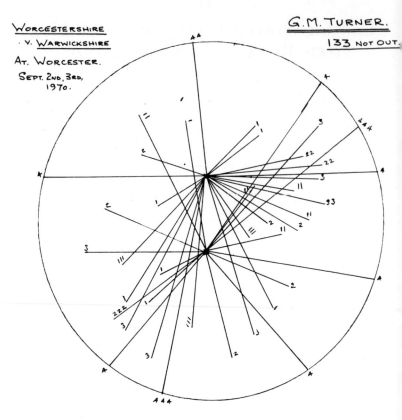

WORCESTERSHIRE
· v. WARWICKSHIRE

At. WORCESTER.
SEPT. 2ND, 3RD, 1970.

G.M. TURNER.
133 NOT OUT.

10TH CENTURY OF THE SEASON   (WORCESTERSHIRE RECORD.)

133 RUNS IN 276 MINS. FROM 244 BALLS.

1ST DAY. 19 NO. IN 46 MINS (36 BALLS)
2ND DAY. 50 RUNS IN 139 MINS. (96 BALLS)
        100 " " 236 " (201 ")

14 FOURS
8 THREE'S.
13 TWO'S.
27 SINGLES.

50 PARTNERSHIP WITH J.A. ORMROD IN 93 MINS.
50   "   " T.W. GRAVENEY " 35 "
100   "   " T.W. GRAVENEY " 80 "

RUNS SCORED OFF WARWICKSHIRE BOWLING.

D.J. BROWN. 41 BALLS - 22 RUNS.   L.R. GIBBS. 80 BALLS - 30 RUNS.
N.M. McVICKER. 35 "   25 "   W.N. TIDY. 24 "   24 "
K. IBADULLA. 44 "   18 "   J.A. JAMESON. 20 "   14 "

By courtesy of Mr. P. Pike, the Warwickshire scorer.

58

It was ironical I should get the record against Warwickshire,
the county I was meant to play for, particularly with Ibadul-
la's record against me, one way and another, in this match.
In fact, after getting him out in the first innings, I think I've
only bowled once more in county cricket. But, you know, I
should have had the century against Lancashire, even after
getting out for 73 in the first innings. We were close to a
declaration in the second innings, and I was conscious we
should get it quickly. Then Jackie Bond, the Lancs captain,
put in an extra slip and left only one off-side fieldsman in
front of the wicket — Clive Lloyd! He was at squarish cover;
I pushed it straight of him, towards mid-off; he came in on it,
and hit the umpire's, the non-striker's, end from square on
with only one stump to hit. He hit it that square, in fact, that
all the stumps hit each other, it was so square on. I wasn't
even close enough to bother grounding my bat. Mind you, it
seemed to bother other people more than me, because I was
confident I still had time enough to achieve it. But I had to
sweat a bit when I missed out Essex and Surrey but, 12 years
on, maybe there was nothing to worry about: I'd always have
to back my chances against Warwickshire! Not that they
necessarily have weak attacks, and there was nothing wrong
with this one. David Brown, a test player, and Norman
McVicker, a very handy seamer, opened, and they were fol-
lowed by Ibadulla, with his medium/off-break mixture, the
great Lance Gibbs, Warwick Tidy and a bit of John Jame-
son.

On the first evening, a sunny finale to the day, Turner scored
19 of Worcestershire's 24 for one, but had not had a happy
time against the sharp and accurate in-swing of Brown and
McVicker. They were the less controlled on the new morning, though they still posed some problems with deliveries
lifting awkwardly from a length: the thighs and the close
vicinity of the ears had the ball as near neighbours on many
occasions. There were, in fact, only 23 runs in the first
three-quarters of an hour, when McVicker mostly held sway;
it was mostly the all-spin of Gibbs, from the off, and Tidy,
from the leg, after lunch.

But Turner, again, was in one of these century-establishing innings. His 50 came in 139 minutes, his 100 in 236 minutes, and another 40 minutes for his last 33 runs. He hit 14 fours, and if the first 50 of the 127-run partnership with Ormrod took 93 minutes, the second was in only 51 minutes. The first 50 with Graveney, perhaps predictably, took just 35 minutes; their 124 came in 90 minutes.

A memorable photograph in many ways. Turner is on the way to his tenth century of the 1970 season, a Worcestershire record. The fieldsman is Billy Ibadulla, the man who enticed Turner to England to play for his county, Warwickshire. The cricketing fates took Turner down the road to Worcester and, as it happened, century upon century against Warwickshire.

16
179 for Worcestershire v Pakistan, New Road, 1 May 1971

Worcestershire 305/5 decl (G. M. Turner 179, J. A. Ormrod 44, B. L. D'Oliveira 40; Asif Masood 3/54) and 251/2 decl (R. G. A. Headley 146*, Turner 76) drew with **Pakistan** 241 (Zaheer Abbas 110, Sadiq Mohammed 59; D. N. F. Slade 3/54) and 256/6 (Aftab Gul 80, Asif Iqbal 63*, Sadiq 32).

First innings: c Aftab b Intikhab Alam 179
Second innings: b Masood 76

It seems faintly unbelievable now that Turner should have gone eight months without scoring a century, especially as he fitted a full New Zealand season into that, and scored 517 runs at more than 34 an innings. Miracles were expected of him, says Turner, after his 10 centuries in England, but there was a natural mental reaction. Two comments were passed to me, of Turner, in the 1970-71 New Zealand season. Brian O'Brien, then editor of *Sports Digest*, offered the view — in October, mind, before Turner was even back from England — that he would believe Turner was a reasonable player if he scored some runs in New Zealand. No matter that his batting had just dominated the toughest competition in world cricket. Basil D'Oliveira saw the problem when he arrived with Ray Illingworth's MCC team, however. 'What's the matter with Glenn, man,' and it wasn't a question. 'He's absolutely stuffed.' Not all of it was directly related to the 10 centuries reaction thing, though.

A lot of people in Dunedin subscribed to a membership or appeal thing to bring me back; they paid a dollar a head. So when I wasn't doing too well, or even when I had scored a few, badly, they would come up to me in a pub and say, 'What's the story? I paid a buck for you.' Another thing was that I had an awful job, nothing like what had been promised me.

So it was, I suppose you could say, a blessed relief to get back into a solely cricketing atmosphere and life. I think I should point out that professionalism was not easily understood or accepted in New Zealand at the time; I suppose I wasn't easily accepted or understood, either, being New Zealand's only professional cricketer.

What a balmy, if breezy, May Day this was, the cathedral calm only interrupted — and then outside the gates; the cricket was not disturbed — by a day-long demonstration by hordes of placard-bearing East Pakistanis, the peoples who would now be called Bangladeshans. The batting was not as glorious, for a start, with Ron Headley no doubt fully cognisant of the fact that it was Sarfraz Nawaz who had broken his left arm less than three months earlier, during a Commonwealth XI tour match in Karachi. Turner, for his part, was undoubtedly desirous of a big and bright innings after his difficult summer of discontent in the southern hemisphere. So when Headley was bowled by the well-built newcomer, Asif Masood, at 12, and his own score at 5, as many as nine overs had been bowled. And it was 50 minutes into the innings before Turner cover-drove the first four.

But then, he and Alan Ormrod started the scoreboard ticking over, Turner producing some sturdy drives. They saw the openers off, and those two great performers for Pakistani cricket, Intikhab Alam (captaining this team) and Asif Aqbal, fared no better; at 80, Intikhab brought the openers back, and they had no joy, either. At lunch, two hours, Worcestershire had scored 89; more to the point, Turner and Ormrod had 77 in 75 minutes. Soon after lunch, too, the 100 came in the 35th over, a most respectable rate after the dogged start, and Turner became the new aggressor. He was 37 to Ormrod's 43 at lunch, but while Ormrod was scoring only a single, Turner slipped past him to a splendid 50 — with five fours — in 138 minutes. Moments later, Ormrod fell to a magnificent gully catch by Saeed Ahmed, from a full-blooded cut off Masood; the stand had been worth 94 in 101 minutes.

Turner, by then, was in full gear, however, as boundary

followed boundary, most of them through the covers. There were five in his first 50; another six of them took him into the eighties. If the earlier part of the innings had been faultless, the second and third scenes were incredible. His second 50 took only 57 minutes, the third 45 minutes, and Basil D'Oliveira, no slug himself, was left with a watching brief. Where the Turner-Ormrod 50 partnership took 55 minutes, the Turner-D'Oliveira 50 came in 35 minutes, the 100 in 62 minutes! And Turner had scored 75 of them. He hit 12 fours in his century, which came in a total of 172, and delighted the crowd of 2000, which had doubled as people scurried along to New Road to see this glorious exhibition, by on-driving Intikhab for six. D'Oliveira himself was whacking Intikhab and Saeed around, but Turner stole the afternoon matinee. Compare the figures: he had 37 of the 89, from 31 overs to lunch; in the session to tea, 35 overs more, Turner scored 113 of Worcestershire's 157. D'Oliveira was out immediately after tea, at 246, and after adding 35 with Jim Yardley (16), and 21 with Doug Slade, Turner was out at 302 for five, those runs coming in 313 minutes, with Turner striking 24 fours and one six, and giving only one chance. The declaration came moments later; the plethora of runs continued for the three days; and note the newcomer in the Pakistani side who had a first innings century. When Glenn Turner became cricket's nineteenth man to score the Century of Centuries, it was Zaheer Abbas who was busily establishing himself as the twentieth.

17

101 for Worcestershire v Essex, New Road, 17 July 1971

Worcestershire 364/7 decl (G. M. Turner 101, B. L. D'Oliveira 97, R. G. A. Headley 78, T. J. Yardley 31) and 214/7 decl (J. A. Ormrod 70, Yardley 44*, Turner 37, D'Oliveira 30; R. E. East 4/32) drew with **Essex** 321 (B. C. Francis 115, G. J. Saville 65, R. N. S. Hobbs 36, K. D. Boyce 32; R. G. M. Carter 6/110) and 183/7 (K. W. R. Fletcher 44, Saville 41; D'Oliveira 4/77).

First innings: c B. Ward b Hobbs 101
Second innings: c Saville b East 37

Turner had started 1971 as though he was to outshadow even 1970, but the fates conspired to make this much less of a season to remember.

I then seemed to be entirely free of injuries, and the most bothersome of them came at a most inappropriate time. With Giffy and Basil D'Oliveira on test duty, I was appointed captain for the first time, in mid-June, for a county championship match. It was against Derbyshire, at Queen's Park, and I even won the toss. Then as I was loosening up in the dressing room before batting, I somehow ricked by back. That may have cost me more in the matter of runs and centuries than I care to think, because after four or five mediocre matches, I had made Worcestershire's first ton in a Gillette Cup match, against Lancashire. Sure, we lost, and I had to graft a bit, even to the stage of going from 79 to 100 in singles. But I felt I was getting back into the right groove, then this back came along.

So Turner could not bat against Derbyshire, and while he did so in the 50 minutes possible before lunch in the next game, against Surrey at Guildford, it was for a painful four runs which persuaded him to retire at the break. That cost

Turner two games, but it was to become oddly typical of him that he returned from an enforced break with immediate results: 90 not out against Warwickshire (who else!) and 74 off the Notts bowlers. Then came Essex, on a firm, fast pitch and in gorgeous weather: a setting to cure all aches and pains.

The batting was a tonic, too, though a fitful one from Ron Headley. He started in scorching style, with 18 from the first nine balls, but after racing to 35 in eight overs, called for a new bat. It was the next over before Turner both hit his first boundary, and reached double figures; and the team's 50 arrived in 10 overs. But then Headley went off the boil — and asked for a third bat! — and Turner became dominant.

He overtook Headley in the forties, and went to a flawless 50, out of 97, in 102 minutes with five fours. The milestone was the signal for Turner's first false shot: a thick-edged attempted off-drive flew to slip and was grounded by Graham Saville. Then another Turner came into the act as a principal: Stuart Turner's first 11 overs cost only 14 runs, and after that hectic start, the 100 partnership ended up taking 31 overs, or 105 minutes. Then it was the turn of the heavy battery of Essex spinners, but they made little impression on Turner and Headley as they steadily, surely, built Worcestershire's highest opening stand of the summer. From 40 overs, it was 129 at lunch, Headley 61 and Turner 62; it went on till 3 pm and 162 in 170 minutes before Headley fell. The stop-start nature of the innings continued: Peter Stimpson hit a boundary from his second ball, but took 40 minutes to reach double figures; Turner took 12 singles and a solitary two to go from 80 to 92, but he had 10 fours in his century, which took 213 minutes. At 204, all sorts of funny things happened: Stimpson was caught at cover from Ray East; the next over from Robin Hobbs, Turner, after 225 minutes, was caught at mid-on, driving; and Ormrod was bowled by his third ball. But Basil D'Oliveira sorted things out in an astonishing solo chase for batting bonus points. He reached his 50 in 35 minutes, going from 16 to 50 in nine balls, and to 97 in only 74 minutes.

There was, sadly, not the same urgency about the rest of

the match. Ormrod battled his way out of a miserable trot and worked his way to what turned out to be his highest score of the county season; Turner batted 150 minutes for his 37. The veil can be quietly drawn across those second and third days.

18
101* for Otago v Wellington, Basin Reserve, Wellington, 9 January 1972

Otago 195/6 decl (G. M. Turner 47, W. L. Blair 44, J. C. Alabaster 33*; B. R. Taylor 3/37) and 170/2 decl (Turner 101*, Blair 50) drew with **Wellington** 103/9 decl (M. G. Webb 7/49).

First innings: c and b G. T. McConnell 47
Second innings: not out 101

Turner quite freely acknowledges that this was one of the least memorable and least important of his centuries, a score which just happened to come along when a match severely interrupted by rain was stumbling towards it conclusion. With the whole of the first day lost because of rain, and on a pitch which made free scoring difficult, Turner and Wayne Blair, 47 and 44 respectively, had another of their sound starts, and Jack Alabaster chimed in with 33 not out. Murray Webb, who had such a violent but brief first-class career, swept Wellington aside, but only three and a half hours remained. Turner and Blair provided some pleasant entertainment, reaching their first 50 together in 68 minutes, the second 50 in only 32 minutes, and after 106 minutes, Blair was out at 112. A little of the impetus was then lost, Turner simply soldiering on for the practice and for the century, and rather unusually, his second half-century took 107 minutes, where the first had taken 101.

Gren Alabaster took a little bit of media flak from this game for batting out the day, which after all, was only about three and a half hours. But it was a no-win situation, the rain had seen to that. I suppose two county captains would have declared a little earlier in the first innings, but first innings wins still mattered in Plunket Shield cricket at this time. No, the game was just a victim of cirumstance.

That did not stop those of the restive crowd who remained for the last rites endulging in some slow hand-clapping. They increased its speed at the quality of some of the Turner shots, especially the drives, and it was just a pity they could not have appreciated the innings rather more in a different situation and setting.

19

202 for New Zealand v President of West Indian Board of Control's XI, Jarrett Park, Montego Bay, Jamaica, 11, 12 February 1972

New Zealand 486/4 decl (G. M. Turner 202, G. T. Dowling 124, T. W. Jarvis 51, M. G. Burgess 51, B. R. Taylor 47*) and 101/0 (Burgess 51*, B. E. Congdon 39*) drew with **President's XI** 364 (I. Shillingford 124, L. Baichan 96, A. I. Kallicharan 51, S. Morgan 32, R. de Souza 32; H. J. Howarth 4/102).

First innings: c de Souza b Morgan 202
Second innings: did not bat

Turner's first double-century was a classic example of how a correct technique and a modest attack could between them lead to semi-permanent occupancy of the crease. But more importantly, this was only the second match of New Zealand's first tour of the West Indies, and Turner had batted very badly in the first, on the other side of the island, against Jamaica. So this was a case of batting into form, and he and Dowling made the most of the generous conditions. They batted all the first day for 226 (Dowling 104, Turner 115), and there were some interesting statistics. They were 52 (Dowling 32, Turner 14) at lunch, after two hours, but in the 105 minutes between lunch and tea, they scored 109 (Dowling 80, Turner 75). Then, in the final 105 minutes, they scored only 65. Dowling was clearly the early pace-setter — his half-century in 150 minutes was an hour quicker than Turner's — but Turner's century in 316 minutes came only 14 minutes after Dowling. The next morning, they added another 42 in 48 minutes, and the opening partnership of 268 was 21 better than New Zealand's previous best by Bert Sutcliffe and Verdun Scott on the 1949 tour of England.

By lunch, Turner had scored 159 in 450 minutes, and when

he was out just before tea, having batted just three minutes off nine hours, he and Terry Jarvis had added 117 in 157 minutes. Turner's 202 included a five and 20 fours and was his longest innings to that point, 12 minutes longer then he batted in scoring his second century, for Otago against Wellington at New Year, 1969.

After my dreadful batting at Sabina Park, when I could not even hit half-volleys, I needed a long innings and this was the pitch to play it, it was that good. But it was a dreadful struggle in another way, for I was far from acclimatised to the heat and I was sometimes that stuffed, I just had to lean on my bat and defend to get my breath back. That explains that slow last session when Tails commented that the vultures were circling! I don't think I would have been very tasty bait at that stage. But it was runs under the belt, a good sight of the ball, and with so many of our batsmen getting runs — as well as those with centuries and half-centuries. Tails got 47 not out in the first innings and Bevan Congdon 39 not out in the second — a good curtain-raiser with the first test a few days away.

Turner was eventually caught at slip by the Trinidadian, Robert de Souza, from a Guyanan seamer, Stuart Morgan.

20
223* for New Zealand v West Indies, Sabina Park, Kingston, 17 - 19 February 1972

West Indies 508/4 decl (L. G. Rowe 214, R. C. Fredericks 163, M. C. Carew 43, C. A. Davis 31) and 218/3 decl (Rowe 100*, Davis 41, Fredericks 33) drew with **New Zealand** 386 (G. M. Turner 223*, K. J. Wadsworth 78; G. C. Shillingford 3/63, U. G. Dowe 3/75) and 236/6 (M. G. Burgess 101, Wadsworth 36*, D. A. J. Holford 4/55).

First innings: not out 223
Second innings: b Holford 21

Unquestionably, this was one of Turner's best and most valuable innings; he saved New Zealand from what could otherwise have been a humiliating defeat. The West Indies, with Lawrence Rowe making an astonishing test debut on his home ground, had butchered the New Zealand attack of Webb, Cunis, Howarth, Alabaster and Congdon: note, no Bruce Taylor, who was to finish with a record series tally of wickets for a New Zealander. The West Indies scored their 508 runs from 153 overs in only 560 minutes, and in 100 minutes to stumps on the second day, New Zealand lost three wickets scoring 49 runs, Turner 20 of them. And at lunch the next day, it was 128 for five (the fifth wicket had fallen at 108), Turner 64 and Ken Wadsworth five. And Turner had been badly dropped, too, by 'Joey' Carew, at extra cover, off Lance Gibbs. But this was Turner's only chance and thereafter he batted magnificently. With New Zealand needing 201 runs from the final five wickets just to avoid the follow-on, Turner took complete charge and was continually on the lookout for runs. Wadsworth had to play an innings much out of character but Turner took as much of the bowling as he could. In their record sixth wicket partnership of 220 — the previous best for New Zealand overseas was 58 years

71

before, by Dan Reese and L. G. Taylor — Gary Sobers gave surprisingly little bowling to his cousin, David Holford, the leg-spinner causing the most problems of any bowler except, perhaps, the low-slung quick deliveries of Uton Dowe.

New Zealand had really had a disastrous start: Dowling out for 4 at 4, Jarvis for 7 at 25, Burgess for 15 at 48, Congdon for 11 at 75, Hastings getting 16 when out at 108. Small wonder that Turner's 50 took a painstaking 204 minutes. But his eagerness for runs, and the ease with which Sobers allowed singles at the end of an over, had Turner reaching his century in 320 minutes, his 150 in 389 minutes — thus 69 minutes for that third 50 — his 200 in 523 minutes, that the period in which New Zealand lost its next four wickets. Wadsworth, a sturdy partner indeed, took 12 minutes short of four hours for his 50, another hour to go to 78, yet he hit nine fours. Together, they batted two sessions, and more, on the third day, and half the pre-lunch session on the fourth day, and while Bob Cunis was out quickly, Turner found another determined partner in Hedley Howarth.

Dowe had this nasty little bouncer which, rather than ballooning at you, tended to skid through at about throat-height. Nice stuff, and he didn't seem to care that Hedley was a tail-end batsman; going in at No 9 on this occasion must have been the highest he ever batted for New Zealand, night-watchman duty apart. I had a chat to Hedley between overs and offered to take Dowe while he went up the other end and looked after any one of the other eight bowlers Sobers used; it really was that easy to command the strike. But Hedley told me not to bother; the gist of what he said was that the worst that could happen to him would be that he would get hit again, and he'd already been hit twice! It was pretty gutsy stuff, just telling me to go on playing my normal game, and not to worry about him.

Turner's and New Zealand's innings eventually came to an end after 572 minutes — easily his longest innings — when Webb was out for a duck, but only after the final wicket added 22. Rowe's second century set New Zealand to score 341 in 310 minutes, but after Dowling (23) and Turner (21)

were both out by 51, it required a century from Burgess and
more defiance from Wadsworth to save the match. But it had
really been saved by Turner on the second, third and fourth
days, when he had all the West Indies team, save Rowe, and
the wicket-keeper, Michael Findlay, bowl at him. The
others, in no particular order, were Dowe, Sobers, Carew,
Davis, Gibbs, Holford, Fredericks, Grayson Shillingford
and Foster.

21

259 for New Zealand v Guyana, Bourda Oval, Georgetown, 1 - 3 April 1972

Guyana 493/4 decl (A. I. Kallicharan 154, C. H. Lloyd 133, R. C. Fredericks 100*) and 202/5 (Lloyd 104*, Kallicharan 51) drew with **New Zealand** 488 (G. M. Turner 259, B. E. Congdon 103, B. F. Hastings 37; R. C. Collymore 6/115).

First innings: c M. Pydanna b Collymore 259

Turner was well and truly in the groove for batting for ever. For the third time in the West Indies, he exceeded his longest innings, this time batting three minutes over 10 hours on the cricket-killing pitch at the Bourda Oval. There was hardly a pitch in the world easier for staying in to the batsman prepared to play straight; nor was there one quite so unyielding of ready runs, so slowly did it play. Guyana had played an innings of strange contrast, reaching 59 for one in the first two hours, but declaring for 493 after just 482 minutes. Terry Jarvis was bowled second ball, but for the rest of the second day, Guyana knew no success as Turner and Congdon carefully and quietly kept the score ticking over. In 12 minutes short of three hours to stumps, they scored 139 together, Congdon 87 of them and Turner 51, but Congdon was out early the next day for 103 in 205 minutes. It was 171 for two when Brian Hastings joined Turner; 300 for three when he was out for only 37, so increasingly dominant did Turner become. He went from 62 to 147 in that partnership, which lasted 146 minutes, before there was another slump, to 373 for six. But Wadsworth was prepared to play Sancho Panza again, and in the seventh wicket partnership of a neat 100, in 140 minutes, he scored 25 while Turner was getting another 68. Turner, out at 473, caught at the wicket by M. Pydanna from the off-spinner R. C. Collymore, batted 603 minutes and the innings was over 23 minutes later. He hit 33 fours, and after he had reached his first 50 in 156 minutes, there was a great evenness about the rest: the second in 107 minutes, the third in 110, the fourth in 110, too; while he batted 123 minutes for his final 59.

22
259 for New Zealand v West Indies, Bourda Oval, 7 - 9 April 1972

West Indies 365/7 decl (A. I. Kallicharan 100*, G. A. Green-idge 50, C. H. Lloyd 43, R. C. Fredericks 41, L. G. Rowe 31; B. R. Taylor 3/105) and 86/0 (Fredericks 42*, Greenidge 35*) rew with **New Zealand** 543/3 decl (G. M. Turner 259, T. W. Jarvis 182, B. E. Congdon 61*).

First innings: lbw b A. B. Howard 259

If the tour had gone on much longer, Turner could have been batting for weeks at a time. For the fourth time in under two months, he exceeded his previous longest innings, this time batting 704 minutes in scoring his second 259 on the Bourda Oval pitch. Rain cut severely into the first two days and with the West Indies not declaring until early on the third day, clearly there was not going to be a result. So Turner and Jarvis took the opportunity, on another easy pitch, to put together test cricket's second-best opening partnership of 387, bettered only by the 413 of India's Mankad and Roy against New Zealand at Madras 16 years earlier. So far as the bare figures are concerned, they reached 50 in the 103 minutes, the 100 in 166 minutes, four minutes after Turner reached his own 50. Jarvis's personal 50 took 181 minutes, but the third 50 of the partnership was slower than the second, 76 minutes, or a total of four hours and two minutes for the 150. At stumps, the pair had scored 163, Turner 87 of them, Jarvis 71. In the pre-lunch period next day, they scored another 83 — which made the score 246 for none! — and Turner had reached his century in 321 minutes, Jarvis, always trailing that shade, in 363 minutes. Another 99 runs came between lunch and tea — this is . . . um . . . the fourth day by now — or 345 for none, and both had passed their 150s, Turner in 428 minutes, Jarvis 58 minutes longer. And so it went on until, after a neat nine hours, Jarvis was out, caught by Gordon Greenidge from the bowling of David Holford, for 182, a 5 and 19 fours among it. But on and on went Turner, now with Congdon as a partner, and together they scored 95 in 159 minutes. Then, at 482 for two, Turner was lbw to the new off-spinner, A. B. Howard. He had hit 22 fours. Mark Burgess was out quickly but that was the only joy for the West Indies, with Congdon and Brian Hastings adding an unbeaten 47 for the fourth wicket. Mere crumbs they seemed, after the earlier riches.

It's not easy to forget these two innings in Guyana, easier because they were precisely the same scores, and I suppose there was statistical satisfaction in that big partnership. Although that was my highest test score, there was not the significance of, say, the first test double-century when that perhaps meant more to do with winning and losing — or drawing — the match than this one ever could have. It was a much more significant match for Terry Jarvis, because I don't think he had many more tests, and this was both his first test century and easily his best first-class score. Jarv really worked hard for that one. It's odd the funny little things you remember from a glut of runs like that. I remember best when I reached 200 and one of the spectators made the traditional jog out on to the field. But instead of bringing out a few dollars to stuff in my pocket, usually the treatment for a local player or if you were a lucky visitor, he brought out a string of abuse. 'You no good bat, you no good bat, man' was all he could shout at me, as he stamped on his white floppy hat. I think it was another case of an unlucky punter, because the West Indian spectators, as has often been said and written, will bet on which cockroach will reach a certain point first, or who will field the ball next. There were two other enduring memories of that match, one faintly amusing, I suppose, one rather nasty. No West Indian test ground is short of what we would call a Scotsman's grand-stand, and hundreds watch for nothing from tree branches. Far too many tested the strength of one branch and all crashed to the ground, which drew the observation from

Keith Campbell that rather than any being injured, the greatest danger to their lives and limbs lay — in the shape of piranhas — in the moat which surrounded the ground. The other incident focused on Clive Lloyd, making a comeback to test cricket on his home ground after missing the early tests. Through one of those crazy, no-blame mix-ups, he was run out while batting with Charlie Davis, a splendid bloke, and almost before we knew it, police and spectators were involved in a vicious bottle fight. We — and poor Charlie — were in the middle of it all.

23

111 for Worcestershire v Cambridge University, Fenner's, Cambridge, 10, 11 May 1972

Cambridge University 243 (H. K. Steele 68, Majid Khan 67; N. Gifford 7/49, R. G. M. Carter 3/70) and 140 (Majid 70, P. Hodson 35; Gifford 7/27) drew with **Worcestershire** 241/5 decl (G. M. Turner 111, J. M. Parker 61; J. Spencer 4/25) and 91/5 (J. A. Ormrod 35*; Majid 3/33).

First innings: c C. R. V. Taylor b Spencer 111
Second innings: c P. H. Edmonds b Majid 4

There's no way I really feel like going straight back to England after that terribly tiring tour of the West Indies. I don't know how long I batted on the entire tour, but just a quick tally up of those four double-centuries comes out to nearly 41 hours — that's just four innings! The cricket was so, so demanding; it was all hard work, and really there were very few actual cricketing highlights, unless, I suppose, you count my batting at No 11 for New Zealand for the first and only time — that was because I had an injured knee; I got 8 not out against Trinidad — and captaining New Zealand for the first time. It was against Barbados, after Graham Dowling had gone home, and I won the toss. But enough of that, I had to go straight to an English summer, and frankly, I was absolutely stuffed. I didn't want to play in the UK, and I said I was buggered if I was going to graft like I had in the West Indies. But here, I batted through the first innings of the season, for 88 not out against Somerset, a good innings by my standards, and my next innings was this one against Cambridge University. Mind you, it's not hard to score runs at Fenner's, but I'd decided after that Somerset innings that I was going to go for my shots more, get after the bowling — a sort of release, if you like, after what was often drudgery in the Windies. I was still prepared to work hard, harder than I expected, in fact, and I found myself in the groove. I proved to myself just in these first couple of innings that the answer to this tiredness, this lack of interest or drive, is not necessarily to have a complete break from the game in order to come back with renewed vigour. Many times in my career I've felt I've had enough, yet I come right, and feel enthusiastic again, for no real or apparent reason. It might have something to do with off-the-field life: good company, good life, good social atmosphere makes Jack a relaxed boy, and it reflects in his cricket. Or Glenn's anyway! But well as I batted this season — and I think I batted as well as I ever had — I was out pretty shockingly in this innings. John Spencer, Spud Spencer, one of their medium-pacers — the other, incidentally, was one H. K. Steele, a New Zealander, from Auckland — bowled me a terrible ball down legside. I went to whack it over square, and all I got was a fine nick, to be caught by the 'keeper, Chilton Taylor. It was a bit of a strangulation shot.

Much as Turner had an inclination to go for his shots, that had to wait some little time in this innings. He and John Parker, who was having his first season for Worcestershire, had a productive second wicket partnership of 165, but the prelude was quite incredibly laboured, especially against a University attack. In the half-hour at the end of the first day, Turner and Peter Stimpson scored only six — Turner none of them — and the first half-hour of the second morning only brought another 13 runs. Spencer was most responsible for the slow progress (Turner took 35 minutes to score), but when he had to be rested, things loosened up a little, though he had removed Stimpson. Worcestershire's 50 took 102 minutes, Parker's first hour brought him only 13 runs, but the partnership 50 was relatively quick at 70 minutes! And at lunch, 150 minutes on, Worcestershire was 82 for one and Turner 44.

The conditions were not encouraging: the morning sun was replaced by thick sombre clouds in the afternoon, and there was always a cold wind. But as the day grew gloomier, Turner's batting brightened. His 50 took 178 minutes — and he can point to precious few three-hour half-centuries — but his 100 only 235 minutes; just as the second 50 of the 165-run partnership with Parker took just 58 minutes. After 260 minutes' batting, Turner fell 10 minutes before tea for 111 — 'Nelson' to cricket people — and that took his aggregate off the University attack to 200 in five days; his earlier 89 had been scored in a Benson and Hedges League Cup game. Turner hit 12 fours, Parker just five in his three-hour innings, and both left at 196 when the second new ball was taken, two overs late at 87, and both fell to Spencer. The other bowlers were Phil Edmonds, later to bowl his left-arm spinners for Middlesex and England; Majid Khan, who had the remarkable figures of three for 33 from 33 overs of his unremarkable seamers; R. J. — Robert — Hadley, with the right initials and pronunciation but not quite the same pace; and M. P. Kendall.

24
156 for Worcestershire v Warwickshire, New Road, 12, 13 June 1972

Warwickshire 165 (A. I. Kallicharan 37; R. G. M. Carter 4/63, J. Cumbes 3/32, V. A. Holder 3/53) and 90/0 (J. W. Whitehouse 51*, J. A. Jameson 39*) drew with **Worcestershire** 375/3 decl (G. M. Turner 156, R. G. A. Headley 94, E. J. O. Hemsley 79*).

First innings: c D. J. Brown b L. R. Gibbs 156

Rain wiping out the first day fated this match to be a draw and the loss of a day did not, of course, help Ron Headley's Benefit season, for this was his Benefit match. There is not the same all-or-nothing financial importance to the Benefit these days however, so Headley was clearly determined on a century to make it memorable in some way. But it was the dash of Turner which made the match memorable.

It was one of the few times I'd outpaced Ronnie Headley to that point, though I was to do it more often later. He was grafting a bit — Benefit match and all that, he wanted to make a few — and if I had as well, I really could have gone on and on for, I think, a double-ton. But I got that sort of thing out of my system a couple of months before, so I had a go at Lance Gibbs, got away with it for a while, then holed out at deep mid-on.

On the rain-affected pitch, and in the overcast conditions of the second day, the Warwickshire batsmen fared badly as the Worcestershire attack found ready lift and swerve in the morning session. But as things dried out, Turner enchanted the crowd there to pay homage to Headley, crashing the bowling of David Brown, Steve Rouse, Norman McVicker, Billy Ibadulla — seamers all — and the great Gibbs. In the 105 minutes to stumps, he raced to 81 of the total of 117; Headley was only 23, from 27 overs delivered before the close.

Turner's 50 had taken 78 minutes; his next took a neat hour; the third 50 came in 55 minutes; his 156 took 217 minutes. Worcestershire was then 259, and that opening stand was just 50 runs short of the county opening record. Only twice were there checks to the Turner scoring rate: he went primly through the nineties, ensuring himself of the century, and lost the strike to the bludgeoning batting of Ted Hemsley at the very end. By then it didn't greatly matter, for Worcestershire was well on the way to an eventual nine batting points — seven was its old record — and 14 bonus points all told, equalling Warwickshire's own record.

The Warwickshire players were probably pleased to see the back of Turner — where they might not have begrudged poor Headley the Benefit century he so narrowly missed — but little were they to know what was to come. That blazing century was simply the preamble to the most systematic and consistent attack on one county by an opposition batsman in the county championship history.

25

122 for Worcestershire v Warwickshire, Edgbaston, 1 July 1972

Worcestershire 380/7 decl (G. M. Turner 122, E. J. O. Hemsley 61, T. J. Yardley 57*, B. L. D'Oliveira 52; N. M. McVicker 3/71, L. R. Gibbs 3/71) and 201/4 decl (Turner 128*) drew with **Warwickshire** 350/5 decl (D. L. Amiss 156*, A. I. Kallicharan 72, McVicker 42; R. G. M. Carter 3/102) and 72/1 (Amiss 34*).

First innings: b McVicker 122
Second innings: not out 128

Bob Willis was having his first championship game for Warwickshire since transferring from Surrey, and he could hardly have had a more auspicious introduction to the county. His first ball for Warwickshire was square-driven for four by Turner, and that set the pattern for a pronounced — if sometimes fortunate — mastery by batsman over bowler.

In those days, Willis used to tell Jimmy Cumbes — they'd played together at Surrey — that he couldn't bowl to me; I used to hammer him, and this was one of those examples, I suppose. I averaged about five an over from the quicks, a bit less off McVicker, and it really was a quick hundred with all those seamers bowling, and doing most of the bowling. I was 88 not out at 1.45, and I was certainly going to make sure of a hundred before lunch for the first time. But at Birmingham, they start at noon, and just when I was thinking of lunch with 100 under my belt, all of a sudden they started walking off the park.

Turner had reached his 50 in 63 minutes in an innings in which he gave both himself and the bowlers every chance! Even Willis, who was to suffer in the years to come, beat him twice in his opening over, and at 32, found an edge but the ball dropped short of the second slip. Norman McVicker, 10 runs later, induced a falsely timed straight drive but could not get his left hand to the shot; a further straight drive, however, was sweetly timed and gave Turner his fifth four, and 51. And just before lunch, Turner had another escape when the West Indian wicket-keeper, David Murray, dropped him in the first over by the West Indian off-spinner, Lance Gibbs.

Just after lunch there was another. Turner, aiming to drive, got his twelfth four all right — but over the head of Dennis Amiss at second slip, and Willis was the sufferer again. But does not such aggression deserve some rewards? For Turner had raced to his fastest century at that time, in just 128 minutes, with 12 fours and out of 142. All told, he batted 170 minutes, and when out at 179 for three — he and Ron Headley had an 81-run opening partnership — he had hit 14 fours.

26
128* for Worcestershire v Warwickshire, Edgbaston, 4 July 1972

Scoreboard as for Century No. 25.

There had been an astonishing preview to this innings: in the John Player League match on the same ground, Turner and Ron Headley had together scored 184 in an amazing 34 overs to equal the then-record for any wicket, held jointly by Mike Denness and Brian Luckhurst, of Kent, and Lancashire's Harry Pilling and Clive Lloyd. Headley was caught on the boundary for 82 to end the partnership; Turner was caught behind by Deryck Murray from Bob Willis, but only after he had hit 108 with seven fours and a big six (from Willis, of course) over long-on.

So I was in the right sort of nick for the rest of the county championship match, but the pitch was too good for a chance of a win, especially as Dennis Amiss was in such good form, opening for one of the first times in first-class cricket. And this innings was against very much a second-string attack: Brown, Rouse and Gibbs all had six overs, McVicker only five, and most of the bowling was done by John Whitehouse and Alvin Kallicharan. It was all a declaration job, and only of statistical interest, in that I scored four centuries in as many innings against Warwickshire, and three in four days.

In three innings against Warwickshire (including the Sunday match), Turner and Headley had scored 522 runs in partnership, but that was not extended, with Headley resting a slightly strained hamstring and Peter Stimpsom opening instead. He had gone at 14, however, and when Worcestershire had scored only 24 — including only one four, cover-driven by Turner from McVicker — from 11 overs, the part-timers were called in.

Instead of accelerating the scoring toward an early declaration, they had the opposite effect. Turner — only 28 out of 59 for two, in 80 minutes to lunch — had his problems timing Whitehouse's floating off-spinners, and Kallicharan was no less inexpensive with his leg-spinners. Strangely, when Turner did score, it was in batches of boundaries. He went from 28 to 44 with four of them, then reached his half-century in 112 minutes, in the course of which he and Alan Ormrod put on 51 in 45 minutes. But it certainly got Turner moving along, and there was far brighter stuff from him and Basil D'Oliveira. With Turner again scoring these 'batches' of boundaries — from 52 to 81 with seven of them interrupted only by a single — and reaching his century in 150 minutes, the pair reached their half-century partnership in 27 minutes, 64 all told — and D'Oliveira only 10 of them! Then there were 47 between Turner and Jim Yardley, as Turner went to 128 in three hours, with 21 fours, in those cool and overcast conditions. The pitch really meant it was a nothing sort of match — if Turner's statistics of 514 runs in four innings, average 171, could be called average — and Norman Gifford in the end set Warwickshire the slightly impossible task of 232 in 110 minutes. Small wonder that Mike Smith politely declined the 'challenge'.

27
170 for Worcestershire v Gloucestershire, Bristol, 12, 13 July 1972

Gloucestershire 228 (C. A. Milton 49, Sadiq Mohammed 47, A. S. Brown 43, M. J. Proctor 33; V. A. Holder 3/52) and 179 (R. D. V. Knight 97; J. A. Ormrod 5/27) beat **Worcestershire** 297/7 decl (G. M. Turner 170, D. E. R. Stewart 40, Ormrod 35; J. B. Mortimore 3/71) and 104 (Mortimore 3/47).

First innings: c R. Swetman b J. Davey 170
Second Innings: lbw b Brown 10

Though Turner and Worcestershire made relatively slow progress, it was quite understandable. A much-weakened attack without Gifford, D'Oliveira, Cumbes and Hemsley had done well to bowl out Gloucestershire in the first innings. Needing a substantial lead, Worcestershire eventually lost by nine runs in a second innings batting display which 'defied credibility', as the county's records put it. But it is the first innings under review.

This was not an untypical Bristol pitch, in that it was pretty placid; it's only when it's wet that it gets awkward. But the atmosphere was awkward: it was overcast and very humid, and of course the seamers had a ball in the heavy atmosphere, with Tony Brown particularly dangerous, though he didn't get any wickets. It was less suited to John Mortimore, who was always a pleasure to play against. There was always, can we say, dialogue exchanged, a bit of banter, and his attitude made the game a pleasure. I would encourage him to not put a man out for a start, and he would usually respond. Or if he didn't, he would usually put him only halfway, so I would accept the challenge. I did, and got away with it, a few times in this innings, but not all the time.

The Worcestershire innings was in the relatively parlous state of 24 for two, from 11 overs at the recommencement, after losing both Ron Headley and Peter Stimpson by the time the score had reached five. So Turner and Alan Ormrod had good reason for taking care, and the first 50 of their 87-run partnership took a slow 81 minutes. But Ormrod and Jim Yardley were both out by lunch, taken after 46 overs at 116 for four — Yardley's dismissal — with Turner 57. His 50 had taken 146 minutes, and soon after lunch, he went to 1000 runs in the season at 63. A profitable partnership with David — 'Jock' — Stewart was also set in progress, 94 all told for the fifth wicket, with the 50 milestone taking 72 minutes, and Turner reaching his century in 266 minutes.

At tea, Worcestershire was 221 for five and Turner 116, and at that stage, he had given only one chance, to slip at 78. There was a second, in the deep, at 150, but by then Turner had ensured Worcestershire of a sound first innings. He had found another willing partner in young Keith Wilkinson, only 17 not out was his contribution, but he held fast while Turner blazed away to such effect that his final 70 runs took a mere 107 minutes. They added 62 together in even time, and Turner went out to a total of 15 fours, the first of them all-run from a cover-drive off Jack Davey, the big left-arm seamer. He, Brown and Mortimore apart, the Gloucestershire bowlers were Mike Proctor, in the early days of a brilliant county career; the slow left-armer, Mike Bissex; and a few overs each of Sadiq's left-armers and Roger Knight's medium-pace.

28

154 for Worcestershire v Essex, Leyton, 9, 10 August 1972

Essex 275 (G. J. Saville 92, R. E. East 89*; V. A. Holder 5/93, N. Gifford 3/59) and 234/6 decl (K. R. Pont 75*, Saville 50, K. W. R. Fletcher 41) drew with **Worcestershire** 303/9 decl (G. M. Turner 154, J. M. Parker 91; K. D. Boyce 5/52, J. K. Lever 3/63) and 93/3 (Parker 39*).

First innings: c and b Boyce 154
Second innings: b Boyce 4

This was Turner's only match at Leyton, a small and not terribly attractive ground in a county dotted with small and attractive grounds, and not one used often by Essex. Nor was it a particularly auspicious occasion for the match always seemed doomed to a draw, especially as Worcestershire in the second innings seemed to be haunted by thoughts of the first innings. Then Worcestershire, having lost only Ron Headley (18), and 264 for one, lost the final nine wickets for 39 runs.

There seemed no real reason for that, unless it was a case of reaction after a long partnership. The Essex seamers and Ray East bowled pretty tightly, but it was a good pitch, and a century was always possible if one was prepared to work a bit. Hence, I grafted pretty solidly for a start, especially with Keith Boyce and John Lever getting a little bit of lift, and East not giving much away, then I feel I played pretty well as the innings went on.

Turner and Headley had two runs from one over at stumps on the first day, but found it difficult to get the scoring moving when they resumed: Headley was out in the eighteenth over with the score at 44. And after the 50 had arrived in 21 overs, East placed a clamp on the scoring again by starting with four successive maidens. Turner broke the spell with a couple of rather fortunate fours, and John Parker broke his own spell of boredom when he finally got off the mark after 40 minutes! It was all graft, and Worcestershire was 79 at lunch, from 35 overs, Turner 46 of them. Four overs later, after 132 minutes, he reached his 50 — a late cut, a shot he plays relatively rarely, from Boyce, and the Worcestershire 100 took 41 overs. But, as Turner had observed, he got after the attack rather more willingly from that point. His 100 took 210 minutes; he was 121 at tea (from 76 overs, 249 minutes); and when he was out at 264 for two, he had batted 312 minutes and struck 16 fours.

Parker scored his highest county championship score to that point, he and Turner reaching 50 together in 62 minutes, 100 in 119 minutes, and 150 in 169. All told, they added 220 in 225 minutes, from 71 overs, and then the rot set in. Boyce had his impressive figures from 25 overs, while Lever had 21 overs, Stuart Turner 19 in taking one for 46, and East 20 overs for 57 runs. The only relief came in the form of Robin Hobbs, his 14 overs costing 60 runs, mainly to a Glenn Turner in full flight, and often quite brilliant.

29

107 for Worcestershire v Nottinghamshire, Trent Bridge, 25 August 1972

Nottinghamshire 282 (R. A. White 59, M. J. Harris 54, M. J. Smedley 48, D. W. Randall 46; V. A. Holder 6/60) and 308/2 decl (Harris 174*, S. B. Hassan 75, Smedley 45*) lost to **Worcestershire** 320/5 decl (J. M. Parker 118, P. J. Stimpson 66, G. M. Turner 53, J. A. Ormrod 31) and 271/6 (Turner 107, Ormrod 46, Parker 42; M. N. S. Taylor 4/74).

First innings: c Harris b Taylor 53
Second innings: b Taylor 107

A fine and sunny day, and a fair and true pitch combined to give Worcestershire a splendid conclusion to a moderately successful season, and Turner his twelfth century of 1972. It was a match for the batsmen, as the scoreboard well indicates, though Vanburn Holder performed wonders in restricting Notts so when they threatened to run riot, but 'Patsy' Harris and Basharat Hassan nonetheless played some powerful innings. Worcestershire was set the daunting task of 271 in three hours, and Turner was actually outscored by John Parker — the latter having scored his maiden county championship century in the first innings — in the opening stand of 70. Then came Peter Stimpson, he and Turner reaching their 50 partnership in 34 minutes, 57 all told, and Turner in that time reaching his own 50 in 85 minutes. After Stimpson had gone at 127 for a valuable 21, there was no let-up, even the often-sober Alan Ormrod pushing the scoring rate along at a merry rate. Their 50 partnership was in only 30 minutes, but just after Ormrod had gone after he and Turner had added 96, and placed their team on the brink of victory, Turner went too. His own century took 153 minutes, but with the loss of Ormrod and the strike, he took a further 21 minutes over his last seven runs. But his combination of bold and booming stroke-making — eight fours and a six — and swiftly taken ones and twos, acted as the springboard for victory.

When the final 20 overs commenced, Worcestershire was 175 for two, and although there were some alarums and excursions around the time of his departure, Worcestershire kept boldly after the victory. At Turner's departure, 41 were still needed in six overs, and that slipped away a little to 19 being needed from the final two overs. No faint-heart, Norman Gifford saw his team there.

30
132 for Otago v Auckland, Eden Park, Auckland, 2, 3 January 1973

Otago 276 (B. E. Congdon 95, W. L. Blair 67, G. M. Turner 34; H. J. Howarth 5/78) and 340 (Turner 132, Blair 75, R. W. Anderson 63; Howarth 5/123) lost to **Auckland** 387/8 decl (R. E. Redmond 131, G. E. Vivian 104, R. A. Dykes 34*, T. W. Jarvis 30; G. A. Powell 3/62) and 230/3 (Jarvis 79, R. M. Harris 44, R. W. Morgan 42, Redmond 30*).

First innings: b R. E. Sutton 34
Second innings: c H. J. Howarth b R. S. Cunis 132

Though Turner was not the designated captain of Otago for this match, he assumed the job for the final session — with Gren Alabaster injured — when Auckland needed 230 to win. Nor was it a victory that Auckland deserved to achieve for, having won a first innings lead, it batted on far too long for there to be much in the game. Alabaster had responded by batting longer than he really should have in the second innings.

But enter the 'new' captain — though he had already led Worcestershire, in the absence of Gifford and D'Oliveira — and a new attitude.

We needed points more badly than we needed another boring draw, simply to give us a better chance in the Plunket Shield competition. In other words, I was not looking at the match in isolation; I was looking at it in the broad sense of a season's performance, the sort of thing that would be done in England. Maybe it was a misconception on my part to try and encourage English beliefs and/or attitudes in the New Zealand scene, then anyway. Our guys weren't playing enough cricket to be able to readily accept a defeat, particularly as it was one I quite easily could have avoided. It turned out it was more criminal on my part to lose trying to win than to draw not trying to win.

Although trailing by 111 runs (a mystic figure, that 111, to cricketers), Turner and his stalwart supports, Wayne Blair and Robert Anderson, removed any chance of Otago losing, at least losing under ordinary circumstances! In the last hour of the second day, Turner and Blair scored 72 together, Turner 49 of them and many scored by hitting Bob Sutton, that very handy fast-medium left-armer, 'over the top'. The next morning, the opening stand was taken to 155 in 167 minutes, then Turner and Anderson added another 101 for the second wicket in 75 minutes, before Turner was out at 256, scored in two minutes over four hours. He hit 17 fours, before being caught by Hedley Howarth, but not in the gully.

I was going really well, hitting Suction (Bob Sutton) in the air, certainly, but never really dangerously, when I tried to drop-kick Bob Cunis. But it was a typical Eden Parker, and the ball didn't bounce a bit; I got it on the toe of the bat and spooned it up to square-leg. I was really pissed off, as I didn't deserve to get out.

Auckland relied on its virtual international attack of Cunis, Sutton, and the Howarth brothers — Geoff Howarth then quite a regular bowler of off-breaks — and its strong early batting line-up. Partly helped by Otago bowlers who did not bowl to their fields, the runs were made in ease before a crowd of 8000.

31

131 for Otago v Wellington, Carisbrook, 9, 10 January 1973

Wellington 322/6 decl (B. R. Taylor 173, J. V. Coney 94; B. Andrews 3/110) and 2/0 drew with **Otago** 338/5 decl (B. E. Congdon 173*, G. M. Turner 131; A. R. Hounsell 4/76).

First innings: c and b Hounsell 131

Although Otago had seen out the 43 minutes to stumps safely enough — 25 for none, Turner 19 of them, Wayne Blair 6 — it was in deep trouble after another 40 minutes on the second morning. The score was 45 for two, Turner 29, and Bevan Congdon coming to the wicket. But that was virtually the end of Wellington's prospects, made all the more difficult with Bruce Taylor unable to bowl because of a knee injury. He had batted in that condition, and poor John Morrison had one of his hardest day's batting: he was the runner while 251 runs were added by Taylor and Jeremy Coney, and got credit for none of them! It was and extraordinarily high century for such a free hitter as Taylor, but Turner had the answer.

Because of his knee, Tails reckoned he couldn't play his dong over mid-wicket, which probably would have cost him on the 'Brook. He had to play a lot straighter, and look at the result. For much of the same reasons of the pitch, though I didn't have Tail's fitness problems, I relished the new ball; that's why I was getting the runs fairly quickly early in the innings, as it is hard to score off the new ball at Carisbrook. I consciously went out there to whack them, and I told Congo my intentions. He took the mickey out of me about that later.

It was not all whack for Turner and Congdon, however, as they had the first priority of securing the first innings lead. So after his early flourish, Turner ground for his runs, so much so that his 50 took 167 minutes. But the subsequent 81 runs took only 151 minutes — the century in 257 minutes — and it included 16 fours and a mighty six from the off-spinner, Bruce Smith, well over the long-on fence. Square- and cover-driving brought him many of his boundaries, and the same area was also the scene of his only chance, a difficult catch to cover when Turner was 29.

In the 167 minutes of the Otago innings to lunch, Turner scored 61, and Congdon was 28 at the interval: they had been together 84 minutes and scored 63. But there was a growing domination of bat over ball: the 100 partnership took 149 minutes, 150 in 196 (better than even time), 200 in 225 (only 29 minutes for that 50), and the 213 in 235 minutes. When Turner's innings came to an end after 318 minutes, at 258 for three, Otago still did not have the first innings lead but a punishing Congdon (three sixes, 20 fours) saw it there. With- out Taylor, Wellington was down to three front-line bowlers, Alan Hounsell, who had 24 overs, the best of them. The others were Richie Collinge, with 22 overs, and Wayne Greenstreet (18); while the four part-timers, 'Bags' Murray, a leg-spinner, John 'Mystery' Morrison, with his left-arm spin, and the off-spinners, Smith and Coney, between them bowled 21 overs. The final day's play was washed out, but an outright decision would have been very difficult to accomp- lish.

32

151* for New Zealand v D. H. Robins' XI, Saffrons, Eastbourne, 25, 26 April 1973

New Zealand 250 (R. E. Redmond 65, G. M. Turner 41, M. G. Burgess 39, R. W. Anderson 38; J. N. Graham 4/25, B. Stead 3/37) and 299/2 decl (Turner 151*, B. E. Congdon 77, Redmond 57) drew with **D. H. Robins' XI** 223 (B. A. Richards 102; R. O. Collinge 4/41, H. J. Howarth 3/66) and 298/9 (D. R. Turner 103, M. J. Smith 66, D. W. Randall 42, C. T. Radley 34; R. J. Hadlee 4/96).

First innings: lbw b R. N. S. Hobbs 41
Second innings: not out 151

This was almost the typical start to a touring team's English expedition, with Eastbourne, rather than New Road, providing the venue, but New Zealand did not make a good fist of the first innings. Only Redmond and Turner (41) made much progress against the 6ft 7in (2m) Norman Graham, the Kent left-arm seamer who had four for 25 from his 25.5 overs. A slow pitch made easy stroke-making a little difficult to a team having its first innings of the tour, but were things really that hard? After all, Barry Richards had only been back from South Africa for less than three days, and here he was scoring a century in almost even time.

Maybe he provided the spur for Turner and Redmond in the second innings, and conditions were in their favour: warm, sunny weather, a good pitch, if a little slow, and a shortish boundary. Also, Derrick Robins had not invited a mean, containing attack: there were Graham and the late Barry Stead, of Notts, to open, and three spinners to back them up: Fred Titmus, Middlesex and England's famed off-spinner; Robin Hobbs (Essex), the last of the English leggies; and a slow left-armer, David Hughes of Lancashire. Turner was the complete master of them. With Redmond so delightfully picking up the reins of his recent test debut — he had made a century and a 50 against Pakistan only two months before, and that remained his only test! — the pair scored 103 together in 90 minutes, Redmond hitting three sixes and seven fours, then Turner and Congdon got 196 in 174 minutes. In his 265 minutes and 225 balls, Turner hit two sixes, both off Titmus and 22 fours, a neat century in boundaries, and only one chance, when he hit Graham straight up in the air at 84. The bowler dropped it himself. Turner's 50 had taken three minutes under two hours — he was 56 overnight — and he reached his 100 in 203 minutes.

On this rather hectic final day, 467 runs were scored in just over six hours, Robins' XI needing 327 at 93 an hour, but falling 29 short, with Graham and Titmus having to play out the final five overs. Richard Hadlee, making his first tour, had a good start with four for 96 — suffering a bit from David Turner — off 21 overs. In the first innings, Richard Collinge had missed Richards's onslaught and had four for 41 from 18 overs.

33
143 for New Zealand v Worcestershire, New Road, 28 April 1973

New Zealand 369/3 decl (G. M. Turner 143, B. E. Congdon 93, R. E. Redmond 79) and 26/0 drew with **Worcestershire** 230 (D. E. R. Stewart 69, R. J. Lanchbury 46, I. N. Johnson 36; R. O. Collinge 6/52).

First innings: b J. D. Inchmore 143
Second innings: did not bat

Worcestershire fielded a much weakened team, without six capped players, Turner and Parker obviously pre-occupied with their New Zealand commitments, and also leaving out three front-line members of the team, Ron Headley, Ted Hemsley and Vanburn Holder. So the attack consisted John Inchmore, playing his first game, Brian Brain of an extraordinarily long (and many counties) career, Paul Pridgeon, Basil D'Oliveira, Norman Gifford and another slow left-armer, Ivan Johnson.

This was the second and last game I played against Worcester, and I certainly wouldn't have been thinking about centuries against all 17 counties at that stage. But it turned out to be a big one to get out of the way, against my own county, and particularly against Brainy: just fancy, none for 80 off only 21 overs! Oh yes, no question there was friendly rivalry there, because I'd played against them so often in the nets, but only once in the middle, in '69 when I was out to D'Oliveira. I said friendly rivalry, I know, but I did distress Giffy a bit. I knocked him for a six over mid-wicket, then a four, and then another four, when he tried to bowl it flatter and faster: I still got enough bat to it, and did he do his nut!

There was another rollicking opening partnership from Turner and Redmond; what a shame this pairing of such potential never really built on those euphoric days of early

1973. They got their 50 in 42 minutes, 100 in 99, and at lunch, 135 minutes, 148. Their 154 partnership took 143 minutes, Redmond outscoring his more illustrious partner, his 50 taking 84 minutes, to the 113 of Turner. Then Turner and Congdon took New Zealand to 305 for one at tea, Congdon passing his 50 in 82 minutes, but Turner was out eight minutes after tea, precisely two hours after Redmond.

They had just taken the new ball, and I thought I should get 200 here — and I wanted to, too! But Inchmore, John Darling Inchmore, yorked me, and that's very unusual, as I don't normally get yorked. It was his first first-class wicket, as he reminded me, and has never failed to remind me! When he went back to his school, he boasted to his class that he bowled me — he never told them that I got 143 first!

Turner had reached his 100 in 220 minutes, and his 143 took 268 minutes (294 balls), with two sixes and 15 fours. It took him to 335 runs before May had started.

34
153* for New Zealand v M.C.C., Lord's, 19, 21 May 1973

New Zealand 259/1 decl (G. M. Turner 153*, J. M. Parker 88) and 63/4 decl (B. F. Hastings 41*) drew with **M.C.C.** 146/2 decl (D. Lloyd 66*, A. R. Lewis 49*) and 37/2.

First innings: not out 153
Second innings: b R. H. M. Cottam 3

John Woodcock, of *The Times*, referred to Turner as a clockwork batsman in this innings, and certainly the runs were still ticking over. It had been three weeks since Turner had scored a century, but he was still scoring runs. Since the Worcestershire match, there had been 85 against Hampshire, failures of sorts against Kent (7) and Gloucestershire (8 and 17*), 81 and 13 against Somerset, 53 and 44 in the Glamorgan match. But the pressure was starting to tell for his total, after Glamorgan, was 643, and one more long innings would place the Thousand within reach. Not that Turner initially cared overly much for the milestone, but the media, the cricketing public and Turner's own team were becoming increasingly conscious of the significance of the chances of the feat. They were almost demanding he do it, for it may never be done again; certainly, the structure of county cricket now is such that a tourist is probably the only player with the opportunity. So, Turner now confesses, he felt quite ill for the early part of his Lord's innings, taking 20 minutes to score against the near-test attack that the MCC invariably puts together: Geoff Arnold and Bob Cottam, of Hampshire, to open, Tony Greig to follow, Jackie Birkenshaw and Derek — 'Deadly' — Underwood to bowl spin. Those worries past, and ignoring the interruptions of rain, Turner proceeded to play his finest innings of the summer, not a demolishing innings, despite the 16 fours and majestic six from Birkenshaw, the subject of a much-published photograph, but one of smooth efficiency, easy stroke-making and no chances. It was a regal innings at Headquarters, and took Turner to 796. He suffered, all told, four different sorts of interruptions, which perhaps explains — along with the agonising start — his 50 taking 154 minutes. But the next 50 took only 53 minutes, the century reached just before tea on the Saturday, when New Zealand was 180 for none in 223 minutes. In the few minutes possible after that break, New Zealand went to 188, Turner to 109 and the valuable John Parker 75. On the Monday morning, the opening partnership went on to 211, in 262 minutes, before Parker was out, and in the final 51 minutes of the innings, Turner and Bevan Congdon (14*) scored 48 together. Turner batted a quarter-hour over five hours all told, and received 285 balls.

I suppose by then, or after that innings, I had to be aware of the Thousand but I was, more, obviously happy to score well at that point as the test matches were drawing near, and because I scored and batted well against such an accomplished attack, four of them test players. It was important, too, to score runs again at Lord's, and it continued my good trot there. I was pleased to score a few off Horse (Arnold) and to be not out to him because he is one of these guys — there are a few of them — who deliberately impedes a batsman running between the wickets. He once got me lbw for 98 in a test in Christchurch, and put on a real performance with a bowing act. Another time, he got me out for 100-odd just after he had returned to the field, having gone off for treatment. He said at the time, he only went back on the field to get me out. I replied that that was all right; I usually got a 100 first. Nothing to do with this innings, perhaps, but an illustration of a little bit of feeling, and the . . . psychological, I suppose . . . importance of getting runs on this occasion.

35

111 for New Zealand v Northamptonshire, Northampton, 30, 31 May 1973

New Zealand 247/6 decl (G. M. Turner 111, B. E. Congdon 72; B. S. Bedi 4/70) and 151/2 decl (J. M. Parker 69*, Turner 42) drew with **Northamptonshire** 163 (R. T. Virgin 50, A. Hodgson 41; B. R. Taylor 4/28) and 139/4 (D. S. Steele 64*, Mushtaq Mohammed 42).

First innings: c Mushtaq b Bedi 111
Second innings: c P. Willey b Bedi 42

After his Lord's performance, Turner appeared well set for the Thousand, and he went to Grace Road needing 133 in five playing days. The opposition was Leicestershire, the pitch was placid, the day beamed fine, and Turner played one of his worst innings. He was at ease enough against the opening bowlers, but when Birkenshaw and Chris Balderstone came on, Turner went off the boil. The ball was not coming on to the bat, and after scratching around for most of the morning, he was out for 30 and lucky to get them. Bevan Congdon went on to 134; that innings to Turner would have made his tally 1001! Rain washed out the last day when Turner, batting rather better, was 10 not out.

That rain was significant, for it swirled round much of central England and Turner thought it had robbed him of all chance. It cost 200 minutes of the first day at Northampton when David Steele put New Zealand in to bat — not because this courteous fellow was giving Turner his chance, but because the pitch was downright dangerous, and Northants possessed a very useful attack. Of the four main bowlers, John Dye, Bishen Bedi and Steele himself were left-armers; the other opener was Alan Hodgson. The other bowlers used were Peter Willey, later to bowl his off-breaks for England, and Mushtaq Mohammed. The run chart of this innings illustrates the type of attack and the huge proportion of runs scored by Turner behind the wicket on the off-side.

G. M. Turner N.Z. v Northamptonshire 30, 31 May, 1 June 1973

NEW ZEALAND FIRST INNINGS 247—6 declared. TURNER, c MUSHTAQ, b BEDI 111.

Opponent	Score	Minutes	Balls Received	4s	6s
D. H. Robins' XI	41	90	87	6	
	151*	265	225	22	2
Worcester	143	268	294	15	2
Hampshire	85	169	168	11	
Kent	7	25	11	1	
Gloucester	8	33	13		
	17*	56	53	1	
Somerset	81	176	152	10	1
	13	49	34	2	
Glamorgan	53	108	105	9	
	44	62	69	3	
M.C.C.	153*	315	285	16	1
	3	6	6		
Derby	2	11	7		
	66*	98	83	7	1
Leicester	30	113	107	2	
	10*	43	32	1	
Northants	111	255	247	15	

TOTAL

11 matches, 18 innings, 5 not outs, 1018 runs,
153* highest score, 78.31 average.
Scored in 35 hours 42 minutes off 1778 balls.

LEGEND

D J.C.J. Dye   W P. Willey
H A. Hodgson   B B.S. Bedi
M Mushtaq Mohammed S D.S. Steele
* runs scored after 93.

GLENN TURNER
1000 runs before the end of May

COMPILED BY I.M. WALTER

It really was a spiteful pitch, bad enough at any time but more so with all the world, and his camera and typewriter, at the ground. I understand, too, that half New Zealand was listening because the Northants secretary kindly let Alan Richards, the New Zealand radio announcer, use his telephone to broadcast a commentary. So with all that, and the ball taking off, a big innings was not only going to be bloody difficult to play, but would have to rate as satisfying as the Thousand. Looking back, though, it was not a terribly classical innings. I was dropped in the slips by Roy Virgin from Dye's bowling when I was 16, and it was around this time, I decided I would have to have a bit of a flirt. So I played pretty freely for that first hour and a half; I got my 50 in 93 minutes, I believe. Then the pitch started flattening out, and I thought: 'Hang on, no sense in taking chances. I'll be bloody annoyed if I get out in the high 900s.' So I grafted for that last hour, and only got 15 in that time. That made me 70 at stumps, 23 short, and I did have to consciously resist the temptation to score the runs that night.

Even so, Turner had outscored the doughty Bevan Congdon, who, Turner says, got more nasty lifters even than he. Congdon took 134 minutes for his 50, and was 55 at stumps. Next morning, he and Turner took their second wicket partnership to 154 in 189 minutes — John Parker was out at 12 — when Congdon was out, Turner then 84. Mark Burgess joined Turner and, tested always by the graceful arc and sharp spin of the magnificent Bedi, he edged to 86. Then there was another of those square slashes which characterised his early batting in this innings, not the 'flat bat' shot he was to make his own; another four, and Turner was 90. Then it was Bedi for another over, with Burgess settling himself in at the other end, and another maiden. Finally, at 11.40 am, Congdon having been out 41 minutes earlier, and 10 minutes short of four hours (around the time for many of Turner's centuries), the bat cracked again at Bedi, and the ball flew, finer than that boundary 11 minutes earlier, to the fence again. The tension was over, the batsman Burgess, and the fieldsmen showered Turner with their congratulations, for they were part of history being made; and the shackles of the innings were leased. He blazed briefly away, 'lapping' Bedi and off-driving Steele for boundaries, snicking the latter through slip for his 100 in 245 minutes, trying to hit Bedi over the top for six, and instead being caught, deep at mid-off, by Mushtaq. He batted, all told, for 255 minutes, receiving 247 balls, and hitting 15 fours. None counted so much as one square slash from Bedi, nor ever in these 100 centuries, has a score in the nineties been of greater significance.

Turner looking for more runs towards that magic thousand, pre-June 1973.

*Turner goes to 93 against Northampton-
shire, 31 May 1973 — and his season's
total to 1000.*

Wicket-keeper, George Sharp, and New Zealand batsman, Mark Burgess, are the first to congratulate Turner, followed by other Northamptonshire players, including Colin Milburn (shaking Turner's hand) and the turbaned Indian, Bishen Bedi.

36

121* for New Zealand v Surrey, The Oval, 30 June, 1 July 1973

Surrey 199 (D. R. Owen-Thomas 59, G. R. J. Roope 30; D. R. Hadlee 4/37, R. O. Collinge 4/53) and 336/4 decl (Younis Ahmed 141*, Owen-Thomas 76, L. E. Skinner 36; R. J. Hadlee 3/70) drew with **New Zealand** 320/4 decl (G. M. Turner 121*, K. J. Wadsworth 49*, J. M. Parker 44, B. F. Hastings 40, R. W. Anderson 30) and 100/4.

First innings: not out 121
Second innings: did not bat

Captaining New Zealand for only the second time on this tour, Turner had had a miserable June. After the Thousand, the reaction that many had threatened had set in, and his three test innings had realised scores of 11, 9 and 4, though twice he and John Parker had virtually seen John Snow and Geoff Arnold off before getting out. After his fine start to the tour, Rodney Redmond had been ignored for test consideration, but he was given a chance in this match. And as all three openers were playing, Turner batted himself at No. 3, coming in at 48, when Redmond was out for 28. June might never have been, so quickly was Turner in full stride. The Surrey attack was perhaps not quite all it could have been, but with Robin Jackman, Pat Pocock, Intikhab Alam, Graeme Roope and Allan Butcher, it was more than adequate.

He reached his 50 in 76 minutes, Parker having been dismissed for 44, when the pair had added 55 in 47 minutes for the second wicket, then Turner and Brian Hastings (40) put on another 87 in 82 minutes. A whirlwind 70 in 47 minutes with Robert Anderson (30) followed, and in the course of that fourth wicket partnership, Turner reached his century in a mere 155 minutes. He went on to 111 before Anderson was out, and Ken Wadsworth then came in to play an extraordinary innings. With Turner scoring another 10 runs, Wadsworth thrashed his way to 49 not out in half an hour; indeed, when 'they' had added 55 in 27 minutes, Turner's contribution was a mere five singles as he sought to give Wadsworth the bowling. He batted 207 minutes, all told, and hit 16 fours to the long Oval boundary.

I'd been told that after the Thousand, there would be a letdown, and it was nice to get back to form. Not that my form was marvellous for the third test, because I dislocated my finger in Surrey's second innings, trying for a first slip catch off Richard Hadlee and going down too late. So I didn't bat in the second innings, and it all meant Rodney Redmond missed out again, because John Parker definitely had to play, to field at slip. I struggled batting too, only 11 in the first innings, then I somehow scraped through to 81 in the second dig, before being out to a dirty lbw to John Snow. I say dirty, because Charlie Elliott, one of the umpires, had a go at Dickie Bird, then pretty new to test umpiring, for not giving me out earlier. We were nine down overnight, and Elliott told Dickie he could have headed for home a night earlier if our innings was finishing. I was looking at the weather, though, because there was every chance of rain on the last day, and our saving the game. There was a personal record at stake, too, because if I'd lasted, I would have been the first opener to bat through three test innings.

That was all to come, however, and the interesting side-issue to look back on in this innings was the toss.

I was certain John Edrich had won it, but the groundsman came out, and said: 'What's the story, which roller?' I said he'd better ask John, but Edrich said: 'I think you won it, didn't you?' I had to say no, but it was a pretty generous gesture. I think he may have been giving me a choice of whatever we wanted to do, with the test the next match.

Although Richard Collinge and the Hadlee brothers made relatively short work of Surrey's first innings, Younis, later to become a rather volatile team-mate of Turner, ensured his team against defeat.

37

109* for Worcestershire v Glamorgan, Sofia Gardens, Cardiff, 26, 27 July 1973

Worcestershire 334/9 decl (J. A. Ormrod 96, I. N. Johnson 53, J. M. Parker 52, G. M. Turner 40, Imran Khan 38; R. Dudley-Jones 3/55) and 171/1 decl (Turner 109*, Parker 48) drew with **Glamorgan** 265/9 decl (E. W. Jones 62*, A. Jones 62, Majid Khan 47; B. L. D'Oliveira 3/60) and 156/5 (Majid 50*, R. C. Davis 40; N. Gifford 3/32).

First innings: c A. E. Cordle b J. W. Solanky 40
Second innings: not out 109

There was a rushed atmosphere to the end of the New Zealand team tour, at least as far as it concerned the Worcestershire players, Turner and Parker. The final Prudential Cup, one-day, match against England was on Friday, July 20 — or was to have been; rain forced its abandonment. Then Worcestershire had its Benson and Hedges Cup, lost to Kent, on the Saturday, and a John Player League match, a rare tie with Surrey at Byfleet, on July 22. But had the B. & H. match not been completed in one day, always a possibility, it would have continued on the Monday, and that would have created a very serious problem.

I was getting married that morning, you see — married twice, even, because I went through the Sikh ceremony as well, to please my in-laws. It all had to be in the morning, too, because the team had an appointment at Buckingham Palace in the afternoon, and I got a bollocking from the Queen for not bringing my wife. Then, on the Tuesday night, it was off to Cardiff — not really an ideal preparation for returning to county cricket.

There was the comforting thought that Malcolm Nash, such a handy left-armer despite suffering six sixes in an over at the hands of Gary Sobers, was not playing. But Glamorgan still had Tony Cordle, of Tiger Bay, and Lawrence Williams to open, and the Tanzanian, John Solanky, to follow, with another medium-pacer in Rodger Dudley-Jones. Off-spin was provided by Barry Lloyd and Roger Davis. Against this attack, Turner got 40 in the first innings, and his second innings was one of those 'declaration jobs' — runs needed in something of a hurry in an effort to win the game. The slow pitch and the slow outfield did not do much for that cause, however, and Turner did well to reach his century in 165 minutes — only an hour for the second 50 — with nine fours. His total innings — and he had scored 13 before stumps — took five minutes longer, and Glamorgan needed 241 in three and a half hours. Even allowing for the difficulty in scoring briskly, it made a feeble effort. The opening partnership of 130 between Turner and John Parker took 150 minutes.

38

110 for Worcestershire v Leicestershire, Leicester, 7 August 1973

Leicestershire 305 (R. W. Tolchard 120*, J. C. Balderstone 61; B. M. Brain 3/64, Imran Khan 3/99) and 66/3 decl (J. F. Steele 32*) lost to **Worcestershire** 171/8 decl (G. R. Cass 42*; R. Illingworth 4/44) and 202/6 (G. M. Turner 110; Illingworth 5/60).

First innings: c K. Higgs b Illingworth 22
Second innings: b Illingworth 110

For the first two and a half days, the match at Grace Road belonged entirely to Leicestershire. Roger Tolchard dominated the home side's first innings, with noble help from Chris Balderstone, and in reply, Worcestershire could do virtually nothing with Ray Illingworth. He took four for 44 from 31 overs, and although Turner made 22, the only real resistance afterwards came from Rodney Cass, with a desperate 42 not out. The Leicestershire declaration left Worcestershire needing 201 in just under three hours, not quite as generous as it seemed for the pitch was one of those that cricketers say was 'turning square'. But in the batsmen's favour was a short boundary on one side — or should it be in Turner's favour? For he was the only batsman who could capitalise on the difficulties posed to a fielding captain, even one as clever and capable as Illingworth. Turner was in quite brilliant form for his 162 minutes, hitting one six and six fours in these difficult conditions, before being bowled having a slash at Illingworth.

I just can't believe that still. I didn't, did I? I can't imagine now that I would fire it away when I could be En Oh, and with only seven needed in 12 balls. I suppose it was some satisfaction for Illy, even if they still lost, and he did not accept defeat lightly; that is typical of a Yorky, but especially Illy. I'll never forget him grizzling and moaning, particu-

larly about the length of the boundary on one side.

I enjoyed the performance, because no other batsman scored more than 25. And although the declaration seemed generous, the number of overs bowled by their spinners was a good indication that it suited slow bowling. As well as Illy, John Steele — David's brother and another slow left-armer — was also very accurate and dangerous. But the truth of the matter of Illy's moaning was that with the pitch turning as it did, he thought he could bowl us out. He was sour that he didn't.

It was not as though the Worcestershire openers, Turner and John Parker, exactly got a flier on this soft pitch. After 10 overs from those skilled test openers, Graham McKenzie and Ken Higgs, careful batting had brought them 24, and the 50 (Turner 28 of them, Parker's 18 including a pulled six from Chris Balderstone) took an hour. Even so, the opening partnership of 73 in 75, Parker out for 25, was a very reasonable start, and at 103 for two when the final hour commenced, Worcestershire was soundly placed. Perhaps as a rather desperate measure, McKenzie and Higgs returned with a limited overs-style field — slips and short legs despatched to the outer — but it was Illingworth who made the dangerous inroads. Certain, there were useful partnerships with Turner of 51 (Imran Khan, 23) and 39 (Basil D'Oliveira, 21), but Illingworth winkled them out, and Norman Gifford, too. But Turner, cutting fiercely, driving strongly, defending primly, had gone to his 50 in 86 minutes, his 100 in a sweetly timed 162 minutes. On the stroke of 6 pm, he was bowled by Illingworth. But two overs remained in which to score the eight runs needed, and one was enough with the final ball scuttling away for four leg-byes.

39

106* for Worcestershire v Essex, Chelmsford, 27 August 1973

Worcestershire 241 (G. M. Turner 76, Imran Khan 40; R. E. East 4/40, J. K. Lever 3/36) and 192/2 decl (Turner 106*, J. M. Parker 63) beat **Essex** 136 (R. N. S. Hobbs 30; B. L. D'Oliveira 4/30, J. D. Inchmore 3/29, B. M. Brain 3/51) and 65 (Imran 4/29, D'Oliveira 3/8).

First innings: c N. Smith b Hobbs 76
Second innings: not out 106

Apart from the very tidy bowling of Ray East in Worcestershire's first innings, four for 40 from 26 overs, there was hardly an Essex player who performed at all worthily. One uncharitable critic said that this display was 'typical of the Essex delinquents of those days'. Turner, more kindly, says they were a 'spirited side of young men'.

They were far from a spirited side in this match, Basil D'Oliveira showing a startling bowling return of seven for 38 from his 25 overs in the match, a quite astonishing second innings analysis of 14-10-8-3! Imran Khan had a fine all-round match, too, with his 40 in the first innings and four for 29 in Essex's second. But if Essex batted dismally, it bowled well with its varied attack of John Lever, Stuart Turner and Brian Edmeades, for seam; East, Robin Hobbs and David Acfield with their differing spin. Turner, however, was masterly in his 195 minutes (63 overs) at the crease. There was a sparkling stand of 142 for the second wicket with John Parker, after Ron Headley had been run out at 39 for 14, and it was Turner who was — as always, dare one say — the dominant partner. His first 50 took a neat two hours, he hit a six and 10 fours, and Worcestershire was able to afford the luxury of giving Essex a complete day in which to score 298. Two sessions of that day, were not needed, as Essex weakly succumbed to its lowest score of the season.

I was still in pretty good sort of form. In the three weeks since the Leicestershire match, I'd scored 29 and 70 against Gloucestershire, a 70 and a 50 against Sussex, 50 against Kent. Now I was back into the century habit and that was a relief, in a way, after this uneven sort of season.

40
140 for Worcestershire v Nottinghamshire, New Road, 1 September 1973

Worcestershire 382/8 decl (G. M. Turner 140, T. J. Yardley 135; B. Stead 4/107) and 108/1 decl (Turner 65, J. M. Parker 37*) beat **Nottinghamshire** 132 (M. J. Smedley 36; B. L. D'Oliveira 3/31, B. M. Brain 3/33, J. D. Inchmore 3/44) and 357 (D. W. Randall 107, Smedley 84, G. Edwards 46*, Stead 41; Brain 3/44, Imran Khan 3/123).

First innings: lbw b G. S. Sobers 140
Second innings: c Sobers b M. Nanan 65

The way Nottinghamshire played, it was keen to get this match and the season out of the way. It was not helped in being without two leading batsmen, Mike 'Patsy' Harris and Basharat Hassan, but it was still a miserable performance which only went into the final day because of a splendid maiden century from Derek Randall.

But more than anything, this match was distinguished by Turner's ninth century of the season, and the first he had scored before lunch; it helped immeasurably to his reaching 1036 runs in county championship matches, in what was only a half-season for the county. Yet it was not a promising start for Worcestershire, Turner himself surviving an lbw appeal from the very first ball, by Brian Stead. He off-drove the next for three, hit a four over mid-wicket the next over from Stead, yet after eight overs, Worcestershire had a mere 14 runs! Stead's left-arm medium-fast was appealing, one could say, and at 27, his fourth and fifth requests for lbw decisions finally fell on kindly ears, and John Parker and Alan Ormrod departed in successive balls.

That was the end of any joy for Notts, as Turner unwound a full range of shots. Stead had had his dual successes in the eleventh over: the next 32 overs to lunch brought Worcestershire 136 runs as Turner raced first to 51 in 63 minutes, from a score of 71, in the nineteenth over; then to 103 — out of 149 — in three minutes over two hours. With Jim Yardley an able and willing partner, the 50 partnership took just 31 minutes, eight overs, the 100 in 63 minutes. At lunch, they had added 136 undefeated, and Turner was 113. He had scored 95 runs while Yardley was carefully garnering 39, but there was nothing wrong with that. For when Turner eventually fell in the rain-interrupted afternoon, after 185 minutes, they had added 190 and Yardley was firmly set towards the highest score of his career to that point.

Turner was merciless towards the attack, hampered by losing Philip Wilkinson with a twisted ankle after he bowled his first and only ball of the afternoon, dull overhead but hardly on the field. A particular sufferer was John Birch, a medium-pace then and having his first game: he struck Turner in full flow and conceded 39 runs in his first six overs. The only blemish in Turner's innings, in fact, was when Gary Sobers found an edge which flew just wide of the wicket-keeper, David Pullan; though Turner was restrained rather more by Bob White than by the medium-pacers. Even so, he was in such touch that he was able to cut White against the off-spin for the twelfth boundary which gave him his century.

41
106* for New Zealand v Tasmania, Launceston, 13, 14 January 1974

New Zealand 216 (K. J. Wadsworth 44, B. F. Hastings 30; L. J. F. Appleton 4/61, M. Leedham 3/43) and 221/4 decl (Turner 106*, J. V. Coney 57, Hastings 43) beat **Tasmania** 178 (J. Wilkinson 49, P. G. Roberts 42; D. R. Hadlee 4/52) and 165 (K. Thompson 35; D. R. O'Sullivan 4/49, G. D. Alabaster 3/32).

First innings: c K. B. Badcock b Leedham 21
Second innings: not out 106

Turner's only century in Australia came late in a thoroughly disappointing tour. By the time the team reached the island state, it had played nine matches, first or second-class, and Turner had taken part in parts of only three of them, for four innings. Twice he had had injured hands or fingers and as he has said, he needed this innings for the practice, even if he was to face a weak attack. Tasmania was still not admitted to the Sheffield Shield competition, and its only bowler of any significance was Jack Simmons, the Lancashire off-spinner and a long-service coach in Tasmania; he took one for 48 from his 14 overs.

Turner's hand injury had not completely healed for this match, but there was a keen desire to get the vice-captain back into the team for the third test. He made a very tentative 21 in the first innings — even so, only Ken Wadsworth's 44 was better. In the second innings, he was still favouring his right hand, but it seemed to matter little — or did it, in fact, enforce and encourage Turner to drive firmly and with exquisite timing straight and to the off? In the last 145 minutes of the second day, New Zealand scored 151 for three, Turner 79 of them, and he and Jeremy Coney scored 113 together in 100 minutes, the last 42 in 28 minutes, for the second wicket. Turner reached his 50 in 90 minutes, and next morning, with Brian Hastings (43) his main assistant, went on to his century in 218 minutes. He batted, all told, 10 minutes under four hours, scoring precisely half New Zealand's runs from the bat, and hit seven fours. It was much more like the Turner of 1973, beginning and end.

42

101 for New Zealand v Australia, Lancaster Park, Christchurch, 9, 10 March 1974

Australia 232 (I. R. Redpath 71, R. W. Marsh 38; B. E. Congdon 3/33, R. J. Hadlee 3/59, R. O. Collinge 3/70) and 259 (K. D. Walters 65, Redpath 58, I. C. Davis 50; R. J. Hadlee 4/71, D. R. Hadlee 4/75) lost to **New Zealand** 255 (G. M. Turner 101; M. H. N. Walker 4/60, G. Dymock 3/59) and 230/5 (Turner 110*, B. F. Hastings 46).

First innings: c K. R. Stackpole b G. S. Chappell 101
Second innings: not out 110

In any review of New Zealand cricketing history and highlights, this match and result will glow like a beacon; and in retrospect, none will shine more brightly than Turner. His first home century, let alone his second; New Zealand's first victory against Australia — those features alone make this one of New Zealand's, and Turner's, most memorable matches.

But he would be the first to insist that his first innings century, though rather brisker than his second, was far from memorable. Rarely has Turner batted quite so long, quite so valuably for his team, yet so badly; he 'scratched around like a bloody ant,' said one relation; he played and missed more than he would in a season. Even John Parker — and that is not meant as disrespectfully as it may sound — looked surer in the opening partnership; some would say that the rest — John Morrison, Brian Hastings, Bevan Congdon, Ken Wadsworth — looked sounder. But they all fell, and in such personal adversity, this was a sharp sign of Turner's ability, his well-honed professionalism. He was struggling, but he could stay there. Seven of the other first eight in the New Zealand innings reached double figures, none of them got to 25. At tea on that Saturday, the second day of the match, New

122

Poise and balance and intense concentration. But this first innings test century was one of Turner's least memorable.

Zealand was 99 for two in 132 minutes, Turner 55 of them, and at stumps, two hours later, he was 99 himself, the second time in a relatively brief test career (Dacca, 1969, was the other) that he sat on a century overnight.

Overnight, too, was not a time for recharging and restoring of the batting batteries, for a personal note must intrude. Twelve months earlier, to the day, Turner had been best man at my wedding and as he was in town for the occasion, a celebration was called for. The dinner was Italian, the evening was long, but not so long that I should be greeted with jibes the next morning, that I was responsible for Turner's slow progress. Turner, indeed, took 29 minutes to advance from 99 to 100, or 34 balls if you like, and a moment after he had reached 100 — and fled from the pitch, to protect it from the children who advanced on him — Turner was out, caught by Keith Stackpole at short leg, dabbing uncharacteristically at the bowling of Greg Chappell. He was out at 213 for six, the innings then having lasted 283 minutes. No masterpiece for sure, but it helped New Zealand to a handy little lead.

*Turner is the centre of youthful attraction
after completing his first home test century.*

43

110* for New Zealand v Australia, Lancaster Park, 12, 13 March 1974

Scoreboard as for Century No. 42.

This was perhaps the high point of Turner's test career for New Zealand, some time still from its conclusion, some time still from the batsman who could take charge of any attack, as he was to prove in county cricket in the late seventies and the dawning of the eighties.

But the occasion made this perhaps his most important innings: he had just made his first home test century, but this completed the illustrious milestone of two centuries in a test match, a preciously rare feat. More, it made possible New Zealand's first win at the expense of Australia, in the face of a doughty attack; it was scored in the face of adversity — for New Zealand was 62 for three, needing 228 to win, and Turner had just seen Bevan Congdon run out — and it was completed amidst a nasty slanging match with Ian Chappell. The attack is worth examining. Max 'Tangles' Walker, then perhaps the finest opener in the world in English or New Zealand conditions, and Geoff Dymock opened; they had Doug Walters (in the first innings only) and Greg Chappell, the latter then a regular medium-pacer, as back-up, and Ashley Mallett, whom many would consider Australia's best off-spinner since the war. Kerry O'Keeffe, a formidable leg-spinner, was also in the team, but on this splendid pitch, which both encouraged the batsmen in stroke-making and the bowlers, for the movement and bounce which it offered, he was not given even one over.

When Turner and John Parker commenced the pursuit of the runs for victory, a whole day and a little over two sessions remained. Australia, 211 for six overnight and Walters still there, had succumbed in short order to the brothers Hadlee,

Dayle and Richard, the four New Zealand seamers enjoying fine returns. For the record, Richard Hadlee had seven wickets in the match, Dayle five, Richard Collinge four, and Congdon had three for 33 in the first innings. Note that this was a pitch on which swing and seam prospered, for Hedley Howarth had only 11 overs, all in the second innings, while for Australia, Walker took six wickets, Dymock and Greg Chappell both three, and Mallett got the other two which fell to bowlers.

In the 40 minutes to lunch on the penultimate day, Turner and Parker were rarely troubled; they scored 21, and went on to 51 for the first wicket. Then the magnificent Walker induced Parker to follow an out-swinger, a few moments later, he had John Morrison lbw without offering a shot, and Congdon came to the wicket. He watched Turner drive handsomely wide of mid-off and heard Turner — whose call it was — insist there was a run. Congdon felt there was not, but too late, for Turner had taken off for what was a perfectly reasonable run. Congdon — was he burdened down with the worries of the situation? — was run out by half the length of the pitch, and the situation had turned from bad to worse.

In the bad old days, that would have spelled the end of the effort, but Brian Hastings was made of sterner stuff, and Turner was completely unruffled by the upset which would have intruded on the composure of a lesser man. He defended calmly, he only rarely followed Walker's wicked out-swinger, and Hastings, whose batting artistry was largely based on the cover-drive and cut, dutifully followed that example. But they were not idle, for the score had to be kept ticking over, and even with the accuracy of the Australian bowlers, and Ian Chappell's restraining field placements, their swift and sharp running for singles brought relatively ready runs. Peerless cover driving took Turner to one milestone: at 27, he reached 2000 test runs, and only four New Zealanders had beaten him to that target. At tea, it was 83 — 62 in two difficult hours, but the rescue operation was launched. It gathered momentum in the hour after tea, the almost giddy heights of 53 runs being put together with strong and precise driving by both players, and Turner going to his 50 in 187 minutes. That rate, furious in these circumstances, slowed somewhat in the final session, but there were still 41 runs and a traumatic final 10 minutes. It all started when Hastings swung Mallett high and firmly to the mid-wicket boundary, and the umpire, Bob Monteith, concurred with several spectators that it was a six. But the ball had bounced from the rock-hard outfield over the fence, and Turner, without a thought to the fact that his was a sporting gesture, told Mr Monteith of the error. As Mr Monteith was about to re-direct the scorers, Ian Chappell rushed up to remonstrate.

It's not really an episode I want to dwell on; enough was made about it at the time, and since. In retrospect, I suppose New Zealanders now tend to think of Ian Chappell only in terms of his abusing me, just as they remember Greg for the under-arm thing. In short, all that happened was that as Ian Chappell ran up, doing his block, I tried to tell him it was OK, there was no need for any drama; the umpire was correcting things. But he was so wound up — more because the match was slipping away than whether or not Hasto had hit a six or a four — that he just let fly. It was pretty disgusting language, and I'm not a prude when it comes to slipping into . . . um, slang . . . and even one or two of his players — Bacchus (Rodney Marsh) comes to mind — tut-tutted a bit and apologised for it. A few of our players thought it was pretty rough too, and Congo felt it warranted an apology. I don't suppose there was much prospect of Chappell saying sorry, even though he was invited to, so there it finished. But I think it may have cost Hasto his wicket, because he had a wipe at Mallett's fourth-last ball and was bowled. It was, I suppose, a crazy shot at that time and in that situation, but he had batted so well and worked so hard that I think the effing and blinding from Chappell had stuffed up his concentration.

For 153 minutes, the pair had battled it out with Mallett and the medium-pacers — Walker had two for 36 from 22 overs, what a feat — and the day closed at 177 for four, Turner 85 not out in 280 minutes. Only 51 were needed on the final day,

Turner despatches Greg Chappell, with Keith Stackpole and Ian Chappell in the slips (note their contrasting fielding styles), Rod Marsh, the wicket-keeper, Jeremy Coney, the New Zealand batsman, and umpire John Hastie.

A no-ball from Geoff Dymock is clipped square, and Turner is the first New Zealander to score two centuries in the same test match; and Turner acknowledges the applause, with Ken Wadsworth as his batting partner.

One of the most published of New Zealand cricketing photographs: Ken Wadsworth imperiously cover-drives Greg Chappell to the eastern boundary of Lancaster Park, and New Zealand has beaten Australia for the first time.

and clearly only the first session, at most, would be used. But nearly 6000 had relatives' funerals and flocked into Lancaster Park on this beautifully sunny day. Turner, too, had seemed to have forgotten all about Ian Chappell and foul abuse, and he was rarely in trouble in the hour and 32 minutes the match lasted this final day. He went quietly but steadily to an inevitable century, it taking 337 minutes, or 150 minutes for the second 50, and it came with a finely timed square drive from a no ball by Dymock. Jeremy Coney, a virtual newcomer to test cricket, was half an hour scoring his first run, in a little more than an hour for 18, but his innings was one of tremendous character and composure. He was out when only 22 were needed, and Ken Wadsworth ensured there were no more alarums and excursions. He, in fact, struck the winning boundary, a healthy whack through the covers from Greg Chappell. Turner had gone to 110, his test average passing 50 for the first time; he hit 11 fours in this innings, which lasted 11 minutes over six hours. He was on the field for all but the last 70 minutes of New Zealand's first innings, in a match that lasted 22 hours and 22 minutes, and had batted only seven minutes short of 12 hours.

44

138* (ret. hurt) for Worcestershire v Kent, New Road, 8, 9 May 1974

Kent 302/8 decl (B. W. Luckhurst 100, G. W. Johnson 58, Asif Iqbal 36, M. C. Cowdrey 35*; J. D. Inchmore 3/76) and 59 (M. H. Denness 35*; N. Gifford 4/2, B. M. Brain 4/29) lost to **Worcestershire** 276/6 decl (G. M. Turner 138* ret. hurt, B. L. D'Oliveira 42, G. R. Cass 39; R. A. Woolmer 3/53) and 88/5 (R. G. A. Headley 52; D. L. Underwood 5/25).

First innings: retired hurt 138
Second innings: did not bat

This first county championship match of the season was one of vivid contrasts, a firm pitch making life relatively easy for the batsmen in the first innings. But when Kent was 10 for three (from 10 overs) in its second innings, bad light and rain brought the second day to a premature close. The same rain meant play started an hour late on the final day, and also turned the pitch into a spinner's delight; Gifford taking four for two from a ball short of eight overs, while Ron Headley's second innings aggression meant Derek Underwood could not bowl Kent to a sensational victory. But, without Turner's own outstanding century of the first innings, Worcestershire would have faced an impossible task. He batted 282 minutes in scoring precisely half Worcestershire's total, not swashbuckling stuff, but good, controlled batting against four men who bowled in test matches: Bernard Julien and John Shepherd of the West Indies; Underwood and Bob Woolmer of England, plus Gordon Johnson's off-spinners. It was off Johnson that Turner hit a six; he also hit 14 fours, before his innings came to a premature end.

We were getting close to the 100 overs, then a compulsory declaration, and fairly close to their total, too, when Bernard Julien, a left-arm seamer, came back with the old ball. I hit him for a couple of fours, then he let me have a bouncer. I started to duck, then thought that I should be attacking, the innings being nearly over. So I ended up with a change-of-mind shot, and I got hit over the left eye — nine stitches: six surface, three deep, I'll always remember. Come to that, though, playing day in, day out, it's often possible to be pinned, and I guess I'm lucky that this was the only time I got a real good whack. But I was still there, in case, in the second innings.

At the time, Turner was batting with Rodney Cass and they had added about 90 for the sixth wicket, Gifford helping take the three-way partnership to 106 before Cass was out for 39. Earlier, Turner had had a third wicket partnership of 65 with John Parker (25) and 88 for the fourth with Basil D'Oliveira.

Turner's first innings form was sorely needed, for in the 21 overs bowled in 75 minutes to stumps on the first day, it lost both Ron Headley and Alan Ormrod, and of the 51 scored, Turner got 22 of them. It was much the same heavy weather the next morning, in not very nice weather, either. A sharp cross-wind kept the Worcester folk at home, and Turner and Parker concentrated on staying at home, in possession of their wickets, for the most part. Mind you, the bounce Julien was able to extract from the hard pitch, and the control of Shepherd, made batting a difficult business and there were only three runs from the bat in the first 20 minutes of the morning. By the end of the first hour, Parker had both been dropped, then caught, after the third wicket partnership had realised 65 in 90 minutes. It was that sort of batting. Turner's 50, for example, took him 154 minutes, with just three fours; the team's 100 did not arrive until after 47 overs; and Basil D'Oliveira scored six in his first 40 minutes — all of this partly because Shepherd spent the first 105 minutes of the morning bowling from the New Road end.

His departure loosened the shackles, even with 'Deadly' Derek Underwood coming into the attack, for D'Oliveira struck the first psychological blow, a straight drive for six from Underwood's first ball. That got the score moving, finally, and at lunch — 66 overs — Turner was 84 and D'Oliveira on 38 in a scoreboard of 165 for three. D'Oliveira went straight after lunch, after they had added 88, and so —

for nothing — did Jim Yardley. But Turner went on remorselessly to his first century of the season, in a shade under four hours, with Rodney Cass as his partner. But after 93 overs, and when the pair had added 80, Julien struck and Turner retired; he had batted 282 minutes.

45

202* for Worcestershire v Cambridge University, Fenner's, 15 May 1974

Worcestershire 388/1 decl (G. M. Turner 202*, E. J. O. Hemsley 120*, J. A. Ormrod 62) beat **Cambridge University** 109 (B. M. Brain 4/25, J. D. Inchmore 3/19) and 211 (R. I. Smyth 55, S. P. Coverdale 52; R. Senghera 3/41).

First innings: not out 202

Worcestershire's only activity between the Kent match and this had been a Benson & Hedges Cup match at Northampton.

*I was very keen to get back into the game, as I'm a great believer in facing the music again as soon as possible. Northamptonshire had Sarfraz, of Pakistan, playing for them at the time, and it seemed he was keen to play the music! He kept trying to hit me, like a boxer whose opponent has been hurt — they keep after the same spot. But I got through that without many problems — stumped off Mushtaq for 41, was it? — and the universities traditionally don't pose too many terrors. You know, against the universities and other lesser opposition, with all due respect to **some** very good players, I've always found it more difficult to motivate myself. But this time, I thought: Bugger it, double-centuries are there to be taken, specially on a pitch like Fenner's, and I should get one. It's not an attitude I have all the time, and there is certainly not the satisfaction in getting a double-ton at Fenner's or The Parks, as there is, in getting a not out ton and a bit in a run chase on a turner. So there was not much to remember about this innings, except that the Cambridge lads did field very well. They had to, because the bowling was pretty average, and considering the opposition, it was a relatively controlled innings by me.*

As is often the case with county teams playing a university

133

side, a couple of key players were rested, on this occasion Basil D'Oliveira and Ron Headley, their replacements being Ravinder Senghera, on his first-class debut, and Jimmy Cumbes, for his first game of the season in the county side. This meant the adaptable Alan Ormrod opened for one of the first times with Turner, and the pair paved the way for many great deeds. One of the finest features of their partnership was the running between the wickets; the 37 they scored in the first half-hour included five threes. It was remorseless stuff, too, with the 50 in 47 minutes, from 13 overs, and 57 in the first hour, Turner 33 of them and Ormrod 23. By lunch, it was 125 in two hours from 38 overs, Ormrod having just reached his 50, while Turner (then 73) had passed his in 87 minutes. But the real run-plundering came in the day's middle session, those 40 overs, in 125 minutes, bringing Turner 86 runs and advancing the score by 163 runs. Ormrod had gone at 143, but Ted Hemsley was not of a mind to mess around, and he was then 64. Turner's century had taken 173 minutes, his 150 in 228 minutes, and in the 80 minutes after tea, there was no more joy for the university bowlers. Turner went to his first double-century, other than on West Indian shores, in 317 minutes, and he batted 325 minutes all told, hitting 19 fours. Hemsley was no less aggressive, batting three hours for the partnership which was worth 245 runs. So far as Turner was concerned, it made his aggregate then 372 runs for twice out; by the end of May, it was 500 for four times out and could have been better but for a leg injury against Derbyshire (when he retired hurt for 83) causing him to miss the match against Oxford University at The Parks.

46
181 for Worcestershire v Gloucestershire, Cheltenham, 3 August 1974

Worcestershire 390/5 decl (G. M. Turner 181, J. M. Parker 61, K. W. Wilkinson 46, B. L. D'Oliveira 43*) beat **Gloucestershire** 142 (A. W. Stovold 44, R. B. Nicholls 35; N. Gifford 5/27, D'Oliveira 3/15) and 122 (D'Oliveira 5/49, Gifford 4/40).

First innings: b P. A. Thorn 181

The great South African all-rounder, Mike Proctor, was often to cause Worcestershire trouble in subsequent matches, but he and his fellow seamers — Julian Shackleton (a son of Hampshire's tireless Derek), Tony Brown (the captain) and Roger Knight — could do little against a solid all-round batting display in which Turner shone most brightly. Nor did the spinners, John Mortimer and Phillip Thorn, enjoy much great success and they must have watched in envy as Gifford and D'Oliveira prospered on a fine pitch turned sour by rain. Gifford had nine for 67 from 41 overs, D'Oliveira eight for 64 from his 33 overs.

The Gloucestershire attack was without Jack Davey, a left-arm seamer, and its regular left-arm spinner, David Graveney, but they would probably have made little difference to a Turner hungry for a century after a long, lean patch. He was in sparkling, stroke-making form, with his 28 fours and a six, and he led Worcestershire to the highest 100 overs total for the season.

It was not with Ron Headley as an opening partner, however. He had a face injury, and a 24-year-old left-hander, Keith Wilkinson, got his chance instead. He responded splendidly, overshadowed by Turner of course, but doing his bit to such good that when he was out, on the stroke of lunch — the second-last ball, in fact — they had scored 148 for the first wicket, in 135 minutes. Turner, in a powerful performance on the comfortable pitch, was then 87 from a ball short of 42 overs, his 50 having come in 80 minutes. Alan Ormrod got 20 towards a second-wicket partnership of 67, and by this time, it was all Turner. His century took 153 minutes of poised and elegant stroke-making, nothing finer than one superb off-drive from Roger Knight. But, as has often proved to be the case in a long Turner innings, the third 50 was the slowest: it took him 90 minutes, but then it was into top gear again and the 181 lasted only 268 minutes. Turner fell to Thorn, trying to cut the left-arm spinner, after he and John Parker had made 91 together in brisk time.

It was his third century of a season often interrupted by injuries, his first in two and a half months. Yet this was one of Turner's best seasons on figures: he averaged 60.5.

47
135 for Otago v Northern Districts, Harry Barker Reserve, Gisborne, 30 December 1974

Otago 312/4 decl (G. M. Turner 135, R. W. Anderson 76, K. O. Campbell 43*, H. C. Sampson 30*) and 292/6 decl (Turner 108, I. A. Rutherford 41, Sampson 37, B. J. McKechnie 34*; C. W. Dickeson 3/95) drew with **Northern Districts** 320/5 decl (R. W. Fulton 106, J. M. Parker 81, A. D G. Roberts 47, G. W. Taylor 45) and 246/7 (G. P. Howarth 137, Fulton 53; S. L. Boock 5/67).

First innings: b Howarth 135
Second innings: c Howarth b Dickeson 108

Gisborne had long had a reputation for possessing the best pitches, and some of the sunniest weather in New Zealand, but this was the debut in first-class cricket of the Harry Barker Reserve. Turner made it an occasion to remember with a handsome, efficient innings against an attack that was no more than steady. The pace was in the hands of Alan Stimpson, Hira Unka, an Indian, and Alan Hounsell, with Rod Fulton also bowling some medium-pace, while the spinners were Cliff Dickeson (slow left-arm) and Geoff Howarth, then a semi-regular off-spinner. Turner went methodically to his 50 in 130 minutes, and 10 minutes later, at lunch, he was 61. His 100 took 211 minutes, Turner going from 98 to 102 with one of many glorious square-drives, and he batted, all told, 294 minutes, hitting 15 fours. For 230 of those minutes, he was partnered by Robert Anderson in a second wicket partnership of 189, before being bowled by Howarth.

48

108 for Otago v Northern Districts, Harry Barker Reserve, 31 December 1974, 1 January 1975

Scoreboard as for Century No. 47.

This was something of a declaration job, but a win was always going to be rather difficult to achieve on this pitch. Two English counties would probably have got a result out of it but as I think I've already commented, New Zealanders play too little cricket in a first-class season to get in the habit of taking a chance on a match. Also, the ND bowlers stuck to a rather better line and length than in the first innings, and we were never really able to get completely on top. I felt I batted pretty well on the second afternoon, but I couldn't quite pick up the threads again on the final morning.

Turner and Ian Rutherford scored 87 in 89 minutes for the first wicket, and at stumps — 125 for two — Turner was 64, in 125 minutes. He had reached his 50 in 97 minutes, and next morning went on to his second century (the third time he had accomplished the feat) in 208 minutes. After batting for 231 minutes, and hitting 11 fours, Turner was caught by Howarth from the bowling of Dickeson, he and Henry Sampson having added 72 in 68 minutes for the fourth wicket.

I had been in Gisborne a few weeks earlier, and John Guy, one of the ND selectors, took me to see the ground which was to make its debut in first-class cricket. He told me then that he expected me to treat the Gisborne crowd to a century to mark the first Plunket Shield game in the district. Well, I hadn't had much of a run against ND, just as I still haven't scored a century against Canterbury, for what it's worth. A double-dose fixed that, and I believe my 189 partnership in the first innings with Robert Anderson was an Otago record for the second wicket.

49
105 for Otago v Central Districts, Carisbrook, 10 January 1975

Otago 295/5 decl (G. M. Turner 105, I. A. Rutherford 58, H. C. Sampson 50, K. O. Campbell 45*; A. B. Jordan 4/78) and 326/2 decl (Turner 186*, Sampson 56*, R. W. Anderson 55) beat **Central Districts** 313 (D. H. Payton 145, D. R. O'Sullivan 49*, D. W. Neal 32, R. A. Pierce 30; G. D. Alabaster 5/122, G. B. Thompson 3/60) and 241 (B. L. Cairns 56, Neal 53, Pierce 41, Payton 38; Alabaster 5/88).

First innings: c G. N. Edwards b Jordan 105
Second innings: not out 186

I felt these were two of my better innings in this country, and they were played on a pitch which was unusual for Carisbrook: it was a little bit grassy, and there was a little bit of seam there, but it allowed you to play shots. Ian Snook must have thought it was an untypical 'Brook pitch, because he put us in.

How Snook must have rued that decision, yet how correct it must have seemed. The pitch, as Turner said, was green and seemed hard, the atmosphere was heavy, and he had Alistair Jordan, so often on the fringe of the New Zealand team, and Lance Cairns, who thrived in such conditions, to open; Richard Ellis to follow, and David O'Sullivan to bowl his slow left-armers. But at lunch — what a splendid start — Turner and Ian Rutherford had scored 113 together, and they went on to a first wicket stand of 145 in a little over three hours. Turner scored his own 50 in 105 minutes, his second 50 surprisingly took a quarter-hour longer, and he was out — caught at the wicket by 'Jock' Edwards from Jordan's bowling, his only loose shot — after 239 minutes, with the score 189 for three. Turner hit eight fours and — that lush outfield — seven threes.

50

186* for Otago v Central Districts, Carisbrook, 11, 12 January 1975

Scoreboard as for Century No. 49.

Mainly due to a determined century from Dermot Payton, Otago actually trailed by a few, but Turner, in a second immaculate century in the match, soon made nonsense of that. He started batting three-quarters of an hour before tea on the second day, scoring 26 in that time. Then, in the day's final session, he scored 103, the first time in New Zealand in which he scored 100 runs or more in a single session, and Otago was wonderfully well placed at 192 for one, Turner having reached his chanceless century in 141 minutes. In the 100 minutes he batted the next morning, Turner went on to his highest score in New Zealand, then or since. He batted 265 minutes, a dizzy rate of scoring, and hit 18 fours, he and Robert Anderson plundering the Central Districts attack, in which Snook and Wayne Burtt were called upon to bolster the four who did all the work in the first innings. Between them, they added 169 for the second wicket in 141 minutes.

I took a lot of satisfaction from that innings, as I was able to show, for one of the first times, some of my England form. I was also pleasantly surprised when the Carisbrook crowd stood up and cheered when I got my fiftieth 100. I was getting stick left, right and centre at that stage, mainly because I had awful trouble coming to realistic terms with the Otago Cricket Association. What do I mean, though? I've always seemed to have had these difficulties.

Turner had given chances on the first day at 107 and 110, but that was inevitable with the flow of strokes. The square-cuts and square-drives, and exquisitely timed on-drives most took the eye, but the rest were all there: the late-cuts, the leg-glances, the off-drives and the hooks. It was superb batting, a double-century in the making before Turner called it off.

140

51
100* for Worcestershire v Nottinghamshire, New Road, 9 May 1975

Nottinghamshire 316/9 decl (D. W. Randall 79, P. D. Johnson 77, R. A. White 71*; Gifford 3/66, B. M. Brain 3/107) and 296 (Randall 100, P. D. Johnson 72, M. J. Harris 49; Gifford 6/77, I. N. Johnson 3/90) lost to **Worcestershire** 379/9 decl (J. M. Parker 133, B. L. D'Oliveira 75, I. N. Johnson 69; C. E. B. Rice 4/64) and 235/3 (G. M. Turner 100*, J. A. Ormrod 47, D'Oliveira 41*, Parker 34).

First innings: lbw b C. E. B. Rice 9
Second innings: not out 100

One contemporary report was rather harsh in suggesting Turner had had a lean start to his eighth season of county cricket. His earlier two games had brought him scores of 0, 55 and 35, and May had barely started. On this grey day, he was in golden touch, however, and masterminded a handsome victory which gave Worcestershire the then-maximum 18 points.

Such a victory seemed most unlikely when a depleted Worcestershire attack took until well into the third afternoon to finish the Notts second innings, and Worcestershire needed 234 from 70 minutes plus 20 overs, six an over in simple terms. But Turner and Alan Ormrod, the latter now cast as Turner's opening partner, had a magnificent start. At tea, just over three-quarters of an hour, they were 80 from 15 overs, Turner 40 and Ormrod 39. When Ormrod was out, caught at the long-on boundary aiming for his sixth four, or better, they had made 105 from 20 overs, and the foundation was laid. After Ted Hemsley had scored all nine runs for the second wicket, John Parker maintained his first innings form and, rare feat, outscored Turner as they added another 56 from nine overs. By this time, Turner had passed his 50 —

in 58 minutes — of course and when the final 20 overs loomed, Worcestershire was 119 for two from just 22 overs: the run-rate was ticking over to perfection. Basil D'Oliveira made sure it did not slacken.

He really was in good nick, Basil, so good we nearly ran out of enough runs for me to get my ton! Not that that was a factor, but it all sorted itself out.

We only needed five or six to win, more than two overs to go, and obviously going to win, and Bas had hit, I think, seven or eight fours in his 36. He could have hit another one, but instead, he just pushed a single to give me the strike, and I got the one I needed. For sort of stage-managing the team's innings, the ton came pleasantly quickly, 136 minutes, and next over, first ball, it was all over. Bas and I got our 65 in nine overs — we even had 11 balls to spare at the end. It was a good win, a very good win, but this rollicking batting at the end tended to obscure Giffy's bowling, which put us in the winning position.

Notts used only four bowlers in this second innings as, indeed, had Worcestershire, with Vanburn Holder injured and Gifford himself opening the bowling. How the Notts men suffered, too: Clive Rice had 13 overs for 68 runs, and his fellow-opener, Philip Wilkinson 12 for 76. The seamer, John Birch, and Bob White had seven and eight overs respectively, for 42 and 45 runs. Not one of them bowled a maiden.

52
214* for Worcestershire v Oxford University, New Road, 25 June 1975

Worcestershire 354/4 decl (G. M. Turner 214*, G. R. Cass 52*, K. W. Wilkinson 46, J. M. Parker 30) and 266/4 decl (E. J. O. Hemsley 143*, Wilkinson 61, I. N. Johnson 30) beat **Oxford University** 339/5 decl (T. R. Glover 117, V. J. Marks 88, Imran Khan 69, A. C. Hamilton 37) and 200 (Imran 91, Marks 36; Johnson 5/74, Parker 3/26).

First innings: not out 214
Second innings: did not bat

Turner's second double-century in England, and his highest score, was almost inevitably against one of the universities, and his first at the expense of Oxford. It was the most rapid of his double-centuries, in only 270 minutes, with two sixes and 23 fours, and Turner himself scored his runs at the rate of three an over. Worcestershire, which went on to bat for 83 overs, was given a splendid start by Turner and the left-handed Keith Wilkinson, and the latter certainly prospered from the bowling of Oxford: 141 and 80 the year before, 46 and 61 this time. Hemsley, to make amends in the second innings, made only five, and Phil Neale four (but he was there for 24 runs), but there were other sizeable partnerships. John Parker and Turner got 93 for the third wicket; Turner and Rodney Cass an unbeaten 106 for the fifth wicket before Turner declared.

The university lads must have thought they were at home on the Parks, such was the excellence of the pitch, and Turner was not too unkind in asking them to score 282 in three and a half hours. He kept the game open, too, by bowling his part-time spinners in long spells with Ian Johnson and John Parker responding appropriately, though not before Imran, then a part-time player for Worcestershire, had completed a splendid batting double: 160 runs for once out, in even time. Trevor Glover, the Oxford captain, batted four and a half hours for his first innings century, and Victor Marks, later with Somerset, helped him add 140 for the second wicket. Apart from Marks and Imran, Oxford used four bowlers: David Fursdon, Charlie Cantlay, Andrew Wingfield-Digby and David Brettell.

This wasn't one of my most satisfying centuries, though the bowling was a little stronger than one often meets in a university match. I was dropped twice (35, 126) and there were one or two streaky shots, because I wasn't consciously trying to play a big innings. But I welcomed having four and a half hours out in the middle, because the first Prudential Cup competition was coming up. As it happened then, this was very good practice for the series and I went on to get the highest aggregate.

53

154* for Worcestershire v Glamorgan, St Helen's, Swansea, 23, 25 August 1975

Worcestershire 300/2 decl (G. M. Turner 154*, J. M. Parker 57*, K. W. Wilkinson 54) and 247/4 decl (J.A. Ormrod 124, Parker 47, Imran Khan 42*) drew with **Glamorgan** 300/3 decl (Majid Khan 170*, A. Jones 65, J. A. Hopkins 33*) and 186/6 (J. W. Solanky 51*, L. W. Hill 40, R. C. Davis 31; N. Gifford 3/66).

First innings: not out 154
Second innings: did not bat

I remember this game not so much for my innings, because the pitch wasn't really that very difficult, as the attitude of Majid. The very last run I took, I injured a muscle in the top of my thigh, and was not able to field at all in Glamorgan's innings. Of course, Majid — perhaps because it's the sort of thing he would have done — thought I was doing a Hanif; you know, run up and down for 154 runs yet not able to field. Actually, the tear was that bad, I wasn't able to take any further part in the match, and I wasn't even really right for the next game, against Essex, though I played. Not that I was needed in the second innings, for the pitch got easier and easier, and Ormers was in good nick. But Majid took a real negative attitude to the match. I mean, his batting was far from negative, but his captaincy was. He got a stye in his eye, but even allowing for that, Giffy set a pretty reasonable target: 248 in two and a half hours, which included 20 overs in the last hour, and it turned out to be about 5½ an over on a pitch which really was very, very good. But Majid just kipped in the dressing room without taking any interest in his team's innings at all, and they were pretty pissed off with him. He eventually had to come in, at No. 8, and naturally didn't want the last half-hour, so Giffy claimed it anyway, just to make him stay out there.

Turner himself was in very crisp form in Worcestershire's innings, hitting 22 fours in his four-hour innings, which had Worcestershire declaring after 84 overs. He, Alan Ormrod (26 — they scored 62 for the first wicket) and Keith Wilkinson had taken Worcestershire to 147 for one by 1 pm when steady rain finished play for the day. But it made little difference to the fine pitch, and after Turner and his team had dashed back to Worcester for a John Player League match against Sussex at New Road, in which Turner kept his eye in with a rather ponderous 57 not out from 35 overs, Worcestershire piled on the runs. He and Wilkinson took their second wicket stand from 85 to 129, then John Parker, for a rare change outscoring Turner, helped his New Zealand colleague add an unbeaten 109. Nor was there anything much wrong with the attack: Malcolm Nash, and Tony Cordle, the West Indian from Tiger Bay, were the openers, followed by John Solanky and Lawrence Williams, with Roger Davis and Geoff Ellis also bowling.

54
177* for Otago v Wellington, Basin Reserve, 26, 27 December 1975

Wellington 302/9 decl (G. P. Bilby 86, M. J. Harris 83, G. A. Newdick 55; B. J. McKechnie 3/72) and 225/2 decl (Newdick 112*, Bilby 56*) drew with **Otago** 298/6 decl (G. M. Turner 177*, W. K. Lees 72) and 113/3 (Turner 38).

First innings: not out 177
Second innings: c Harris b B. W. Cederwall 38

It was almost entirely thanks to Turner that Otago not only avoided a heavy defeat, but also could have secured a first innings lead. Such events did not look at all likely early in the second day, for Otago, 31 for one at stumps after 45 minutes (Turner 16), was quickly 31 for two, and half an hour before lunch, 85 for five, Turner having reached his 50 in 136 minutes. But the Wellington bowlers — Ewen Chatfield, Christopher Ross, Brian Cederwall and Mike Coles did most of the work — then had nearly a whole session without reward. Turner and Warren Lees together put on 165 for the sixth wicket in 146 minutes, Turner going to his 100 in 208 minutes, and when he declared at tea, he had batted 315 minutes for 20 fours. The weather conspired to foil the efforts of the captains — Grahame Bilby led Wellington — to achieve a result, however. Rain cost two hours 46 minutes on the final day, and Otago finished a mere 17 runs short of its target.

55

104 for Otago v Auckland, Carisbrook, 30 December 1975

Otago 276 (G. M. Turner 104, H. C. Sampson 90, B. J. McKechnie 30; H. J. Howarth 4/58) and 194 (R. W. Anderson 53, Turner 34; Howarth 7/75) beat **Auckland** 276 (R. W. Morgan 81, J. D. Riley 80, M. G. Burgess 33, R. E. Redmond 31; P. J. Petherick 5/104, D. E. C. McKechnie 3/71) and 184 (Redmond 52; D. McKechnie 6/65, Petherick 3/86).

First innings: b Howarth 104
Second innings: c and b R. J. Hunter 34

Dunedin provided unusually hot and tiring conditions for one of the most even of Shell series matches, and in retrospect, Richard Matthews must have suffered agonies for his dropping of Turner at mid-off from the medium-paced bowling of Warren Stott when the opener was only nine. Even so, Otago was struggling a shade at 60 for two, before Henry Sampson joined Turner and the pair added 113 in 112 minutes. When Turner was bowled by Hedley Howarth, drawing away and trying to cut the slow left-armer, he had batted 208 minutes and faced 205 balls. He hit 15 fours, usually in batches of two or three at a time and with fluent drives and cuts, before having to lapse into frequent inactive periods as he battled to contend with the masterly bowling of Howarth. Turner's footwork was equally masterly.

It was obvious that someone of Howarth's skill had to be handled carefully, and it was a pretty demanding, but very enjoyable battle we had. I guess honours were pretty even: I got my ton, and he got me out and finished, I see, with four for 58 from 38 overs.

Turner took 103 minutes for his 50, and the same time for his second 50, reaching his century with a straight drive from the off-spinner, Ray Hunter. He was out at 173 for three, Auckland's bowlers being Matthews and Stott to open, followed by Howarth, Hunter, Ross Morgan with his dart-like off-spinners, and Austin Parsons, with some medium pace. After the first innings were tied, Otago won a dramatic victory thanks to its two 'country' spinners, Peter Petherick and Don McKechnie.

56
115 for Otago v Northern Districts, Carisbrook, 8 January 1976

Otago 319/8 decl (G. M. Turner 115, R. W. Anderson 69, K. O. Campbell 36; R. O. Collinge 5/30) and 168/2 decl (Turner 80*, H. C. Sampson 51*) drew with **Northern Districts** 172 (B. Dunning 32; P. J. Petherick 9/93) and 109/2 (A. D. G. Roberts 45*).

First innings: c M. J. E. Wright b Roberts 115
Second innings: not out 80

There's always been a certain amount of friction between 'town' and 'country' in Otago cricket. On the one hand, there were the Dunedin (and Mosgiel) players and competition; on the other, Southland, south and central Otago, and North Otago, with Southland especially often providing the bulk of the representative side. This season, with Gren Alabaster just having finished, Peter Petherick came into his own and it was a pretty big step for a guy who had been around a long while but never far away from Alexandra. He stayed with me during our home matches, and it was then that I found he had been warned to be careful — or to ignore — what the 'townies' said; 'they'll try to stuff you up' was the gist of the message, which was absurd, with me as captain, and obviously wanting to get the best return possible out of my bowlers. I think his returns, notably in this game, were an adequate sort of answer, but it does underline the politics of Otago cricket. Ironically, now I have my holiday home in Central Otago.

Otago was always handily placed in this match, Turner and Ian Rutherford getting the side away well with 79 in 103 minutes, then Turner and Robert Anderson adding 130 for the second wicket in just 109 minutes. But a quarter-hour after Anderson was out, Turner fell too, 'caught' at the wicket by Mike Wright from the bowling of Andy Roberts, hitting a six and 15 fours in an innings lasting a minute short of four hours. Six years after the event, that dismissal brings a chuckle.

If I was out then, I was never out, but Ernie Currie put his finger up, so I had to go. Andy Roberts, of course, loved it; he had me on then, and has done ever since. I think he knew it wasn't out.

Otago just failed to enforce the follow-on, and that failure probably cost it the game. Turner declared at stumps on the second day, Otago and he having batted 182 minutes, and when he reached 51 in that innings, Turner's season aggregate became 703, breaking the record he set the previous season. He left Northern Districts a full day to score 316, but rain played a critical part in the tame finish.

Turner, incidentally, reached his 50 from only 68 balls when he straight-drove Brian Dunning 'like a bullet' (as Brent Edwards described it at the time), while his complete innings lasted 202 balls, many of them from the test opening pair, Richie Collinge and Bob Cunis, who were far from impressed at the slowness of the pitch.

57

121* for Otago v India, Carisbrook, 1 February 1976

India 304/5 decl (D. B. Vengsarkar 130, B. P. Patel 73, A. Rao 34; B. J. McKechnie 3/64) and 144 (P. Sharma 45, Vengsarkar 32; P. J. Petherick 6/36) drew with **Otago** 252/9 decl (G. M. Turner 121*, R. W. Anderson 66; S. Venkataraghavan 5/87, B.´S. Bedi 3/73) and 116/2 (H. C. Sampson 57, Turner 55).

First innings: not out 121
Second innings: c Venkataraghavan b Bedi 55

I was talking last century about the politics of Otago cricket, but this one really involved me in the problems of dealing with totally inflexible amateurs who happened to be employing me, a professional. I had asked to be left out of this game: I was rooted, mentally tired. At Carisbrook, if you got hundreds — and I'd already got two that season — it took more out of you than anywhere (or anyone) else. So by the time this one came round, I was shagged out, and not only that, I didn't think it was vital that I played. I was captain of the team but my responsibility was surely towards the meaningful competition, not what was a fill-in game for both us and the Indians. I pointed out that this was what was done in England, that capped players are frequently left out of the touring team's games, or the non-competition games, to allow qualifying players or youngsters to have a match. But they were totally unsympathetic, and said I should be no more tired than anyone else; they ignored the fact that I had scored twice as many runs as anyone else, or thereabouts and had batted — or worked — twice as long. All they could counter with was that I was employed to play, and I should. Then along came a crazy lack of logic. We were already through to the Shell final, and they came to me, said I didn't need to go to Auckland; that didn't follow, because I should have been playing all the competition games. Ken Deas, *from Auckland, even got in touch and offered $100, a fair sum, then, or an air fare for my wife, but Sukhi wasn't all that fussed about going. In the end, they even insisted I go, which was really my feeling, anyway. But back to this Indian game, I played of course; I really had no option, but it had to be one of my most difficult centuries. I had not had the mental build-up, what with all the hassling, and I gave three chances as well as Syed Kirmani, their very good wicket-keeper, missing an extremely difficult stumping chance. They didn't really worry too much about their opening attack — Ian Rutherford and I put on 42 — because they had Sunny Gavaskar opening with Mohinder Amarnath, but they had their full line-up of spinners, Venkat, Chandrasekhar and Bishen Singh Bedi. Venkat, an offie, and Bedi, a left-armer, were orthodox enough, but Chandra was something different.*

Though he was mainly a top-spin and googly bowler, if it was taking spin, he was able to get the legger to go, and this was very dangerous. He was very difficult to play in these conditions and that meant hard runs. It took all my skills and effort to overcome the best spin attack in the world in this innings, and I don't think those chances detract from the innings.

Turner took 291 minutes over this innings, his first 50 taking 118 minutes, his second 109. He hit eight fours, and shared a second wicket partnership of 148 in 160 minutes with Robert Anderson. Interestingly enough, the next best partnership — apart from the 42 with Rutherford (13) — was 23 for the third wicket with Henry Sampson, who scored five. Otago, needing 196 to win the match, was perhaps deprived of one of its best international results by rain on the third day.

Turner's first chance was at 10, a caught and bowled to 'Sunny' Gavaskar, of all people, and he was put down by Chandrasekhar at 26. He went from 95 to 100 with a dicey sweep for four, then a pushed single next ball, from Bedi, and three runs later gave his third chance, a difficult catch to Patel.

58

177 for New Zealand v India, Lancaster Park, 5, 6, 8 February 1976

India 270 (G. R. Viswanath 83, M. Amarnath 45; R. O. Collinge 6/63, D. R. Hadlee 3/76) and 255/6 (Viswanath 79, S. M. Gavaskar 71, D. B. Vengsarkar 30, M. Amarnath 30) drew with **New Zealand** 403 (G. M. Turner 117, B. E. Congdon 58, J. M. Parker 44, R. J. Hadlee 33, J. F. M. Morrison 31, M. G. Burgess 31; Madan Lal 5/134, Amarnath 4/63).

First innings: c S. M. H. Kirmani b M. Amarnath 117

This was probably the least memorable of Turner's seven test centuries, one scored when he was probably not quite himself after being 'forced' to play against the tourists for Otago. It was an innings, however, in which the approach was dictated by the toss and the strengths of the opposing team. India won the toss, scored usefully if not brilliantly against the all-seam — Richard Collinge, Richard and Dayle Hadlee and Bevan Congdon — attack employed by Turner in the first innings, and had New Zealand batting before stumps on the first day. So obviously a moderately long occupation of the crease was as important as securing a useful lead, for New Zealand faced fourth innings against the world's best spin attack. Such a relatively negative approach consigned the match to a draw; but New Zealand could retrospectively claim correctness, for Richard Hadlee's fiery bowling in the next test, at the Basin Reserve, gave New Zealand a series win.

In the 40 minutes New Zealand batted on the first day, Turner (9) and John Morrison (11) scored 26 together, and in a further 54 minutes the next morning, took the partnership to 56. That was the only wicket to fall in the morning session, by which time New Zealand was 91 for one, Turner just 28 in the morning, 37 all told and Bevan Congdon his partner. The 65 runs in that session came from 25 overs.

So it went on the afternoon, the bare details being that Turner and Congdon added 114 in 168 minutes before Congdon was stumped just before tea (172 for two), when Turner was 73. That session of 28 overs brought 81 runs; the final session was breakneck speed by comparison: 65 from 17.2 overs, 39 of them to John Parker in only 81 balls.

By then Turner, all fierce concentration and dogged defence, interspersed only occasionally with flowing cuts and drives, had gone to his century in 351 minutes, with eight fours. All told, by the time stumps were drawn a half-hour early — Bedi hurried the decision, mercifully, by bringing back Madan Lal with the new ball — he had batted 363 minutes and faced 304 balls.

His resumption was delayed until nearly three hours on the Sunday by rain and Turner was not of a mood to hurry things along. After all, New Zealand still trailed by 33 runs, and still trailed when Parker was out at 254, the 84-run partnership taking 135 minutes. Finally, New Zealand still 10 behind, Turner was caught at the wicket by the excellent Syed Kirmani from Mohinder Amarnath, and he must have counted himself unlucky. He played a very deliberate leg-glance, only to look round not to see it racing to the boundary, but nestling in Kirmani's left hand. Turner batted 415 minutes, in which he faced 346 balls, and hit nine fours. New Zealand went on to a lead of 133 in an innings which lasted a total of 644 minutes, and India ended up averaging close to 12½ overs an hour only because Bhagwat Chandrasekhar, Bishen Bedi and Sriniva Prasanna between them bowled 61 overs. When Amarnath and Madan Lal were operating, it was pitifully slow: a ball a minute for the first hour of the third day. New Zealand's innings actually went into the fifth day, and by then the game was as dead as a dodo. Surprisingly, the people of Christchurch were tigers for punishment for 10,000 or so were there most days.

The toss, the other team's attack, and the situation of the series really tell it all, don't they. Much as one might like to entertain, and to get some personal satisfaction, the whole series could have been finished if we had played irresponsibly. So it's sorry to those who felt they were not entertained, but no apologies at all for drawing a game that could easily have been lost.

59
169 for Worcestershire v Nottinghamshire, Trent Bridge, 12, 14 June 1976

Nottinghamshire 281 (M. J. Harris 74, C. E. B. Rice 56, S. B. Hassan 52; R. Senghera 3/63, Imran Khan 3/70) and 242 (P. A. Todd 60, R. A. White 39; N. Gifford 4/86, Senghera 4/97) lost to **Worcestershire** 367/6 decl (G. M. Turner 169, B. L. D'Oliveira 106*, J. A. Ormrod 35) and 158/3 (E. J. O. Hemsley 37*, P. A. Neale 36, Turner 34).

First innings: c Harris b B. Stead 169
Second innings: c Harris b White 34

Turner and the in-form Basil D'Oliveira contributed mightily to Worcestershire's first win of the season, and one which lifted it then to the dizzy heights of thirteenth in the county championship. Conditions could not really have been much better when Worcestershire set off in pursuit of Nottinghamshire's 281, Imran Khan making the early breakthrough, and the good work being carried on by Ravi Senghera and Norman Gifford. From the 17 overs by the Notts bowlers on a lovely, sunny, summer's Saturday evening, Turner and Ormrod went to 44 in 55 minutes, Turner 39 of them. In between the first and second days, there was a Sunday bleak in terms of results and performance: Notts cruised home in their John Player League match by seven wickets. But Turner (43) and D'Oliveira (56) had been the major run-scorers for Worcestershire, and they were in similar mood and form on the Monday.

There were the preliminaries to get over, however, and under a more cloudy sky, Turner and Ormrod took their opening partnership to 118 in a further 100 minutes before Ormrod was bowled. Turner, then 79, had reached his 50 in 83 minutes, in the 26th over, and while Phil Neale (14) and Imran (3) were coming and going, he passed his 100 in 163 minutes. At lunch, 60 overs, Worcestershire was 179 for three, Turner by then 118 and 'Dolly' a mere five.

An hour after lunch, they reached their century partnership, just 65 minutes, and the fourth wicket stand had gone to 133 before Turner was out at 269, passing his 150 in 235 minutes, batting four hours all told and hitting 22 fours.

Turner was eventually caught by Mike 'Patsy' Harris, who had had some cricket in Lower Hutt, from the left-arm quickish bowling of Barry Stead, now sadly dead of cancer. But his own innings was recalled less easily to mind than the misfortune of Harry Latchman, the West Indian Cockney who had shifted from Middlesex to Notts.

He got pinned, lapping, sweeping at Giffy. Although it really was a very, very good track, it did wear as the game went on and was taking turn, a lot. The ball popped a bit, came off the shoulder of the bat, and next thing, Latchman was away for stitches above the eye, and just when he was getting a bit awkward to move. He actually came out and had a bowl at us in our second innings, but he wasn't himself and that was rather fortunate for us, with the pitch going. That meant Notts really only had Bob — 'Knocker' — White to bowl his off-breaks at us, and with all five of us getting a few, Ted Hemsley getting them the best, we got there pretty easily.

Stead and Clive Rice were the Notts opening bowlers, Philip Wilkinson to back them up, and White and Latchman the spinners.

60

135* for Worcestershire v Somerset, Bath, 18 June 1976

Worcestershire 160 (J. A. Ormrod 30; G. I. Burgess 4/43) and 206/3 decl (G. M. Turner 135*, Imran Khan 31) drew with **Somerset** 148 (P. A. Slocombe 42; J. D. Inchmore 5/53, B. L. D'Oliveira 3/23) and 179/8 (M. J. Kitchen 32).

First innings: b C. H. Dredge 9
Second innings: not out 135

'Cricket perfection' was one contemporary view of Turner's second innings in this match haunted by rain and low cloud until the sun and Turner brought a rosy glow to the final day. Only two hours of play were possible on the first day; the second was 45 minutes late starting; yet Worcestershire still got to the brink of victory. But the Somerset captain, Brian Langford, and a lanky 21-year-old opening bowler in his first game, Colin Dredge, contrived to survive the final eight overs with fieldsmen clustered round the bat. Dredge made his debut match memorable in all ways, as he bowled Turner in the first innings for his first wicket in first-class cricket.

This was one of Turner's finest, most flowing innings. The Worcestershire innings commenced half an hour into the third day but a glittering Turner and the obdurate Alan Ormrod had 94 together in only 88 minutes, Turner 64 of them, Ormrod only 29, and Turner had reached his half-century in only four minutes over an hour. At lunch, 103 for two — Phil Neale was brilliantly caught in the gully for one from the first ball of the final over — Turner was 72 in 103 minutes, or 32 overs. The same tempo was maintained after the break, as Turner, with elegant off-drives and masterly square-cutting predominating, went to his inevitable century in 131 minutes. There was an 82-run partnership for the third wicket with Imran Khan, a quick 21 unbeaten with

Basil D'Oliveira (4*), and when Norman Gifford called a halt — setting Somerset 219 in 142 minutes — Turner had batted 176 minutes and hit 25 fours.

I've often had batches of two or three boundaries together in a longish innings, but this innings was unusual and distinctive for the numbers of groupings. I went from 21 to 49 with seven fours, then from 60 to 80, and from 109 to 129 each time with five boundaries. Mind you, provided one was in good nick, and we'd just finished that match at Trent Bridge where I got a couple of hundred in the two innings, it wasn't too hard to score well and quickly. Bath is a pretty small ground, and even with the rain on the first day, the outfield was very quick.

61
150 for Worcestershire v Sussex, Hove, 24, 26 July 1976

Sussex 195 (P. W. G. Parker 58; A. P. Pridgeon 4/46, Imran Khan 4/54) and 246 (J. R. T. Barclay 79, A. Long 39, J. D. Horley 34; Imran 5/63, J. D. Inchmore 3/50) lost to **Worcestershire** 325 (G. M. Turner 150, J. A. Ormrod 72, H. G. Wilcock 41; R. D. V. Knight 4/46, J. Spencer 4/89) and 117/4 (Ormrod 45; Spencer 3/45).

First innings: lbw b Knight 150
Second innings: c Long b Spencer 18

Sussex became the sixteenth of the 17 English counties to concede a century to the bat of Turner, and only Lancashire remained after this innings. A gently battering innings, it was too, with some glorious driving among the 24 fours. But not all those boundaries were in front of the wicket.

There was this left-arm seamer, Alan Marshall, and he kept trying to bounce me out, especially on the first day, the Saturday. It was a gloriously hot, sunny day, and not too much of the movement that you can get on those seaside grounds in Essex and Kent. So this Marshall kept bouncing me, and I kept hooking him for fours, one of those contests that neither principal will give up, but I tend to think I won. I got an even ton in 160 minutes that day, and Marshall finished with one (Norman Gifford, at the end of the innings) for 98.

There was certainly a buoyant start to the Worcestershire innings, Turner and Alan Ormrod scoring 169 in 153 minutes before a brilliant throw from Paul Parker ran Ormrod out. Before the resumption of the county match, the two sides also met in a John Player Sunday League match, a gripping affair in which Gifford struck 6, 4, 2, 2, 2, 1 from Roger Knight's last over, failing to win an astonishing victory by just one run. Turner made 38 to hold his good form for the Monday, but he was not quite the same commanding figure of the Saturday. With Ravi Senghera, the nightwatchman, as his partner, Turner took Worcestershire past 200 — himself 112 — in the sixty-first over, for a change cover-driving Marshall for four.

Turner and Senghera had 38 together for the second wicket, the off-spinner 13 of them, then Phillip Neale got 11 in the 30-run — at a run a minute — partnership for the third wicket. Imran Khan contributed just two towards the nine for the fourth wicket, and at 257, Turner was out. He square-cut Knight for four — his eighth boundary of the day — to reach 150, and next ball was lbw. He had batted for 248 minutes, and in the light of this assured batting display, 'Spud' Spencer's bowling was deserving of the highest praise. He bowled 44.3 overs — all but nine at his end — in taking four for 89. Marshall should have learned something from watching him.

62

120 for Worcestershire v Northamptonshire, Northampton, 22, 23 August 1976

Worcestershire 313 (Imran Khan 166, G. M. Turner 53, J. A. Ormrod 31; B. S. Bedi 4/78, A Hodgson 3/76) and 328 (Turner 120, Ormrod 92, D. N. Patel 47*, N. Gifford 37; Bedi 4/65, Sarfraz Nawaz 3/72) lost to **Northamptonshire** 395/7 decl (D. S. Steele 92, Mushtaq Mohammed 82, G. Cook 71, R. T. Virgin 54, P. Willey 36*, J. D. Inchmore 3/83) and 247/6 (W. Larkins 83, Cook 45, Mushtaq 42; Gifford 5/106).

First innings: c and b Hodgson 53
Second innings: c G. Sharp b Bedi 120

An injured hand suffered by Imran Khan and an astonishing batting display from Wayne Larkins gave Northamptonshire a dramatic victory in its quest for the county championship — it was to finish second to Middlesex — and Worcestershire one of only three losses in the season. Imran made light of his injury in his amazing first innings, which lasted only 150 minutes, and which included a 127-run ninth wicket stand with Norman Gifford, who got just 10 of them in 75 minutes. But in his absence at the bowling crease, Northants scored plentifully and well to send Turner and Ormrod in again facing a deficit of 82.

How well they responded to the challenge on the hot and cloudless late Sunday afternoon, and on this pitch, already taking considerable turn, and against such spinners as Bedi, Mushtaq and Willey. In only two minutes over two hours, they raced to 169, and for once Ormrod kept pace with his younger, more aggressive partner. At stumps, both were 81 and they had the Northants attack in tatters. The next morning, an equally hot day, Turner raced to his century in 142 minutes, scoring 20 in the first 20 minutes — while Ormrod was getting seven — from Mushtaq and Bedi. Turner had then hit 14 fours. When he was 114, from 50 overs, the opening stand was broken with Ormrod's dismissal: their 213 partnership had lasted only 150 minutes. With that, Turner lost a little of his impetus, and when he was out at 230, scored in 185 minutes, he had 17 fours. But the personal century does not loom largest in his memory.

More, it was this innings from Wayne Larkins. The ball was turning even more when we left them 247 in not much over two hours and they still needed 135 in the final 20 overs, six wickets in hand: they got the runs with seven minutes left and four wickets in hand, thanks to Larkins. He went mad. He kept hitting Giffy over long-on, and they weren't just sixes; they were going for twelves! He hit five sixes, or twelves, or whatever, and six fours, and got 83 in 50 minutes. Poor Giffy couldn't do much about it and he was averaging six an over. The other vivid memory is that this was the game in which Dickie Bird, not quite at the top of the umpiring tree then, broke down in tears after John Inchmore — hardly John Darling! — barrelled him for turning down an lbw.

Very little remained for Worcestershire in this season, though it had a thrilling and unexpected victory at Cardiff against Glamorgan, Turner making 87 in the first innings and Ormrod paving the way to the win with his second innings 166. Then the heat-wave broke and only four hours play was possible against Middlesex, and in the final match, against Gloucestershire, Turner was out for 11 and 2. So he, strangely, finished the season without a home century, and equally strangely, none of his tons came in the second innings chases at which he had become so proficient.

63

113, for New Zealand v India, Green Park Stadium, Kanpur, 19, 20 November 1976

India 524/9 decl (M. Amarnath 70, G. R. Viswanath 68, S. M. Gavaskar 66, S. M. H. Kirmani 64, B. S. Bedi 50*, A. V. Mankad 50, A. D. Gaekwad 43, S. Ghavri 37; P. J. Petherick 3/109, D. R. O'Sullivan 3/125) and 208/2 decl (Viswanath 103*, Gaekwad 77*) drew with **New Zealand** 350 (G. M. Turner 113, A. D. G. Roberts 84*, M. G. Burgess 54, J. M. Parker 34; Bedi 3/80, S. Venkataraghavan 3/102) and 193/7 (W. K. Lees 49*, Turner 35; Bedi 3/42).

First innings: c Viswanath b Bedi 113
Second innings: c Venkataraghavan b Bedi 35

The bare bones of the innings first, commenced an hour before stumps on the second day after India had established a record with all 11 players reaching double-figures. Even Bhagwat Chandrasekhar was 10 not out! But Turner and Geoff Howarth seemed undismayed for they raced to 50 by the close, Turner 31 of them, Howarth 17, but Howarth was quickly out the next morning. Turner and John Parker took the score from 54 to 118, then Burgess took part in a 106-run stand for the third wicket before Turner was out at 224, scored in 216 minutes. He had hit 14 fours, and even though Burgess followed immediately, Andy Roberts was to play his highest innings in a test career rather oddly scantily encouraged by New Zealand selectors, and to guide his team past the follow-on mark. That was to prove the saving of the game. Turner, however, had greater battles.

This was the ill-fated tour, and one on which I very nearly didn't go. I was the captain, yet, with the other two pros of the time, John Parker and Daffy O'Sullivan, I was going to be the lowest paid. I was only on the same terms as the amateurs in the team, expenses and basic wages, but the likes of Peter Petherick, for example, got $1500 from the Alexan-

dra community. Don't take me wrong; I don't begrudge him
that at all. But just across to the east of Alex, I was employed
by the Otago Cricket Association. I'd been employed by
the OCA that long that it was my southern hemisphere
employer, but it was not prepared to pay me for these two or
three months.

So it became the responsibility of the New Zealand Cricket
Council to make up the difference; it refused, even though in
all modesty it could not risk me pulling out as well. Already,
Bevan Congdon and Hedley Howarth were unavailable,
then Ken Wadsworth pulled out with the first illness from
the cancer that was to take his life. And when we arrived,
Geoff Howarth wanted to go home, he just couldn't live
there.

Then there was the big barney in Lahore because Wal
Hadlee, back in quiet old Christchurch, found out I was
going to write for a newspaper, the Sunday Times in Wellington. As chairman of the NZCC board of control, he said
no way. Murray Chapple, the manager, confronted me with
this news and edict, and my argument was that I needed some
employment as the council had shown me no consideration.
I mean, it was just a principle as the money wasn't that great
and Murray reported back to New Zealand that my participa-
tion was crucial to the tour and strongly recommended that I
be allowed to go ahead. Nothing more was heard to the
contrary, not that it mattered, because I was going ahead,
anyway. I did feel a commitment to continue with the tour,
all along, though, because my in-laws live in Bombay, my
wife Sukhi was there for two months, and they all considered
my presence very important.

Then, along came the second big crisis. In the second test
against Pakistan, at Hyderabad, I got hit on the forearm, my
left arm, by Imran Khan. That had happened to me before, in
England, and I'd tried hydrocortizone without it having any
useful effect. The next test was in Karachi, and I found I
couldn't hold the bat. I depend so much on my top hand that
if I can't grip the bat tightly, I'm not half the player. So I
declared myself unfit — the hardest decision I've had to make
and the most unpopular. The side were as grizzly as hell;

165

Chapple wouldn't talk to me for two days. It was the old New Zealand attitude: Colin Meads plays with a broken arm and is to be admired; my attitude was that my playing, in my condition, would have been an insult to the substitutes.

After all that trauma, I worked very hard in Bombay in the nets; even a special session on my own to get into form. So it was a great relief to get a hundred, and pleasant too: a little over 23 degrees, against the mid-30s and 90 per cent humidity in Bombay. It made batting and playing generally a great deal more comfortable.

I wasn't so comfortable when I was out in the second innings. Rather, I was **given** *out, caught in the gully off Bedi by the guy with the longest name in test cricket, and usually abbreviated to Venkat. The ball pitched on my toe and lobbed up to gully, and that is the only time I can remember throwing a bit of a wobbly. Bedi reckoned I walked off the field like Ian Chappell, and I do remember that as I went past the umpire, I had a few things to say to him. Incidentally, that was the test when the Indian press said we refused to eat with the Indian team. In fact, they usually ate in their dressing room, and so much happened in this game that we felt we were better to eat in private!*

After that controversial second innings dismissal, New Zealand struggled to save the game, but did so with Warren Lees and David O'Sullivan — he scored 23 not out — staying together for the final two hours. Examine the flattering figures of the home team spinners: Bedi three for 42 from 40 overs, Venkat — we'll stick with the diminutive! — two for 46 from 34 overs, and Chandra two for 61 from his 33 overs.

177* for Northern Districts v Central Districts, McLean Park, Napier, 7 January 1977

Northern Districts 278/8 decl (G. M. Turner 177*; D. R. O'Sullivan 5/82) and 194/3 decl (Turner 63, J. M. Parker 34*, J. G. Wright 32; A. B. Jordan 3/88) beat **Central Districts** 206 (M. J. F. Shrimpton 51, D. H. Payton 45; A. D. G. Roberts 5/30, R. O. Collinge 3/72) and 261 (G. N. Edwards 62, G. J. Langridge 36, P. J. Holland 36, Shrimpton 35; G. P. Howarth 3/34).

First innings: not out 177
Second inning: c Shrimpton b Jordan 63

Rather surprisingly, Turner had returned from all the hassles of the India-Pakistan tour like a lion refreshed. Perhaps it was the relief of being out of a tour that is always difficult, with its attendant problems of sickness and sub-standard almost-everythings: hotels, press relations, umpires, decent cricketing pitches. Not to mention again, of course, the problems mentioned in the previous chapter. Equally surprisingly, though, Turner made only this one century for Northern Districts in this season which was almost certainly the most pleasurable he spent in New Zealand cricket.

Northern Districts had been the poor relation of New Zealand cricket for so long, merely because it was the youngest and thus the least successful. But as far as I was concerned, it was the most professional of the New Zealand associations, a real pleasure to deal with, nothing a real problem — treating me as a real person, and not an object who should be engaged grudgingly because I could bat. But for having my roots in Otago, I would have found it very easy to head more permanently for the far north.

But though Turner had not made a century for Northern

Districts before this match, he was certainly in the right sort of form. His previous Shell Cup scores — this was in the days when the first round was for the Cup, the grand final-type play-off was for the Trophy — had included 93, 89 and 97 not out when he declared against Wellington.

This was all put to rights on this curious pitch, one which no doubt encouraged Central Districts to bowl first, for it was grassy and damp. But Alistair Jordan and Dennis Kay got surprisingly little life or movement from it, except that the occasional ball was inclined to pop off a good length. Conversely, it took turn on the first morning — accordingly, David O'Sullivan, in his home town, had all but eight overs from one end, 29 all told, and had five wickets. In this rather limited attack — the fourth and only other bowler used was the off-spinner, Doug Bracewell — he regularly winkled out the talented Northern Districts line-up, and Turner found himself fighting a lone action. The partnership figures tell all: 33 with John Wright (15), 17 with Geoff Howarth (6), 43 with John Parker (17), 32 with Andy Roberts (8), 27 with Rod Fulton (9), 11 with Mike Wright (7), 76 with Cliff Dickeson (8) for the seventh wicket, 31 with Richard Collinge (13), an unbeaten eight before the declaration, all of them to Bob Cunis. A talented line-up indeed, but those many failures drove Turner to a grafting innings: 268 minutes for his century. But at 163 for six and the tail well exposed, the situation demanded runs while they could be taken, and Turner set after the bowling in glowing fashion. Nothing brutal about the last 77 runs, in a mere 79 minutes: simply persuading the ball that asked for it to the boundary, stealing singles with ease to shelter Dickeson from the strike, until he called it a day, in the interests of the ultimate victory which gave Northern the Shell Cup, with a double-century beckoning. And in the end, the captaincy aggression of Turner brought his team a 5-run win, flattering to Central Districts as he had Geoff Howarth continuing to bowl no-balls by way of bait to the Central batsmen. It worked . . . just.

65

153 for Worcestershire v Hampshire, New Road, 18 June 1977

Worcestershire 308/5 decl (G. M. Turner 153, E. J. O. Hemsley 79, B. L. D'Oliveira 48*) and 127 (P. A. Neale 31; J. M. Rice 7/48) lost to **Hampshire** 284/7 decl (D. R. Turner 69, N. G. Cowley 60*, Rice 34) and 152/4 (B. A. Richards 78*, C. G. Greenidge 30).

First innings: c R. B. Elms b J. W. Southern 153
Second innings: b Rice 2

I'd had a strange sort of season, one way and another. For one thing, for the first time since Graham Dowling shoved me down the order in 1969, I didn't open regularly. Not that it worried me as much as eight years earlier. Then I was still fighting to make my way, to prove myself to everyone's satisfaction. This year, however, I went down without much persuasion because of the all-round situation of the team. We only had four capped batsmen, only seven capped players altogether, and one of the youngsters in the side fairly regularly was Barry Jones. The poor lad didn't have much of a season at all, mainly because he wasn't too good against spinners. So we thought we'd try him opening, with me at 5 or 6; it didn't really make a great deal of difference to me and I think I did much the same there as opening. I remember I had an 89 against Lancashire, which naturally stuck in the mind as I still hadn't scored a ton against them. But for this match, I was back to opening.

It was as well for Worcestershire at the outset, for Bob Stephenson won the toss for Hampshire and on this dull and damp day, and with this dull and damp pitch, brightened only by its greenness, had no hesitation in telling Worcestershire to bat. The correctness of that decision was quickly brought home to the local side, with Alan Ormrod out to the first ball he faced from Trevor Jesty, and Phillip Neale was out soon afterwards: three for two wickets.

But Turner and Ted Hemsley were nothing if not dedicated to the task of sorting out Worcestershire's problems, and they aschewed all risks for the next half-hour while the pitch was at its most venomous: it was not until the eleventh over that the score moved into the twenties. This was the Turner of his fledgling days: settling into the 'V' until his touch was such that the compass of attack could be broadened. So it proved with the pair of them, and as the pitch eased a shade, they moved into their drives more fluently, and Turner reached his 50 in 103 minutes — three minutes quicker than Hemsley — with seven fours. So juicy was the pitch, too, that five medium-pacers had been used by the time the score was 70. At 91 for two, Jimmy Southern, a slow left-armer, was given his turn but Turner (67) and Hemsley (55) were still together at lunch: a respectable 128 for two from 41 overs.

Strangely, Turner scored only another 67 from a further 43 overs in the second session and his second 50 took 109 minutes. But the score was always ticking over in difficult circumstances, for the 179 he and Hemsley scored together took just 150 minutes, then Turner and Basil D'Oliveira put together a further 88 for the fourth wicket in 93 minutes, before Turner was out at 270. He had hit 18 fours and a six, and the final 53 runs came in 69 minutes, but the cost was high. For Turner strained his back, a re-occurrence of that suffered in the previous match against Surrey, and it not only prevented him opening in the second innings — he batted in difficulties at No. 7 — but missed the following game, against Middlesex at Lord's. And despite the batting heroics of Turner, Hemsley and D'Oliveira in the first innings of this game, a second innings disaster cost it the match.

66

141* for Worcestershire v Glamorgan, Swansea, 29, 30 June 1977

Glamorgan 309/4 decl (M. J. Llewellyn 91*, G. Richards 74*, A. Jones 48; N. Gifford 3/91) and 142/7 (R. Ontong 56, J. Hopkins 45; J. Cumbes 3/30, V. A. Holder 3/48) drew with **Worcestershire** 169 (G. M. Turner 141*; A. E. Cordle 5/53, M. A. Nash 3/51).

First innings: not out 141

This had to be one of Turner's most astonishing innings. By definition, this was so, for Turner's incredible domination of the Worcestershire innings brought him 83.4 per cent of the score, a world record, and eclipsing the 79.8 per cent by the Indian, V. S. Hazare, for the Rest against Hindus at Bombay in 1943/44.

Firstly, the details, the chronology of the innings, which started in the final hour of the first day after Glamorgan had scored heavily and well. Barry Jones and Phillip Neale were out in this time, after having played fiddle to Turner: Jones lbw at 18 for 1, Neale caught at the wicket for 3 when the score was 35, just before stumps. So Jim Cumbes was sent in as nightwatchman, though search Wisden and the county yearbook and that will not be apparent, for the more usual scoreboard is listed, with Cumbes in his customary position at No. 10. More of that later. At stumps, Worcestershire was 42 for two, Turner 39, and next morning, the overnight pair added 33 for the third wicket before Cumbes was out for 5. Then there was a horrible middle-order collapse, going like this: 71 for four (Hemsley 3), 71 for five (D'Oliveira 0), 82 for six (Patel 4), 87 for seven (Humphries 0), 93 for eight (Holder 4 — and that was a nick through slip, according to Turner). Avoiding the follow-on seemed a distant impossibility, though nothing was impossible with the remarkable Turner still there. He had reached his 50 — actually 52 out of 59 — in the 23rd over, or 70 minutes with his eighth four, and when David Humphries was out at 87, Turner was 70.

But he needed someone to stay with him, and that prop came in the predictable form of Norman Gifford, and with his reassuring presence at the other end, Turner went to 101 — out of 127! — in 173 minutes, and he had 14 boundaries. There had been one blemish in this one-man spectacular, however, when Rodney Ontong, a South African, dropped Turner on 92, at slip from the bowling of Malcolm Nash. He was given cause to rue this miss, for Turner took to his off-spinners with great gusto, and the ninth wicket partnership was worth 57, in only 50,minutes, before Gifford was caught at short-leg. But the first target, 160 to avoid the follow-on, was then beckoning, and though Paul Pridgeon scored no runs, he managed to stay there while Turner scored a further 19 for the tenth wicket and to pass the follow-on target. Finally Pridgeon was lbw — the fourth dismissed in that fashion in the innings — after the innings had lasted 216 minutes, Turner finishing with 20 fours and one six. His own display and the inept performance of the rest, made batting look easy. But he had his problems.

Bob Blair, who was just finishing his test and first-class career as I was starting, arrived in Swansea with a couple of young Aussies who were playing in the leagues with him. They called in to see me, and we ended up having a rather heavy session of G and T's. (Turner's standard refreshment is gin and tonic.) Next day, I was still suffering from a hangover and I didn't remember being like that during a match since I was at school.

Turner is not the only one who remembers that occasion. He was nearing the end of his school days in 1964, had indeed already scored a century for Otago against Southland in a Plunket Shield trial that was to propel him into first-class cricket. I had not long finished my own school days and was covering the match between Otago Boys' High School and Christ's College. Turner, batting at No. 3 those days and captaining his team, scored a painstaking 109 in about a day, and actually got slower the longer he batted.

*Turner at full stretch, as indeed he was for
the duration of this innings, 141 not out
for Worcestershire v Glamorgan and a
world record of 83.4 per cent of his team's
score.*

Then, too, he was suffering from that not-rare form of Bacchus disease, inflicted as a consequence of choosing to be billeted with older brother Brian, then at the University of Canterbury, in preference to a fellow-schoolboy. He was, he says with a considerable element of truth, 'a real blocker in those days'. Back to the Glamorgan century, though.

I can't understand the other batsmen. As each of them came out, in what looked like a disaster area, I told them there was nothing wrong with the pitch, but they didn't seem to believe me! Swansea has always been a good ground for me, and there wasn't really anything different about this one, except the statistics. But for something like that to happen, the circumstances must fall right. We had that situation for a start, losing two wickets, then Jimmy Cumbes, being a nightwatchman, was content to let me do the scoring. Next came the middle-order collapse, and with us trying to avoid the follow-on, the tail was playing for me. It all ended up designed for me to score the runs, but I remember Giffy nicking one down leg-side and getting a four. That was one of 14 scoring shots by the other batsmen in their 27 runs. The longer it went on, the worse I got, but I played one or two good shots, particularly through extra-cover, which is a shade unusual for me. And, no, I didn't get another bottle of gin into me after that game!

67
131 for Worcestershire v Somerset, New Road, 8, 9 September 1977

Somerset 383/6 decl (M. J. Kitchen 143*, B. C. Rose 81, V. J. Marks 55; C. N. Boyns 3/98) and 58/1 drew with **Worcestershire** 174 (D. J. Humphries 53*, G. M. Turner 37; G. I. Burgess 4/38, C. H. Dredge 4/42) and 403/7 decl (Turner 131, Boyns 77*, B. L. D'Oliveira 72, Humphries 40; Burgess 3/110).

First innings: b Burgess 37
Second innings: c D. J. S. Taylor b Burgess 131

It is an oddity of the tons of Turner that very few of them have come in a second innings, other than in a chase for victory. This was an exception, a rare case of Worcestershire following on and scoring heavily, and of Turner briefly finding himself a new and aggressive opening partner, one willing enough to outscore him, in fact.

David Humphries, the Worcestershire wicket-keeper, was a handy man with the bat too, and he had top-scored in the first innings with his second half-century of the season.

Barry Jones had been opening in the absence of Alan Ormrod, who was injured, but when David came in after having batted so well, Giffy told him he might as well keep his pads on. Not really surprisingly, Brian Close — this was his last match in first-class cricket, and we made him a presentation — told us to have another bat, and Humphries was in the right sort of nick. So out we went again, and in he came less than an hour later, 17 overs actually, but not until we had put on 73 for the first wicket and Humphries had got most of them. It really was a heartening way to start a fightback, and I think it was significant for the whole of our innings. Not so much that Basil and I got runs, but it seemed to generate more confidence in the likes of Cedric Boyns and young Barry Jones, and they batted very, very well.

The start of the saving of the game did come from the experienced men, however. Humphries and Patel were out overnight, when Turner was 76 and Worcestershire 174 for two, still 35 behind. After the early blazing-away of Humphries, Turner had quietly gone to his own 50 in 94 minutes, 21 minutes after losing Humphries, and much still needed to be done. In those circumstances, it was predictable that he should have taken a further 100 minutes to complete his century. By then, he had 13 fours, mostly with handsome driving, and there was an even more handsome on-drive from the bowling of Vic Marks, one of the Oxford University sufferers of 1975. It went for six to wipe out the overall deficit faced by Worcestershire, but the county was not then out of the wood. D'Oliveira, painstakingly 142 minutes over his 50, brighter later, helped Turner add 165 in 236 minutes and when he was out at 277 for three, Worcestershire at least had a fighting chance. At lunch, it was 293 for four, but Turner fell soon after, at 298 for five, after hitting 16 fours as well as the six from Marks. With Boyns and Jones later playing their parts, Worcestershire comfortably saved the match.

68

127 for Worcestershire v Northamptonshire, Northampton, 10, 12 June 1978

Northamptonshire 312/4 decl (W. Larkins 170*, T. J. Yardley 45*) and 265/7 (D. S. Steele 117, R. G. Williams 46; N. Gifford 3/67) drew with **Worcestershire** 308/3 decl (G. M. Turner 127, P. A. Neale 74, J. A. Ormrod 65, E. J. O. Hemsley 31*) and 77/6 (B. L. D'Oliveira 30*; G. J. Griffiths 3/30).

First innings: c G. Cook b P. J. Willey 127
Second innings: c G. Sharp b Griffiths 2

They always seem to be nothing sort of games against Northants. Well, maybe not always, because they were the setting for that 1000 in May, but the pitch is often dead and slow, and batting can be a drag there.

Even so, Worcestershire needed an innings of some substance, for it faced a healthy total, after the compulsory declaration, in which Wayne Larkins loomed large. The distant 300-odd was never a problem, though, for Turner (33 not out) and Alan Ormrod had 54 in the 63 minutes by stumps, from 19 overs, and that set the pattern for the innings. The pair were still there by lunch on the Monday, Turner by then 79, Ormrod 53 and the score 140, rather brighter than the cool and sullen day. Forty-five minutes after lunch, 227 minutes all told, they were parted when Ormrod was caught at the wicket after he and Turner had scored 163. Then 93, Turner went on to his century in 235 minutes, rather slower progress than his first 50, which took 102 minutes. There had been one easy chance, when Ian Richards dropped him at mid-off from Peter Willey, the England off-spinner to-be, at 64; no others until he was out at 233 for two, Phillip Neale bringing a little more colour into the batting than there had been.

Northamptonshire's bowling was opened by Jim Griffiths and Tim Lamb, with Willey, Bob Carter — later to coach and play in Christchurch — David Steele and Richard Williams, an off-spinner, the other bowlers.

69
155* for Worcestershire v Hampshire, Portsmouth, 8, 10, July 1978

Worcestershire 250/2 decl (G. M. Turner 155*, E. J. O. Hemsley 36*, P. A. Neale 36) and 193/9 decl (J. A. Ormrod 74, B. L. D'Oliveira 31; N. G. Cowley 4/74) drew with **Hampshire** 238/8 decl (M. N. S. Taylor 67, C. G. Greenidge 46; G. G. Watson 4/56) and 104/4 (D. R. Turner 41*).

First innings: not out 155
Second innings: c Greenidge b K. Stevenson 23

In three matches, and six innings since his previous century, Turner had had a relatively miserable time: 70 runs only, but to many, that was only to be expected in a Benefit season. But overshadowing all that was the greater drama of the announcement by the-then chairman of the New Zealand Cricket Council's Board of Control, Walter Hadlee, on June 28, of Turner's ' suspension from cricket activities in New Zealand until he meets his financial obligations to the board. ' It is grossly understating the situation to note that the announcement created a storm in cricketing circles, both in New Zealand and in Worcestershire. And in my view, it was a classical case of ill-timing, conflicting personalities and poor communication. It is over-simplification, indeed inaccurate, to suggest that the fault lay wholly with the board or with Hadlee; Turner acknowledged at the time that his was a bloody-minded attitude, but one born of frustration in his dealings then with the board in general and Hadlee specifically. But it underlined the insensitivity then of the board of control of what was essentially an amateur cricketing country, towards its only true professional. Things have improved, though they are still far from perfect, and the lots of New Zealand's professionals these days — one of them a son of Walter Hadlee, rather ironically — are directly attributable to Turner, to his patience in insisting that he not be treated as a man who played cricket, but as a man whose business was cricket. People in England found his 'suspension' incomprehensible; in New Zealand, where the business of professional sport and the professional sportsman is still far from understood — Richard Hadlee and the short run could testify to that! — Turner actually copped flak.

Walter Hadlee issued the statement through the office of the New Zealand Cricket Council. It was handed over by the-then secretary, the late Bob Knowles, to me, and in response to a query on whether Hadlee could add to it, Knowles said that Hadlee wished only to say what was in the written statement; he would add nothing. Events indicated quite strongly that the board — or Hadlee — expected the statement to appear unaccompanied. Instead, I telephoned Turner in Worcester, and confronted him with the news that he was 'suspended'; the board had apparently not felt it had a requirement to advise him personally. Turner reacted quite vigorously, both then — when he was still waking up from a Benefit function the previous evening! — and a few days later in an interview with Jack Godfrey, in the *Worcester Evening News,* an article reprinted — to the displeasure of Walter Hadlee — in *The Press* in Christchurch a little later.

The alleged reasons for the 'suspension', incidentally, were that Turner was in breach of a contract with the cricket council as a result of unlawfully witholding moneys advanced to him for the purpose of returning to New Zealand in October (1977) to play during the past season. Firstly, Turner's initial reaction:

It doesn't affect me; in fact, it almost makes me smile. I have no intention of returning to New Zealand to play cricket next season whether or not I am suspended.

The background of this financial arrangement with the council is that normally I pay a return air fare between New Zealand and England in March, in New Zealand. Usually, it takes about six months before I get it back and I have told the board that this is unfair. It is unfair that an individual should be out of pocket for this period of time; it is quite a lot of money.

Because I had kept on about this, last year they forked out during the British summer, for the first time before my intended departure from the United Kingdom. At one point I had intended returning to New Zealand to play; the work-load falling on the beneficiary in a Benefit season soon made

179

that impracticable, and when I did not go back to New Zealand, I saw no particular need to rush about sending the money for the fare back. It was not a question of not repaying the money; it was more a case of the pupil learning from the teacher. Subsequently, I have been quite amazed at the way it (the board) has gone about trying to get the money back, at the people it has used. I have even been amused. But I must emphasise that I intend to return the money when I get a chance. It is a very busy year, after all.

The intended silence of Hadlee, outside the statement, was broken by the Turner comment on the time he had to wait for repayment. The day Turner's comments were published in *The Press*, the board responded with a further brief statement insisting that Turner was, in fact, always paid in good time and in advance. The original statement also noted, variously, that Turner had 'indicated that he did not wish to continue dealings with the board'; that he had declined an invitation to be represented at the board's meeting of a few days earlier; that he had a right of appeal and would be advised accordingly; that it imposed the suspension 'reluctantly, but mindful of its obligations to New Zealand cricket generally'; and that it failed to understand Turner's stand on the matter. The statement also attempted self-justification by diversionary comment: 'No barriers were put in the way of him enjoying his Benefit year with Worcestershire in 1978, even though New Zealand was touring the United Kingdom in the same year. Had the board exercised its right (sic), it could have required Turner to play for his country, in which case he would not have been permitted by the Test and County Cricket Board in the UK to play for Worcestershire.

'Rather than adopt an arbitrary attitude, the board invited him to state his availability, for the full tour, or for test matches only. He declined to play at all, stating that he wished to devote his time to his benefit and the board was quite willing to abide by his wishes in this regard.'

But Turner, I wrote at the time, scotched any suggestion that he might have been 'required' to play for New Zealand, and asked if he was aware of any attempt by the New Zealand board to use the influence of the TCCB, responded thus:

Oh, yes, that's obvious. They tried in many different ways to get people over here to make me do my will. But they had, and have, no right over me; they have no power at all in this respect. Worcestershire, for example, were quite happy to release me, as they always do, but they always respect the view of the individual. They took the attitude that if I wanted releasing for the New Zealand tour, okay, but they were certainly not going to insist on it.

*Obviously, cricket authorities throughout the world try and organise harmony between themselves. But the people here don't believe they should bully me; the New Zealand Cricket Council thinks it should. And I think the word 'bully' is appropriate. In this country, I am in a respected profession. In New Zealand, I am not, and I will no longer accept that and the abuse that goes with it. That means that next season, we will be going back to New Zealand so we can re-assess the place, so we can see it as ordinary people, in the case of Sukhi, not just as the wife of a cricketer. The winter I spent **not** there, in the northern hemisphere, was as though I had been let out of jail. I was able to live a normal sort of existence. But there was still this continual harrassment from the board and I did not enjoy it. I told them to call off this intrusion of my privacy. And as far as I am concerned now, I don't have to appeal against this suspension. Who the hell do they think they are?*

Jack Godfrey, in his *Evening News* article stated: 'So, for a matter of a few hundred dollars, New Zealand have kicked out the best batsman that (sic) has ever played for it. Probably the most knowledgeable captain that has ever led their test team . . . Turner will be flying back to his native country in January, when he will personally hand back to the New Zealand cricket board the money he owes them . . . But why all the hullabaloo over such a small sum? It typifies the small-mindedness of the people who are running cricket out there (New Zealand) to bring into the open a domestic squabble . . . (Turner) doesn't like the way cricket is run in his country. He makes no bones about it. Never has. The administrators resented being told during Turner's captaincy where they were going wrong. The air fare matter is the

181

excuse for kicking him in public. But there's much more to it than this. One day, perhaps, Turner will be proved right and some of the advice he has offered as a bonus to ungrateful authorities for the mere pittance of his playing expenses will be heeded . . . It has been suggested in New Zealand that Turner is a loner in whom the patriotic flames burn low. Perhaps the decision of the board to drag the air fare squabble into the open may have implied this. But Turner's brushes with officialdom were always made with one aim in view — a better test team and a better deal for those players striving to achieve this end.'

Turner made some important comments to Godfrey, a man who spent a journalistic lifetime writing of the 'Worcesters':

If you are a professional cricketer in New Zealand, they tend to look upon everything you do or say with a great deal of suspicion. They feel you must have an ulterior motive and self-interest. I fought for years to try and make the cricket council understand that we have to think big to be big. To treat people right to get the best from the resources available. But instead, they allow themselves to be kicked around and to treat their players little differently. I have stressed very strongly to the board the importance of putting the best possible team into the field when we play test matches. The only way we can do that is to be more realistic in the expenses paid to players.

Our ridiculous programme over the past 10 years, since I have been playing, has meant a tour every year, or someone touring New Zealand. Yet the board makes it impossible for some of our established players to give up work in order to play, because they will be out of pocket. Then we tend to tour countries when it suits them and not ourselves. We go to India and Pakistan too soon after the monsoons when the pitches are at their worst and before what they consider a major series to follow. We agree to play at non-test match venues. They try us out on them. And only once since 1969 have we played a five-match series. All others have been three or two. So many things are against us — and me. Once, the chairman of the board said to me they wished I had been born somewhere else because they can't afford to have me.

Think Big. *My Way* was the title of his book, long before anyone else used it. Is Turner the 'ideas' man for Robert Muldoon? However, it was with this background, and struggling form, that Turner approached the Hampshire team of Roger Gilliat.

There was another problem, too, in the form of Andy Roberts, arguably then the fastest bowler in the world, and Turner was dropped from him, at slip by Gordon Greenidge, when he was only seven. Not that things, generally, were easy for the Worcestershire batsmen, for there was no play before lunch on the Saturday, and it was a broken afternoon in which Turner scored 84 not out, bad light sending the players off and on the field. The sea 'fret', in fact, hung round for the whole match, so Turner was contending with rather more than just the extreme pace of Roberts and his supporters, Keith Stevenson, Mike Taylor and John Rice. Even so, his 50 took the respectable time of 100 minutes; the second 50 took 116 minutes, as Turner struggled on the second morning against Roberts again. He scored only eight in the first 50 minutes of the Monday, but a pulled four — his fourteenth boundary to that point — from Taylor, and a dangerous, briskly taken single next over fom Rice took him to his century. That freed the shackles, rather, for Turner then gave his attention to the medium-pace of Rice, extracting such a heavy toll with hooks, pulls and square-drives — and an on-drive for six from the left-arm spin of John Southern — that his final 55 runs contained a further eight fours and that six. So his third 50 took only 78 minutes, and the unbeaten 155 was made in 296 minutes, the declaration coming after the only ball after lunch yielded Ted Hemsley a single.

Turner had added 106 with Hemsley, the 100 taking 103 minutes, while he had earlier put on 109 for the second wicket with Phil Neale in two hours. The opening partnership with Alan Ormrod (14) had produced 35 runs, and the 250 runs — that extra ball being necessary for a third batting point — took 84 overs. But too much time had been lost on the first day for a result to be possible.

70

150 for Worcestershire v Surrey, New Road, 29 July 1978

Worcestershire 438/7 decl (J. A. Ormrod 173, G. M. Turner 150, D. N. Patel 42; R. D. Jackman 4/94) drew with **Surrey** 30/2.

First innings: b Jackman 150

As the brief scoreboard shows, this match was severely curtailed by rain. In fact, the start of the next week was a dismal time for all after the sunshine of the Saturday. The John Player Sunday League match between the same teams was reduced to 13 overs, and that performance is certainly worth noting as it does have a little to do with the first-class match. Note the successes above for Turner and Ormrod; the next day, Turner scored 41 from 19 balls, Ormrod was out for 50 from the final ball of the 13-over innings and Worcestershire scored a remarkable 127 for three. Next day, there was no play in the county championship match, only 17 minutes on the Tuesday. But let's not forget the Saturday, made memorable for Turner as he scored, for the second time in his career, a century before lunch.

Two of the Surrey bowlers, both of them test players, come quickly to mind from this innings. Robin Jackman was captain for the game because Roger Knight had the flu and, I'm pleased to say, lost the toss. It really was a good track and so was the day, and I suppose my luck was too. I had a couple of good shots off Jackman, an on-drive and the tucked one away to fine-leg. Then there was another one, trying to drive and the ball eluding Intikhab's fingers as it flew through gully. A bit later, Jackman had me in a little trouble around the off-stump, playing and just missing; and Inti, trying to bowl his leggers round the wicket, almost bowled me. I guess that had me thinking it was my sort of day, so I took to him and the century seemed to come naturally. Once I had the ton, I decided I was going to slog; it was not one of those innings where you can check yourself and play . . . properly, I suppose. It was one of those innings where you can become spent, bored with success.

So away went Turner, slogging maybe, but playing well enough to drive Jackman to note that 'I didn't realise you could play so many shots.' The record set in 1901 by F. L. Bowley — note the name and the innings — and H. K. Foster for a Worcestershire first wicket, 309 against Derbyshire, was under stern pressure when, at 254, Turner played across the line and — spent, bored? — was back in the pavilion. He had been dropped in scoring his final run. Some facts and figures, then, on this plundering of an attack which boasted three test bowlers in Jackman, Intikhab and Pat 'Percy' Pocock, as well as a stand-in opener, Hugh Wilson. The 50 came, out of 94, in 92 minutes, from 82 balls. The other 100 took only 81 balls more: 100 in 144 minutes (with a six and 17 fours), and there were another nine fours in the third 50, which took just 43 minutes. All told, Turner batted 192 minutes, three hours and 12 minutes of not the sort of perfection he would like, but the crowd purred. They had to be pleased; they got no more satisfaction from Surrey's four days in Worcester. The 250 partnership, incidentally, came at a rate of nearly five an over and maximum — four — batting points had been secured with 25 of the 100 first innings overs still to be bowled. Fancy getting bored, spent, with that!

71

101 for Worcestershire v Essex, Chelmsford, 11 August 1978

Essex 265 (S. Turner 55, B. R. Hardie 45, N. Phillip 40, M. H. Denness 37, R. E. East 36; A. P. Pridgeon 4/38) and 128 (M. K. Fosh 32; D. N. Patel 4/33, Pridgeon 4/48) drew with **Worcestershire** 118 (G. M. Turner 30; East 6/34) and 199/8 (Turner 101; East 4/46, D. L. Acfield 3/59).

First innings: c Hardie b Acfield 30
Second innings: c Acfield b East 101

The century before, only a matter of days earlier, was all froth and bubble on a lovely day and a lovely pitch at the start of a match; this one was absolutely essential for Worcestershire's self-preservation in a match which had had it forever on the back foot. Maybe some of it was of Worcestershire's own making, for Norman Gifford 'invited' — quaint expression — Essex to bat first on a damp pitch. Well justified, it was too, with four out and 80 not reached, but the middle and tail responded to the challenge as the bowlers laboured with a damp ball and still-damp pitch as the rain kept flitting back.

Ray East was one of those to respond, and the left-armer certainly featured in this match in all sorts of ways. It is worth noting here that he bowled 42 overs, 24 of them maidens, to secure his startling first innings figures; there were another 43 overs (22 maidens) in the second innings: 10 for 80 from 85 overs, what figures! At the other end for much of the match, David Acfield had five for 105 from his 70 overs. In Worcestershire's first innings, it had useful contributors in Turner, Alan Ormrod (27) and Ted Hemsley (25), but the follow-on was only just avoided, and bowling Essex out for a similarly mediocre score was not of much use, for it left Essex 290 minutes in which to bowl out Worcestershire, rather than the visiting side having that time to score 276. That target was never within reach.

The umpires for this match appear in Wisden as Lloyd Budd and David Halfyard, but Turner was adamant that Fred Goodall, then and currently New Zealand's outstanding international umpire, was standing in this game during his half-season in and around the county game. The Worcestershire Year Book confirms, indeed, that 'J.' Goodall officiated with Jack Crapp, and Turner has good reason for questioning the majestic reputation of Wisden.

I felt certain it had to be this game, because Easty played such a key part. I padded one off from him, and it didn't turn, for a change. He screamed for LBW, which Fred turned down, and then he was into Fred. Verbally vigorously, I think we could say it was, and it all boiled down to Fred being blamed for a 'bad' decision purely because he was a Kiwi. That was nonsense, not just because someone has researched the subject of home umpire bias and come up with the conclusion that New Zealand umpires err on the side of the visitors, and they're unique in this! Quite aside from what they do with figures, Fred of course is as straight and particular as a die. And quite aside from that, I feel this was one of the much better innings I played, not only was it saving the game, but I feel it was one of the most skilful I had to play with the ball turning square. It didn't compare for excellence of technique, or whatever, with that one early in the seventies against Northants, but a pretty good one, I felt.

Turner has probably told it all, except for the detail that reveals that when he was out, driving at East and slicing wide of slip where Acfield took an outstanding catch, Worcestershire was 155 for six. That it held out was thanks to dedicated defence from Gifford and Greg Watson, having his only full season, principally as an opening bowler. Turner reached his 50 in 92 minutes, with only four fours, and there were only five more in his century, the second 50 taking a minute more than the first.

72

202* for Worcestershire v Warwickshire, Edgbaston, 26, 28 August 1978

Warwickshire 303/2 decl (D. L. Amiss 155*, T. A. Lloyd 93) and 390/4 decl (Amiss 112, A. Kallicharan 101*, K. D. Smith 59, G. W. Humpage 46*, Lloyd 38) drew with **Worcestershire** 395/2 decl (G. M. Turner 202*, E. J. O. Hemsley 106*, P. A. Neale 70) and 84/0 (Turner 45*, J. A. Ormrod 35*).

First innings: not out 202
Second innings: not out 45

The perfection of the Edgbaston pitch was such that in the first two days, only four wickets fell while 852 runs were scored; 1172 for eight wickets was the final total. Dennis Amiss started it all with his 5½-hour innings, his second wicket partnership with Andy Lloyd being worth 228, but Turner and Neale, and Turner and Hemsley, especially, made light of that. In beautiful conditions, overhead as well as underfoot, Turner and Neale scored 139 together for the second wicket in the 110 minutes for which Neale batted. With Alan Ormrod out early, edging an outswinger from Steve Perryman into the clasp of Alvin Kallicharan, at slip, Turner and Neale raced to the first 50 in 34 minutes, from just 8.3 overs. At stumps, 73 minutes, they had taken the score to 93 from only 20 overs; they took the John Player League match the next day quietly (only 18 runs between them), but slipped back in the groove the next morning. The 100 came and went in 78 minutes; the 150 took only three minutes over two hours, or 35 overs, then Neale went the same way as Ormrod, only caught at the wicket by Humpage. He lit 11 fours, 10 of them in his first half-century.

But that was the end of any joy for the Warwickshire bowlers, for Turner had been delivered an incentive bait by his captain.

The pitch was that flat that Giffy said to me to just look at the fact of Amiss getting 155 in the full 100 overs. If you can bat out the 100, was the gist of the message, you'll get 200 and make him look slow. So the idea was put in my mind, and I suppose outscoring another test opener, and outscoring him in time by a lot, was incentive enough. So really, it was just a matter of going out there with the right attitude and not doing anything silly. And with a target of sorts, there wasn't the same problem of getting spent or bored!

The run-glut went on when Neale had departed, with Ted Hemsley playing a full part. Turner, strongly established by then on 72, outscored his new partner, but only by the margin of 130 to 106. They put on 243 in 64 overs, just two minutes under three hours, and while the first 50 of their partnership took 64 minutes, the next took 26, 27 and 29 minutes. It was not all boundary chasing boundary, however, though Turner had 22 of them in his 303 minutes — what a splendid over rate from Warwickshire, 20 an hour. Indeed, there was the picket-fence look to the score-book, with there being 11 singles from 166 to 177; the 14 runs were also from singles.

It was Turner's highest county championship score to that time; his seventh double-century. But the excellence of the pitch — the abbreviated scoreboard underlines that — makes it not quite one of the most memorable.

73

115 for Worcestershire v Gloucestershire, New Road, 31 August 1978

Gloucestershire 367/5 decl (Sadiq Mohammed 176, P. Bainbridge 66, M. J. Proctor 48, J. C. Foat 30*; C. N. Boyns 3/92) and 184/7 decl (Bainbridge 76*, Sadiq 38; D. N. Patel 4/63) drew with **Worcestershire** 256/6 decl (G. M. Turner 115, P. A. Neale 39, S. P. Henderson 37; Proctor 3/37, B. M. Brain 3/83) and 49/1.

First innings: c N. H. C. Copper b Proctor 115
Second innings: did not bat

I suppose this century was a little bit special in that it was the only one of my Worcestershire career in which I did not open. There were two reasons, one being the Barry Jones experiment again and his preference — or better prospects — against the mediums and quicks than against spin; and the other was the injuries which kept Ted Hemsley and Basil D'Oliveira out of the game. The idea was that I could provide some stiffening for the middle-order, and I don't know just who was psychic, because we were 35 for three when I went in! Quite aside from our not-very-good position, it was interesting for me. I had been waiting to play against Brainy, after playing in the same side for so long, and it was novel to face the likes of him and Mike Proctor with the ball 12 or 15 overs old. I certainly noticed the difference: they had just lost that sharpness, but so had the ball to a degree. It didn't race away quite so readily, yet this was a pretty brisk innings for me.

Indeed it was, very nearly as rapid as anything Turner had played to that point. He did not start his innings until 11.35 am but in the 115 minutes he had before lunch, Turner raced to 96, and while it is probably not unique for a No. 5 batsman to score a century before lunch, it is assuredly most unusual. Yet, as mentioned, Worcestershire lost three wickets at 35, in the space of five balls, after starting the day at 25 for none.

Proctor and Brain had their tails up, but the shine going from the ball, and after Turner and Neale saw them off, they proceeded to pursue the far-off Gloucestershire total. Well, Turner did, for Neale had some early moments of uncertainty; their partnership was worth 143 in 119 minutes, the point at which Turner reached his century. He was quite majestic and if three fours in one over from Brian Shantry, three straight-drives from Phil Bainbridge, caught the eye most, the other 18 boundaries were not far behind. One would hardly have thought this was a murky day, hampered by rain and twice stopped for bad light, so brightly did Turner bat, and when he finally fell, at 197 for five, it was to a square-leg boundary catch when trying to hook Proctor. Had it been missed, it would have been a six.

The various meteorological problems cost three hours in the day, and Norman Gifford showed considerable enterprise in declaring 111 behind on the third day. Imagine the chagrin of the crowd then, and the disappointment of his own spinners when Proctor failed to declare at any sort of realistic target. He eventually asked Worcestershire to score 296 in 109 minutes; what a strangely defensive move and mood from one of cricket's great aggressors.

74

148* for Worcestershire v Yorkshire, New Road, 26 June 1979

Yorkshire 393/4 decl (J. D. Love 170*, K. Sharpe 80, D. L. Bairstow 52*, J. H. Hampshire 48) and 195/5 decl (C. W. J. Athey 79*, R. G. Lumb 39) lost to **Worcestershire** 260/9 decl (J. A. Ormrod 56, G. M. Turner 47, J. D. Inchmore 32*, D. J. Humphries 32, E. J. O. Hemsley 30; P. Carrick 4/93) and 329/5 (Turner 148*, P. A. Neale 43, Hemsley 35, Younis Ahmed 31; Carrick 3/103).

First innings: lbw b G. B. Stevenson 47
Second innings: not out 148

Turner had had a very chequered early season. The calls of New Zealand, and the lure of limited-over cricket, had him playing in the second Prudential Cup contest, where once again he was an outstanding performer. But it meant that before this innings, he had played only three matches, and four innings, for the county. Nevertheless, his return — 176 runs in two completed innings, batting in the middle-order for New Zealand — had played Turner into sparkling form, and this match launched one of his best seasons.

Yet Worcestershire struggled all the first two and a half days. Jim Love, especially, led a Yorkshire plundering of the full-strength Worcestershire bowling attack, on a perfect pitch. In reply, Worcestershire always struggled, particularly against Phil Carrick, despite a sound start of 91 from Turner and Ormrod, and faced the very real danger of having to follow on, with the compulsory closure at 100 overs. Then the Yorkshire batsmen again scored freely and set Worcestershire 329 to win in what turned out to be 255 minutes.

I felt they were far from generous in what they set us, especially the way we had batted in the first innings and with the pitch wearing a bit. But I said to Duncan Fearnley, a good Yorky, that I'd give it a fling and see where I could get us. So I crashed it around, dominated early and got us close enough for it to be considered a winning position. Then I set about organising the chase 'from the other end'.

I feel that's my greatest strength in cricket now, the ability to organise, to let the guys at the other end just go on playing while I look after the run-rate, pick up the rate if they're having a bit of a struggle, leaving them to it if they're in good nick. You'll see from the partnership details that I got that flier at the beginning, so I tended to dominate Phil Neale. But Ted Hemsley, Younis and Dipak Patel all outscored me, partly because the bowling was a bit in tatters, partly because they had the form, the confidence and the encouragement to get after it. I take a little bit of pride in my ability to do this organising thing, you know, but it's always a difficult decision when you've started the way I had in this innings. Do you keep blasting away and be brilliant, look good, get the applause and plaudits, or do you make sure of it, percentage stuff? I started one way in this innings, finished the other and it all must have been right, because it was a damned good win for us.

'Paced to perfection' was Wisden's term for the innings, but it was top pace for a start. Steve Oldham, opening the bowling for Yorkshire, yielded five fours from seven successive balls he bowled to Turner. The first wicket fell at 31, but Turner and Neale put Worcestershire well on the road to victory with their 134 in 102 minutes for the second wicket, then the middle order came to light: 54 for the third wicket with Hemsley, another 54 with Younis, 44 for the fifth wicket with Patel, who scored 27. David Humphries came in to see the final 12 runs scored, with Worcestershire — or should it be Turner? — having eight balls to spare when it was all over, Turner having hit another 12 fours after that initial outburst at Oldham's expense. Paced to perfection: Turner's 50 took 80 minutes, his second 50 another 80 minutes, and his final 48 took 97 minutes, 17 singles in a row towards the finish. Earlier, there had been another 'picket fence' of 15 singles — organising from the other end — and it was both Yorkshire's first loss and the first century conceded of the season.

75

109 for Worcestershire v Lancashire, Southport, 30 June 1979

Worcestershire 342/9 decl (G. M. Turner 109, E. J. O. Hemsley 63, Younis Ahmed 50; D. Hughes 4/77, J. Simmons 3/91) and 148 (P. Allott 5/39, Simmons 3/23) lost to **Lancashire** 303/7 decl (D. Lloyd 116, J. Abrahams 73, C. H. Lloyd 43; G. G. Watson 4/49) and 191/2 (D. Lloyd 104*, C. H. Lloyd 57*).

First innings: c and b R. Ratcliffe 109
Second innings: c Simmons b Allott 6

No little publicity was given to the information before this game that while 16 counties, including Worcestershire, had suffered a century or more at the bat of Turner, Lancashire had escaped such punishment. It should have come much, much earlier; in fact, the fifteenth century of Turner's career and his record-breaking tenth of the 1970 season, should have been at New Road, against Lancashire. Turner has already made reference to the innings in his comments of the fifteenth century, but it is worth noting that he had batted very quickly in that innings, spectre of the record or not hanging over his head. Indeed, he and Basil D'Oliveira had scored 150 together in just over two hours. So it was with this innings, again a record beckoning, that of the first man to score a century or more against all 17 counties.

I felt I'd become a little over-cautious against Lancashire, conscious that I hadn't scored a century against them, and the previous year, I became aware that I not only hadn't scored a ton, but that I was deliberately playing for one. As well as that 99 run out nine years earlier, I'd been out another occasion in the nineties. So what the hell, I thought, and I just blazed away. I hit a lot over the top, especially from the seamers, rather more from Paul Allott, who was to have a test the next year, than from Peter Lee and Bob Ratcliffe, I seem to remember. Anyway, Ormers and Phillip Neale were content to let me have my head, and I got to 99 in the last over before lunch. I like the milestone centuries to be something a

194

little different, and I suppose I should have made this one another century before lunch. But I couldn't forget the other 99, and I blocked the last four balls — OK, not me, maybe, but it had been a very long nine years since Clive Lloyd had thrown me out, and I wasn't of a mind to have to sit through another wait for the complete set.

Turner, as he has observed, was given his head by Ormrod at the start of the innings, and it is an interesting statistical fact that when Ormrod was out at 70, in 70 minutes, Turner was 52, having reached his 50 in 67 minutes with nine fours. He had treated the three seamers with equal disdain, though Allott, who was perhaps treated even more 'equally' than the rest was also the closest to dismissing Turner when an out-swinger eluded second slip. Ormrod eventually went to a mis-hook off Lee — the ball 'sat up' on him — for 15, though it is one of the mysteries that the Worcestershire scorebook gives his tally, in order, as 2 2 3 1 1 1 1 1 2, and that adds up to 14. Then Neale was the willing partner in a stand of 67, he getting 18 of them while Turner scored 43 in 53 minutes, that adventurous period seeing Lee out of the Lancashire attack with a hamstring injury recurring, and Turner being dropped off David Hughes at 69.

When lunch was taken after 44 overs, at 145 for two, Turner had hit 14 fours in his 99, and his century was completed immediately after lunch, one or two noting that only Geoffrey Boycott had preceded Turner in scoring a century against every other county. Turner, of course, went one better, because he had then scored tons against all 17 counties; Boycott — seventh in the all-time list at time of writing — has still not made one against Yorkshire; only Viv Richards has since equalled the Turner performance. There was only one more boundary by Turner after he had completed the set; Ratcliffe was hooked for six, then got his own little revenge by holding on to a screaming straight-drive return. Turner was out at 170 for three, but Worcestershire could not repeat the exhilarating batting in the second innings and lost badly, David Lloyd becoming the first Lancashire batsman since Harry Pilling in 1970 to score a century in each innings.

76

118 for Worcestershire v Sussex, New Road, 14, 16 July 1979

Sussex 300/8 decl (P. W. G. Parker 81*, K. C. Wessels 76, J. R. T. Barclay 56; D. N. Patel 4/74, N. Gifford 3/75) and 274/8 decl (Imran Khan 81, Barclay 77, Wessels 54; Gifford 4/54, J. Cumbes 3/60) drew with **Worcestershire** 320/8 decl (G. M. Turner 118, P. A. Neale 108; Barclay 6/101) and 113/8 (D. J. Humphries 34; C. E. Waller 3/34).

First innings: c G. D. Mendis b Barclay 118
Second innings: c C. P. Phillipson b Waller 18

There was an acrimonious side to this match, for when Imran Khan batted — briefly, caught and bowled by Dipak Patel for 4 — in the first innings, he was accompanied by slow hand-clapping. That was an unusual greeting for such an aggressive and attractive player, but it was his first return to New Road, since leaving — being enticed from? — the county in 1977. Even with Imran's meagre contribution, however, Sussex, through Paul Parker (briefly required by England), Kepler Wessels and John Barclay, set Worcestershire a stiff first innings target.

But Turner chose the occasion to make his third century in five matches, and it was also to herald the first of centuries in four successive matches, and Phillip Neale passed 50 for only the second time of the season. Alan Ormrod was out for 21 and Worcestershire was 74 for one over the weekend, when Turner's 68 steered his team to a five-wicket Sunday League match win over the same opponent. But in the three-day match, it was not all easy progress against an attack which relied on Imran's pace (15 overs), Chris Waller's left-arm spinners (40 overs) and the off-spin of Barclay (29 overs) for 84 of the 100 overs. Not out 36 in the 83 minutes, or 23 overs, to stumps, Turner took 28 minutes to score on the Monday morning; and while Worcestershire's 100 took a neat two hours, Turner took 14 minutes longer for his 50, with seven fours. Neale took 17 minutes less for his 50, with one four less than Turner but completed in style with a six off Barclay, later the Sussex captain and one of whose christian names was the unusual Troutback.

The century partnership between the pair took 154 minutes, not startling progress, but then some measure of control and care was demanded, for Neale had been dropped very early in the morning session by Wessels, and Turner, when 80, was also to be dropped at long-on by Waller, from Barclay's bowling. Undaunted, he struck high and hard again to move to 99, and his century came with a single after 212 minutes' batting, 21 minutes before lunch, when Neale was 72 and Worcestershire 214 for one. But 18 minutes, and 17 runs after the break, Turner was Barclay's first victim, caught by Graham Mendis, after hitting 12 fours and the six, and the Sussex off-spinner was on the way. Neale, Ted Hemsley, David Humphries — after the next best score, 29, of the innings — and Greg Watson all fell to Barclay and so, in most freakish circumstances, did Basil D'Oliveira. He crashed a drive straight on to the knee of Peter Graves at silly point, and while Graves, soon to be helped from the field, was writhing on the ground, Barclay was calmly picking up the rebound!

Imran Khan, well favoured or not by the crowd, led a respectable Sussex second innings in the face of deadly spinning from Gifford: 42.4 overs and 23 maidens in his four for 54. Then the Worcestershire captain had to turn dogged batsman, and hold out for one run in two hours to save Worcestershire from certain defeat. Barclay in this innings had a further two for 28 to give him eight for 129, and 133 runs in his two innings.

77

131 for Worcestershire v Surrey, Guildford, 25 July 1979

Worcestershire 446/7 decl (G. M. Turner 131, Younis Ahmed 107, D. N. Patel 56, P. A. Neale 55, E. J. O. Hemsley 33; P. I. Pocock 4/120) and 48/1 beat **Surrey** 183 (J. Cumbes 5/46, N. Gifford 3/53) and 309 (G. R. Roope 87, G. P. Howarth 58, D. M. Smith 34; Gifford 4/67, Cumbes 3/48).

First innings: c Intikhab Alam b R. D. V. Knight 131
Second innings: c Roope b Pocock 14

After a start delayed because of overnight rain, Turner and Neale quietly butchered the Surrey attack before lunch, and Turner was, for a change, outscored by his younger partner. When Ormrod was out at 28, Turner had scored 16 of them. But by lunch, when Worcestershire was 98 for one in 90 minutes from 24 overs, Turner had advanced only to 40, Neale was 40. But Turner found his partners were in willing attacking mood this day, and he was content to let them go while he was hitting a couple of fours here and there, pecking away with the singles, nudging the occasional six. So in the 107-run partnership for the second wicket, Neale scored 55, Turner 37; Turner got 21 of the 57 for the third wicket, Ted Hemsley 33. But all the while, Worcestershire was scoring at four an over, five an over for the latter part. Turner scored his 50 in 124 minutes, with a six and five fours; and went to his century, in 197 minutes, with his ninth four — not his fourth six, as Wisden noted. When he was out, mishitting Roger Knight to the mid-wicket outfield, he had batted 253 minutes, striking 11 fours and five sixes.

We were all whacking in this innings, and but for the rain, and the general slowing it created, I think a hundred before lunch would have been very much on. I remember I hammered Hugh Wilson; I just kept picking him up and there was one big six well over square-leg.

Turner and Ormrod scored their 28 in 41 minutes; Turner and Neale 107 in 99 minutes; Turner and Hemsley 57 in 34 minutes; and the neat 100 between Turner and Younis took only 76 minutes.

78

120 for Worcestershire v Leicestershire, Leicester, 30 July 1979

Leicestershire 295 (D. Dudleston 68, B. F. Davison 66, K. Shuttleworth 35; V. A. Holder 4/79, J. Cumbes 3/74) and 131/5 (D. I. Gower 32; J. D. Inchmore 3/38) drew with **Worcestershire** 404 (G. M. Turner 120, E. J. O. Hemsley 93, Younis Ahmed 47, J. A. Ormod 44, D. J. Humphries 39; Shuttleworth 3/100).

First innings: c R. W. Tolchard b N. G. B. Cook 120

For the fourth time in five matches, Turner struck a century, another superbly dominating effort in conditions which, it must be noted, were in favour of the batsmen.

But the conditions at Grace Road were not favourable enough for a result, for bad light meant the Leicestershire innings stretched into the second day. So brisk batting was demanded from Worcestershire, and Turner and Ormrod were not slow to respond. Ormrod, almost naturally one could say of this admirable servant of the county, was markedly the slower: at lunch, 75 for none, Turner was on the brink of his 50, which he reached, with six fours, in 85 minutes. And even though Ormrod got but 44 in 131 minutes, the first wicket partnership was worth 133 with Turner crashing fours all round the ground, and a mighty six as well, off Chris Balderstone.

Phillip Neale came and went for 11, but they had 25 together in his 18 minutes at the crease, and Turner continued to plunder the bowling with Ted Hemsley. Rather, with Hemsley watching, for when Turner was out in the 59th over, he had scored 21 of the 24 for the third wicket. Indeed, such was the the mastery exercised by Turner — 120 of 182 for three when he was out — that from the time Ormrod was out, he scored his final 39 runs in even time. As well as the big six, there were 14 fours, boundaries taking him to both his 50 and his 100, and the run-plundering was continued by Hemsley, Younis and Humphries. But the bad light which was a constant hassle, and a thunderstorm, between them cost so much time that a result was never possible.

199

79
150* for Worcestershire v Nottinghamshire, New Road, 2, 3 August 1979

Worcesterhire 400/2 decl (P. A. Neale 163*, E. J. O. Hemsley 81*, J. A. Ormrod 73, G. M. Turner 56) and 273/1 decl (Turner 150*, Neale 84*) drew with **Nottinghamshire** 328/7 decl (C. E. B. Rice 91, P. A. Todd 86, B. Hassan 46, B. N. French 37*; N. Gifford 3/122) and 208/9 (M. J. Harris 53, Todd 33, Rice 31; Gifford 5/57, D. N. Patel 4/94).

First innings: b M. K. Bore 56
Second innings: not out 150

New Road was at its most benevolent for this match, a tribute to Richard Stevens and his staff but a pitch which took the teeth from a visiting attack which relied heavily on its seamers. Indeed, for differing reasons, neither of the Notts 'foreigners', Richard Hadlee and Clive Rice, bowled in the second innings, but that still left the left-arm seamers of Peter Hacker and Mike Bore (a former Yorkshire player), and the little in-swinger, H. T. Tunnicliffe, to move the ball about, and Eddie Hemmings and John Birch to bowl their off-spin. Don't the bare figures tell a batting story, though, with just over 1200 runs for 19 wickets (and nine of those in the last innings), and Worcestershire actually losing only three wickets in scoring 673 runs.

Not just because Hadlee and Rice were missing from the bowling crease, Turner was on a profitable batting situation when the Worcestershire second innings started an hour and 50 minutes from the end of the (second) Thursday's play. His team had secured a comfortable first innings lead after the compulsory declarations, Turner himself having an opening partnership of 99 with Alan Ormrod before Phillip Neale and Ted Hemsley really made Notts suffer with their unbeaten 230. This time, Ormrod went early, at 44, by far the most shabby partnership of the match for Worcestershire! That took 51 minutes, but thereafter, Turner and Neale were well up with the clock, as the expression goes.

They brought up the 100 in 97 minutes, from 28 overs; the second 100 took five balls more than the first, but only 74 minutes and in between times, Turner had reached his own 50 in 95 minutes. His next 50 took 74 minutes and the third 50 in 78 minutes, though the Worcestershire scorebook — not in the regular hands of Jim Sewter, who had succeeded the kindly (and now late) Arthur Ross-Slater — rather indicates that it was Neale who was the big scorer! Maybe the memory of his outstanding first innings batting was still floating around. But no question, it was Turner who was the dominant partner in the 229 unbeaten partnership. On the first evening of the Worcestershire second innings, he struck eight fours in his 65, but as the field spread wider on the Friday morning, so Turner kept pecking away. There were only another six fours, and a six in the other 87 runs he scored — only three of those fours, the six, after his century — but he and Neale took singles with almost ridiculous ease.

An end was called to the slaughter when Turner reached his 150, with Neale himself little short of a century in each innings for the first time, and Notts set 346 to win in 152 minutes and the final hour's worth of 20 overs. They had a rich prospect of success at tea, 144 for two, but Norman Gifford and Dipak Patel broke through; Younis Ahmed — fancy him not having a bat in a match not affected by rain? — dropped a sharp chance at nine down; and Notts survived.

And this innings, quite incidentally, took Turner past 1000 runs for the season, the twelfth successive English season in which he had done so.

80

108 for Worcestershire v Warwickshire, New Road, 27, 28 August 1979

Worcestershire 300/7 decl (Younis Ahmed 152*, G. M. Turner 33; A. M. Ferreira 4/70) and 259/2 decl (Turner 108, P. A. Neale 101*) lost to **Warwickshire** 264/5 decl (A. L. Kallicharan 107*, G. W. Humpage 96; V. A. Holder 3/47) and 298/6 (K. D. Smith 69, C. W. Maynard 47*, Humpage 38, Ferreira 33*; N. Gifford 4/91).

First innings: c J. Whitehouse b Ferreira 33
Second innings: c Maynard b C. C. Clifford 108

On the run-gorging pitch of nearly four weeks earlier, Turner had scored his sixth century in eight games, his fourth in as many successive games. But he had gone through a lean trot from that time, with only 81 runs in the four matches, six innings, and a highest score of 29. Trust trusty old Warwickshire to come to the rescue.

I suppose you could say that; Warwickshire always seem to feature, one way or another! By this stage of my career, though, I wasn't tending to worry too much if I was having a run of outs. It can't keep happening, and the runs tend to come back. But I had missed out too often for comfort, and it was a great relief to get back into form and among the runs.

Turner was certainly back into form and if this was not a century before lunch — for the three overs to stumps yielded 11 runs to Turner and Alan Ormrod — he still scored 100 in the pre-lunch period. There can be no doubt that this was 'declaration bowling' fom Warwickshire, in that it did not bowl Bob Willis at all on the final morning. Then again, in the light of his past and future suffering at the hands of Turner, it might have been 'declaration bowling' to have given him the ball!

So Turner and Phillip Neale bowled merrily along,

against the seam of Steve Perryman and Anthome — Anton for ease — Ferreira, and the less regular attack of Chris Clifford, Geoff Humpage and Alvin Kallicharan. Ormrod had gone at 65, in 61 minutes, but Neale was swiftly and violently into his stride and he ultimately outscored Turner. Not that the opener was a sluggard: he reached his 50 in 85 minutes, with eight fours, and his century — with five more fours — took only 48 minutes more. He batted 139 minutes for his 108 before being caught at the wicket by Chris Maynard. The Turner-Neale partnership was worth a startling 147 in 30 overs, which took 77 minutes to deliver, this after the 50 partnership took 13 overs, the 100 in 20 overs or 53 minutes. Neale was quite effervescent. He went to 53 with his tenth four — he had hit Clifford for a six as well! — and there were another six fours and two sixes in his century, which took only 93 minutes, and Worcestershire then declared.

But Warwickshire responded splendidly to the target of 298 in 219 minutes, despite the excellence of Norman Gifford's bowling and losing all the first morning to rain. The pitch, and the consistency of Warwickshire's batting, were too good for Worcestershire: all eight Warwickshire batsmen reached double figures.

81

135 for Worcestershire v Glamorgan, New Road, 7 September 1979

Glamorgan 341/6 decl (A. L. Jones 83, J. A. Hopkins 83, R. C. Ontong 78, P. D. Swart 44) and 241 (A. Jones 108; D. N. Patel 5/95, N. Gifford 3/71) lost to **Worcestershire** 304/6 decl (Younis Ahmed 77, P. A. Neale 74, G. M. Turner 70) and 279/4 (Turner 135, E. J. O. Hemsley 59, Younis 47).

First innings: c Swart b A. Mack 70
Second innings: b N. Perry 135

Since winning the championship in 1974, Worcestershire had never really been close to a title victory and, indeed, Essex had already assured itself of first place before this match. But a win would give Worcestershire second place.

In fact, we had to win to be second, so we asked for a sporty wicket; we wanted a result wicket. Our groundsman, Richard Stevens, won 'groundsman of the year' that season, but he didn't really win many marks from us for this pitch: he prepared a low, slow nothing and Glamorgan — he used to be the Glamorgan groundsman, incidentally — got to a stage of not having anything to play for.

Nor did Worcestershire look to have much to play for when Glamorgan, on this pitch which offered the bowler nothing, scored heavily, and Worcestershire replied in kind. But despite the obstinance of the veteran Alan Jones — not to be confused with the first innings top scorer — who scored the forty-eighth century of his career, Dipak Patel followed up Norman Gifford's bold declaration with a potentially match-winning bowling performance. Interestingly enough, Patel owed his regular place in the first team to a decision inspired and encouraged by Basil D'Oliveira that, as he was to retire at the conclusion of the season, his main successor and any of his secondary successors should play as often as possible. It was a move which contributed much to the development in this season of young Patel.

So, after his penetrative off-spinning, Worcestershire had 154 minutes, and 20 overs, in which to score 279, and Turner and Alan Ormrod made their customarily sound start: 45 in 48 minutes, with Ormrod getting 15 of them. After Turner and Phillip Neale had put together a further 35 in 34 minutes, Neale was run out, but not out of the innings, for Turner was struck on the left foot and required Neale to run for him after tea, when Turner was 80 and Worcestershire 142 for two from 36 overs. That perhaps explains a steadily decreasing tally of boundaries the longer Turner batted, except it is a truism of his batting that in these recent years, he tended to reach the boundary with more frequency early in his innings than later. The presence of the quicker bowlers and the new ball early, the need to 'organise' later, probably both played their parts.

So it happened that Turner's 50 arrived in 78 minutes, with eight fours; his 100 took a further 82 minutes, with another six fours; his last 35 runs took another 64 minutes, with but two fours more. But the additional factors in all this were Ted Hemsley and Younis Ahmed, the latter Worcestershire's 'player of the year', the former failing to even reach 900 runs for the first-class season; for all that he had some golden days as a shock attacker with the bat. This was one of those days, with the lustily hitting Hemsley playing a leading part in the partnership of 111, in 81 minutes, he shared with Turner for the third wicket. Then Turner and Younis put together 85 in a minute over an hour, so only three runs were needed for what Turner describes 'a damned good win'. But Turner himself had a slash to finish the job, was bowled, and it took an agonising eight minutes more, and a further nine balls, before Younis finished it off from the penultimate ball. Turner by this time had left centre-stage, annoyed with himself for not seeing the job through to the end, though he had effectively done so, and to a crowd giving him a standing ovation. There was no such satisfaction for Glamorgan: for the first time in its 58-year history, it completed a season without a win.

82

136 for Otago v Auckland, Molyneux Park, Alexandra, 31 December 1979

Otago 325/4 decl (G. M. Turner 136, W. L. Blair 82*) drew with **Auckland** 135 (P. N. Webb 57; J. G. Bracewell 5/16, S. L. Boock 3/41) and 164/6 (Bracewell 3/65).

First innings: lbw b L. W. Stott 136

The last of the 100 centuries to be made before a New Zealand public was far from one of the most memorable. Turner gave chances at 3, 17 and 35, but a happy holiday crowd in the brilliant sunshine of Central Otago cared little for that. His batting, and the events of the first two days, placed Otago in an outstanding position from which to secure a comfortable victory, but rain on the final day put paid to all the frantic efforts by Otago to bowl out Auckland for the second time.

This was certainly not one of my better innings, and I remember having a not very successful battle with 'Tube' (John McIntyre, the slow left-armer). I chanced my arm pretty often, and was dropped, and kept miscuing. I just didn't play him very well at all. But the runs all counted, because the century snuck in before the end of the decade and gave me a few more towards the record for the most runs scored in the 1970s. It was a pretty easy-paced pitch, and I did bat rather better as the innings went on; I just hope the Central people got some pleasure out of that and forgot some of that early stuff!

There was a solid effort, all-round, from Otago, with Turner and Stuart McCallum scoring 65 together for the first wicket, then Turner and his old opening partner, Ian Rutherford, putting on 68 for the second wicket. Finally, there was 101 for the third wicket with Wayne Blair, before Turner was out at 234, Blair later being denied his first century by the compulsory declaration.

83
228* for Worcestershire v Gloucestershire, New Road, 1, 2 May 1980

Gloucestershire 250/6 decl (B. C. Broad 62, D. A. Graveney 42*, Zaheer Abbas 33, M. D. Partridge 32*, Sadiq Mohammed 30) and 62/0 (Broad 35*) drew with **Worcestershire** 361/5 decl (G. M. Turner 228*, E. J. O. Hemsley 61, D. J. Humphries 36*; Graveney 3/102).

First innings: not out 228

The April showers of musical fame, were April showers of mythical fame this April. For three weeks, there had been dry, sunny weather — just the right sort of prelude for the opening match of the season. But come the final day of April and only 41 minutes of play was possible, and while the rain went away for the Thursday's play, it was still cold and blustery. In such conditions, it was perhaps surprising that Mike Proctor should have declared when 12 of the permissible 100 overs still remained for the match was surely fated to the securing of as many bonus points as possible. What subsequently became more surprising, in such circumstances, was that Norman Gifford should have also declared at 88 overs when, with Worcestershire's remaining 12 and the 12 Proctor had not used, 24 overs were still available.

There was a potential 300 there all right; certainly, I could have gone on to my highest score, which then stood, twice, at 259. As it was, it was my second double-century in the championship — I'd got one against Warwickshire in 1978 — and with those against the two Universities, my fourth all told in England, and all of them not out. It's odd how I often have a big innings first up in a season, especially as early in the season — and this was definitely no exception — one doesn't often strike an on-the-up wicket. I had to put bat to ball to get it anywhere, but it helped a bit that the pitch had a short side; it was cut on the edge of the block nearer the Ladies' Pavil-

ion. It followed that most of my sixes, and the nine I hit were the most I have struck in an innings, were to the short side.

In fairness to myself, however, I continued to accept the challenge, even when Gloucester put a man out there, once I was well established. Some of the sixes just made it; others would have been sixes on normal-length boundaries, so all round I was pretty satisfied.

Proctor had Turner's old team-mate, Brian Brain, to share the new ball, and a left-armer, Alan Wilkins, and David Partridge to follow up with seam. But the county which produced the great Tom Goddard, and which for so long had John Mortimore and David Allen bowling together, this time had no off-spinner, only David Graveney with his left-arm spin. From them, Turner smote 18 fours as well as his nine sixes — 126 runs in boundaries — in his 315 minutes or, put a far more flattering way, he faced only 237 balls. That happens to be an even more striking rate than later was his first triple-century.

There was little early hint of heavy scoring at the start of the Worcestershire innings. Alan Ormrod and Barry Jones were both out by 36, but Ted Hemsley came in ahead of Younis Ahmed and he and Turner put on 184 in 165 minutes. Younis did not last too long; Dipak Patel stayed while 46 were added for the fifth wicket, taking the score to 287; then David Humphries and Turner had 74, unbeaten, together.

Nor was there any hint of spectacular scoring by Turner himself. His 50 took 122 minutes, and 90 balls, with only three fours. Look at the rest though: 100 in 165 minutes (125 balls), with nine fours and two sixes; 150 in 231 minutes (165 balls), and by then 11 fours and five sixes; two more sixes and four fours more going to 200; another two of each after the double-century, which took 289 minutes. Weariness was setting in, though Turner still managed to keep pace with David Humphries as he whacked four fours and three sixes in his 34-minute 36 not out.

Before leaving this innings, it is appropriate to look at the mad May it heralded for Turner. After a mediocre match (0 and 7) at Old Trafford, he was required to play against the

West Indies, when he had made quite clear he did not wish to. In the off-season, Turner had been back to New Zealand, not to play — it was the first southern summer in which he had returned to Dunedin and had a break from the game — but not out of touch, either, for he was signed on as a television commentator. An exceedingly good one, too, and in that first season in front of a microphone, Turner won an enviable reputation. It was a far better reputation than that earned by the churlish West Indians who toured New Zealand after taking a hammering from Australia. It was the tour of the famous photograph of Michael Holding kicking a stump from the ground at Carisbrook and New Zealand winning; of Colin Croft deliberately charging into the umpire, Fred Goodall, at Christchurch, and the unmannerly Clive Lloyd of that occasion refusing to move from slip to see to Goodall; and the fantasies of Willie Rodriguez, for whom the soubriquet of manager is ill-fitting, becoming wilder by the kilometre he travelled away from New Zealand. Turner wrote of the disgusting exhibition:

What I couldn't forget was the West Indies abusing their opponents in New Zealand by not trying. It is the biggest insult in cricket to ignore the players you are competing against.

One of the most insulted was Richard Hadlee, virtually handed his first century and his first test century on a plate; what a disappointment to that gifted player on what should have been a memorable occasion.

Turner had no wish to play this team, this country, which within a year was cancelling an invitation to New Zealand to tour. The official reason was Springbok rugby tours, South Africa and apartheid — suitably moralistic and acceptable to many, myself included. But was it really embarrassment?

Turner felt no embarrassment at being required by his employers to work in this match, but he felt keen displeasure. So he declined to work properly. The man with one of the most finely honed techniques in world cricket and who has frequently commented that he likes important things to be done in style, slogged his way quickly through this match.

Out in Malcolm Marshall's first over in the first innings, but not before he had taken 17 from the first over, delivered by the body-checker, Colin Croft, the man who did not know how to apologise to Fred Goodall. The second innings, he slogged a little longer, this time to 45 before hitting his wicket while Joel Garner was bowling. Deliberate? Turner's not saying, but he makes no bones that his batting was deliberately designed to insult the West Indies. It almost seemed that he had trouble getting the West Indies and the 'funny' batting out of his mind, for in the next match, Turner hit 95 in just under two hours against Lancashire. It has been said that some of his shots were as bizarre as those against the 'Windies'.

But it seemed to get all this discontent out of Turner's system, and it was on with 'proper' batting against a very strong opponent in Middlesex.

84

100 for Worcestershire v Middlesex, New Road, 30 May 1980

Middlesex 252/6 decl (C. T. Radley 114*, R. O. Butcher 50; J. D. Inchmore 4/91) and 225/8 decl (Radley 48, J. E. Emburey 43*, M. W. W. Selvey 31*, I. J. Gould 30; H. L. Alleyne 6/94) drew with **Worcestershire** 203/9 decl (G. M. Turner 51, B. J. R. Jones 30; P. H. Edmonds 3/44) and 234/8 (Turner 100, J. A. Ormrod 45; V. G. Merry 3/42, V. A. P. van der Bijl 3/73).

First innings: c Gould b Merry 51
Second innings: c G. D. Barlow b Merry 100

Even allowing for the loss of three hours' play on the first day, Worcestershire could consider this a match that got away from it. Middlesex was in trouble, deep trouble, at 136 for eight in the second innings, a mere 185 ahead and five hours left. But two bowlers, John Emburey and Mike Selvey, together added 89, undefeated, and the eventual target was 275 in three and a half hours. And that was required from an attack — the seamers were Vincent van der Bijl, Selvey and Bill Merry, the spinners Emburey and Phil Edmonds — with four test bowlers. Take in Mike Brearley and there was a test captain to manipulate them.

Brearley made me work for my runs, too, as I'd crashed around a bit in the first innings for a 50 in just over an hour, with 10 fours. He just worked on containment of me and getting the rest out, and he was helped a bit in that players like Phil Neale, Younis Ahmed and David Humphries weren't in very good nick in this game. We had pretty severe injury problems, too; they must have been really bad, because we had to call up Basil D'Oliveira at 50 or so. He actually batted not too badly in the first innings, for 21 in an hour and a half, and he and Barry Jones put on 45, the second-best of the innings.

But we kept letting this game slip. Hartley Alleyne had all but bowled Middlesex out in the second innings and finished with his best figures till then in first-class cricket, but they got away on us.

Then Ormers and I got 123 for the first wicket in 85 minutes, and the win was really on. Younis, up at No. 3, didn't come off but Phil Neale and I got 34 in 43 minutes and we needed 107 from the last 20 overs. But Neale got out, so did I a few runs later, and then we weren't in the hunt.

It wasn't easy mind you. The pitch was a slow seamer again, and even on the third day, it did seam around a bit. While I was going, we were in with a chance of winning, but I never found it any easier, even after being in for a while. This huge guy van der Bijl — six foot eight, whatever that is in metres — tries to do you off the deck, and he was hard to get away. Brearley made it hard, too, and my last 15 runs came in singles, mainly because of van der Bijl, after I had hit 13 fours earlier. So I got the century, sure, then fired it trying to get things going again — played too freely at Merry outside the off-stump,and caught at slip by Graham Barlow, normally a cover field.

Turner, strangely, was at his best early in the innings. The 50, with seven fours, took only 63 minutes, and he scored 77 towards the first wicket partnership. But the complete century took 160 minutes, Turner's final 14 runs a painful 65 minutes. He faced 186 balls, while at the end of the innings, 41 runs short, Alleyne and Norman Gifford had to survive the final seven overs.

85

115 for Worcestershire v Yorkshire, Bradford, 18, 19 June 1980

Yorkshire 334 (R. G. Lumb 118, C. M. Old 89, G. B. Stevenson 62; V. A. Holder 4/77, A. P. Pridgeon 4/86) and 101/0 (Lumb 51*, C. W. J. Athey 45*) drew with **Worcestershire** 363/9 decl (G. M. Turner 115, J. D. Inchmore 64, P. A. Neale 46, J. A. Ormrod 41, N. Gifford 35*; P. Carrick 6/138).

First innings: c Old b Carrick 115

Turner had had a strangely contrasting few innings since his century and its abortive bid for victory against Middlesex. He had failed in three first-class innings, and the Swansea game against Glamorgan had been abandoned, but in between times, there had been two astonishing innings in limited-over games. Firstly, the man who is now 1000 runs a heavier scorer in the John Player League than any other, got his highest score of all, 147 against Sussex at Horsham. The century took 95 minutes, or 86 balls, but Worcestershire lost the match by 32 runs because, on this little ground, it was set to score 7.4 runs an over and was out with 22 balls left. Without another innings in between, he won the Gold Award from Fred Trueman in the Benson and Hedges Cup quarter-final for a quite flawless 122 against Lancashire. Arguably, this was the most astonishing of all Turner's centuries, though it was not accorded first-class status. He reached his 50 in a mere 29 minutes; how surprising that his second 50 should have taken another 81 minutes. So he was in quite remarkable form for this match in cheerless Bradford, a climate which once drove Geoffrey Boycott to remark to me that did I not come from Dunedin (Turner's real home and birthplace, of course)? 'Dunedin! Like bloody Bradford in winter,' said this most tactiturn of Yorkies, so maybe Turner had a reason for feeling at home in Bradford. But he had his reasons for not feeling quite at ease.

I took out a new stick with me for this innings, one that had been prepared just down the road in Dewsbury by Crown Sports. It was a real heavy one, but I usually use a heavy bat anyway. But this one was a real plank, one of the few I've had from them, so it won't be any surprise that this was the only time I used it. It wasn't a very easy innings in any respect, because the pitch was so slow that I was going for straight hits from the seamers. But I found on numerous occasions that when I was getting it over the top, it was only just clearing mid-on or mid-off; other big hits were only just getting to the boundary, for which I blamed the bat, rather than my timing.

Turner had 47 minutes on the first evening, and four minutes short of three hours the second day, certainly far from one of his faster rates of scoring in England, but the aforementioned reasons played a major part in that. He and Alan Ormrod had 98 together, from 30 overs, or 101 minutes, Turner getting 57 of them. Then Turner and Phillip Neale took the score to 202 in 99 minutes, or 36 overs, more; Younis was out at 212, and Turner at 215 for four. He took 77 minutes for his 50, 193 for his century, and hit 13 fours, none of them after his 100, actually finishing off with nine singles. The weather put an end to any prospect of a result, with all the third day being washed out.

86

101 for Worcestershire v Warwickshire, Edgbaston, 23 July 1980

Worcestershire 324/9 decl (G. M. Turner 101, T. S. Curtis 59*, J. A. Ormrod 55; D. R. Doshi 5/76, C. C. Clifford 4/110) and 330/5 decl (Younis Ahmed 121 *, Ormrod 106, Turner 42) beat **Warwickshire** 300/3 decl (T. A. Lloyd 130, J. W. Whitehouse 50*, D. L. Amiss 49, G. W. Humpage 31) and 258 (Amiss 99, Humpage 49; H. L. Alleyne 4/63, N. Gifford 3/70).

First innings: st Humpage b Doshi 101
Second innings: c Amiss b G. C. Small 42

Turner has always reserved a modicum of his best for Warwickshire, and this innings was no exception, the master scoring a century before lunch for the third time. In fact, he was even out before lunch!

It was the last over before lunch — taken at the slightly late hour of 1.45 — and I was well aware that some of the best lunches in the country are to be had at Edgbaston. That doesn't mean I wanted the afternoon off to savour it, but I'm afraid to say that we were in such a healthy position that I charged Dilip Doshi. Of course, he saw me coming, threw it wide outside the off-stump, but I was confident enough, cocky enough maybe, that I backed myself to flat-bat slash it through the covers, instead of retreating. But it just turned enough to elude the bat and left me stranded. Not often I'm stumped, but I suppose I had to be, because the mediums weren't going to get me out on this good, flat wicket. I played what some call full range of shots; I was particularly severe on the quicks — Gladstone Small, a West Indian Brummy, Dennis Hopkins, Phil Oliver, with his off-cutters, and Anton Ferreira. Between them, they cost about four an over.

As it happened, however, the Worcestershire middle-order

A century scored before lunch on the first day, as one of Dilip Doshi's left-arm spinners is sent fine, despite wicket-keeper Geoff Humpage getting quickly into position.

Another boundary shot as Turner races to his eighth century off Warwickshire.

did not really repay the efforts of Turner and Alan Ormrod, who scored 140 from just 33 overs, in 106 minutes. Strangely enough, too, Turner again scored his first 50 in a faster time — 54 minutes — than his second, which took a further 74 minutes. It was a fine illustration, perhaps, of the degree to which he would get on top of an attack at the outset of an innings.

But when Turner had given Geoff Humpage the simplest of stumpings on the stroke of lunch, at 169 for three, there was a scant follow-up from the middle-order. The Worcestershire innings slumped to 233 for eight, before Tim Curtis, a local product then at Durham University, got together with Norman Gifford, and the pair of them put on 81, Curtis going from 11 to 57 while Gifford was scoring 27. That may have been the turning of the match, for Warwickshire virtually matched that effort, but then conceded second innings runs readily — in the course of which Turner passed 30,000 runs in first-class cricket, crashing nine fours in his 42 — and were bowled out with four overs left in the match. Note that Dennis Amiss twice missed personal milestones by a single run, something about getting nervous on 49 and 99?

87

182* for Worcestershire v Derbyshire, New Road, 26, 28 July 1980

Worcestershire 301/1 decl (G. M. Turner 182*, P. A. Neale 54*, J. A. Ormrod 53) and 204/8 decl (Turner 50*, D. J. Humphries 46; G. Miller 3/60) drew with Derbyshire 254/4 decl (J. G. Wright 155) and 193/2 (B. Wood 101*, Wright 50).

First innings: not out 182
Second innings: not out 50

Though the bare bones of the scoreboard indicate an idyllic match for the batsmen, particularly the two New Zealanders — between them, Turner and John Wright scored 437 runs for twice (both times Wright) out — the Worcestershire openers had a difficult time of it. Certainly, at the end of the first day they were 138, Turner 89 and Alan Ormrod 39. But only 19 minutes over two hours had been possible in a day scheduled to last six and half hours. In the cloudy, humid conditions of the first day, the start was delayed an hour and a half; the rain descended again at 83 for none. But the second day rolled out fine and sunny, and the declaration came at 301 after only 273 minutes of actual batting. There was nothing much wrong with the Derbyshire attack, either: Mike Hendrick, with his pace, Geoff Miller (off-breaks) and David Steele (less so, with his slow left-armers) all bowled in test cricket; Steve Oldham, formerly of Yorkshire, and Colin Tunnicliffe were more than useful seamers, and there was further variety in the leg-breaks of Tim Barrett. But Turner more than had their measure.

I'd developed this restrained way of hitting bowlers in general, but spinners in particular, chipping them over the inner ring but short of the outer ring, the boundary fieldsmen. So I was hitting into gaps and the first few times I did it to Miller, he thought I wasn't getting on to him. Then he realised it was placement — it became obvious, as when I was playing the shot, I was looking for twos. If you can dead-weight the shot, the boundary fielder has to make a lot of ground in to it — it's often a two, not just a one.

Maybe Turner was 'pulling' the shot on occasions, but he still went through with the shot well enough on three occasions to hit sixes, and there were 23 fours. The difficult, stop-start first day is reflected in a few figures. Turner's first 50 took 101 minutes — but he only faced 67 balls, precisely the number he faced in scoring a 64-minute second 50, and both half-centuries included seven fours. His third 50 took 77 minutes, or 57 balls, and he took 31 minutes — 34 balls — for his final 32 runs. Turner and Ormrod scored 165 for the first wicket in 169 minutes (50 overs), Turner 102 of them. There were another 134 for the second wicket between Turner and Phillip Neale in 103 minutes, or 31 overs.

The two teams contrived to do their best to achieve a result, Derbyshire declaring 47 behind and having Worcestershire 55 for four when Turner came in. Because of a — not successful, as it happened — Gillette Cup quarter-final against Middlesex two days later, the order was changed to try and get as many batsmen as possible in batting form. So Ted Hemsley and Younis Ahmed went up the order — but still it was Turner, with David Humphries, to the rescue.

Then it was a thunderstorm to the rescue, Derbyshire — Wright and Barry Wood — having scored the first 100 in 16 overs and needing 55 runs from the final 11 overs when the heavens broke. Before that happened, however, the scorers and the press were working in the dark. They were the only ones who could not — because of their and the wicket position — use lights as the storm clouds rolled over!

88

168 for Worcestershire v Essex, Colchester, 27 August 1980

Worcestershire 388/5 decl (G. M. Turner 168, P. A. Neale 66, Younis Ahmed 60*, E. J. O. Hemsley 49) and 91/5 (J. K. Lever 5/34) drew with **Essex** 300/8 decl (K. W. R. Fletcher 75, K. S. McEwan 57, M. S. A. McEvoy 55; A. P. Pridgeon 4/86).

First innings: run out 168
Second innings: lbw b Lever 23

On the surface, Keith Fletcher's decision to insert us when he won the toss might seem ridiculous as there was a good pitch for my only match at Colchester. But to be fair to Fletch, there was a green patch at one end, and the ball bounced a bit and seamed when it hit it. Despite the scores, too, the ball did beat the bat quite a lot, but the Essex bowlers, those there and those not, didn't really help themselves a lot. John Lever tried to bounce me out, maybe because he reasoned I hadn't been in much form since the Derbyshire match: a count-up tells me I'd scored 262 in 10 innings. But I was prepared to hook him, not a shot I play a lot, and hit a few fours, and indirectly he helped play me back into good nick.

I was in an aggressive mood, anyway, being pretty well settled in my mind that when you've been around regular cricket as long as I had, that you can't keep missing out. Ormers plays a pretty important part in my success when I have this attitude, too. Here was another example: we got 101 in 100 minutes, he got 26. Then I was able to keep blazing away, because Phil Neale played the patient part, and it wasn't his fault I was run out — I was looking for a third and Mike McEvoy hit my stumps with a direct throw. I'll admit I sometimes get a shade ... what, greedy some would call it ... but only when a little target is begging to be reached. I should have walked a 200 here, but ... my fault.

Essex had a moderately fearsome bowling line-up, with the

West Indian, Norbert Phillip, to open with Lever, the dependable Stuart Turner and David Pringle to follow, the latter then known better as the son of an East African Prudential Cup player and himself to play for England against India in 1982 when the 'dirty dozen', 'filthy fifteen', whatever they were, were banned from test cricket for touring South Africa. There was also Rueben Herbert, a coloured South African himself, but only David Acfield as a first-choice spinner: Ray East had had a row with the county.

They all suffered as Turner raced to 168 from 204 balls, in 238 minutes, but none more so than the batsman's bowling namesake: Stuart Turner had one for 90 from his 19 overs, with Herbert the worst of the rest with 10 overs for 43. Turner's first 50 took 80 minutes (70 balls, six fours), the next 78 minutes (54 balls, another nine fours), the third 61 minutes (60 balls, a six and another five fours). He finished with 23 fours and that six, and had partnerships of 101 with Ormrod, from 26 overs, and 162 in 137 minutes with Neale, from a further 41 overs. When Turner was done, Younis and Hemsley kept up the good work, but Essex batted solidly too, and when the same rain that ruined the Centenary Test at Lord's came along, an intriguing finish was looming with the whole last afternoon remaining. What gave it added spice was that the Hartley Alleyne of Essex's first and only innings was as quick as he ever bowled.

89

103* for Worcestershire v Kent, New Road, 1 September 1980

Kent 200/6 decl (A. P. E. Knott 49, C. S. Cowdrey 42, G. W. Johnson 39*; M. Saunders 3/47) and 276/5 decl (C. J. Tavare 144*) drew with **Worcestershire** 168/3 decl (G. M. Turner 103*) and 260/7 (J. A. Ormrod 103, Younis Ahmed 53*, P. A. Neale 51, G. M. Turner 33; D. L. Underwood 4/57).

First innings: not out 103
Second innings: c Knott b K. B. S. Jarvis 33

Turner hardly gave any hint that this was to be his last match of the season and he was heading home to New Zealand for a summer of rest, recreation and television commentating. The end of a difficult summer it was, one in which Worcestershire finished in a sort-of-regular position, eleventh, and with rain following the counties around for most of the poorest summer in years.

Nor was there any relief offered from the rain for the final few days of the season, with it seriously curtailing the first day — when Kent could score only 101 for five — to the extent that both first innings were declared early. Turner's exhilarating batting, yet again, made it possible for Norman Gifford to call a halt after only 43 overs, or 148 minutes. The outfield was still a little holding when the Worcestershire innings started, which helps explain Turner hitting five threes as well as five fours in his first 50, which still took him only 57 minutes (59 balls). But when Alan Ormrod was out soon afterwards, when they had scored 75 for the first wicket, from 19 overs in 70 minutes, Turner found his run-rate frustrated by losing the strike for long stretches. In the 47-run partnership with Phillip Neale (16), the latter faced 41 balls, Turner 25 — from which he scored 29, incidentally. Younis (6) faced 29 balls while helping add 15; Turner 13. So while Turner's second 50 took another 87 minutes, he only faced 55 balls. All told, he faced 121 balls in his 148 minutes and hit 11 fours from Keith Jarvis, Neil Kemp, Derek Underwood and Gordon Johnson.

90
104* for Worcestershire v Sussex, New Road, 6, 7 May 1981

Sussex 252/8 decl (G. S. Le Roux 49*, G. G. Arnold 46, I. A. Greig 46, G. D. Mendis 31; J. D. Inchmore 4/65) and 163/2 decl (Mendis 79*, J. R. T. Barclay 55) drew with **Worcestershire** 158/0 decl (G. M. Turner 104*, J. A. Ormrod 45*) and 145/4 (Younis Ahmed 44, Turner 38, P. A. Neale 31*).

First innings: not out 104
Second innings: c I. J. Gould b Le Roux 38

For the second successive season, Turner kicked off the county championship with a century, and a flowing innings it was in rather difficult conditions. Not usually, of course, for that time of year, the pitch was a slow seamer, and Sussex had a strong attack for such conditions: Garth Le Roux, the big South African who once all but signed for Worcestershire before he was seen disappearing in the direction of Hove, and Imran Khan, who did participate for the county, opened and had Geoff Arnold and Ian Greig as back-up — test players all, with the exception of Le Roux. The only other bowler used was John Barclay, like Turner just taking over the captaincy of his county team and it was Barclay who spared Turner, his only chance, when he failed to grasp a difficult over-head catch at mid-wicket when Turner was 67.

Sussex eventually finished second in the Schweppes county championship and in Turner's view, was perhaps the strongest all-round side in the land. So it spoke volumes for his early-season form that Turner should reach his century in 187 minutes, from 146 balls for the heavy Sussex reliance on seam meant a rather mediocre over-rate. In the 38 minutes before stumps, Turner and Alan Ormrod scored 29 together, and there were a further 111 in the two hours 20 minutes to lunch — Turner 95, Ormrod 38 — before the rain descended. So Turner had a long wait for his three figures, 125 minutes being lost, and he and Ormrod had only a further half-hour before the elements — bad light this time — sent them back to the pavilion.

Turner called the innings off first thing in the morning, but despite the best efforts and intentions of the new captains, too much time had been lost to provide a result. Turner's own innings included 10 fours and his century came up with the fifth three of the innings. He batted 208 minutes and faced 158 balls, eight fewer than Ormrod, taking 78 balls for his first 50 — which came in 110 minutes — and 68 for his second.

91

101 for Worcestershire v Essex, New Road, 9 June 1981

Essex 308/4 decl (K. W. R. Fletcher 127, B. R. Hardie 76, K. S. McEwan 51) and 187/4 decl (N. Phillip 80*, S. Turner 46*) lost to **Worcestershire** 221 (J. A. Ormrod 84* ret hurt; D. L. Acfield 4/34) and 276/4 (G. M. Turner 101, Younis Ahmed 65, J. D. Inchmore 40*).

First innings: c K. R. Pont b J. K. Lever 26
Second innings: c Lever b R. E. East 101

Worcestershire faced a difficult task in this match. Quite aside from some public criticism of selection policies, two successive matches being reduced to one innings games by rain, and the indifferent form — 53 runs in five innings — of Turner himself, Alan Ormrod's season came to an end in the first innings. He suffered a fractured left arm when hit by Norbert Phillip with his innings score at 80 and his career tally at 19,999 runs. He returned long enough to drive Phillip for four to go into the 20,000s, then retired for the match and the season. So, that valuable player short, Worcestershire faced the formidable task of scoring 276 in 205 minutes and from the very handy attack of Phillip and John Lever, to open, Stuart Turner to follow with his nagging medium pace, and the spin of Ray East and David Acfield, two very experienced campaigners. But Turner got away to a booming start, with fours from four consecutive balls in Lever's second over, and was then dropped, at 17, from a difficult chance offered at mid-wicket to Alan Lilley, the substitute for an injured Keith Fletcher, who had scored his fiftieth century in the first Essex innings. But that was the only chance offered in a sparkling display which placed Worcestershire firmly on the path to its very exciting victory. After Dipak Patel, the makeshift opener in Ormrod's absence, was out at 39, when Turner was 27, the captain and Younis

Ahmed scored 132 together in 110 minutes. Phillip Neale stayed for 29 minutes, and 19 runs, while 32 were added, then Turner himself was out at 215 for four, splendidly caught low at square-leg.

It's always satisfying to score a hundred and to win the game — it's even better to see it through to the end, something I've mentioned before and tied up with finishing off the job. But while I would have much preferred to have been there at the finish, there was the satisfaction that at least I'd got us off to a good and substantial start.

After that good and substantial start, there was a good and substantial finish to the innings, with some bold hitting from John Inchmore, promoted in the order, keeping the rate — 67 needed from 10 overs when Turner was out — up to the mark. At the other end, faithful Ted Hemsley played his part by giving Inchmore the strike with quickly taken singles — 10 of them in his 18 when the final over started and Worcestershire still needed nine to win. A single to Hemsley, another to Inchmore, nothing from the third ball, a two to Hemsley from the fourth. Then he hit a mighty six to bring the house down, and to see his side home. That was the great climax, but it was Turner's paced innings which made it all possible. That early flurry, and let-off, apart, there was no wild slogging, so his 50 took him 99 minutes, and 84 balls. But his second 50 took only 50 balls, even if it took another 84 minutes, and all told, he struck 11 fours from the 140 balls he faced in 189 minutes at the wicket.

92

168 for Worcestershire v Yorkshire, New Road, 27, 29 June 1981

Yorkshire 319/7 decl (J. H. Hampshire 94, C. W. J. Athey 64, J. D. Love 44, G. B. Stevenson 33) and 251 (D. L. Bairstow 73*, C. M. Old 55, R. G. Lumb 45, Love 34; N. Gifford 4/82, A. P. Pridgeon 3/27) lost to **Worcestershire** 303/3 decl (G. M. Turner 168, P. A. Neale 102) and 271/7 (M. S. Scott 68; J. P. Whiteley 3/72).

First innings: lbw b Stevenson 168
Second innings: lbw b Stevenson 11

Turner's third successive century from a Yorkshire attack was characterised by easy, effortless driving on both sides of the wicket from an attack which relied heavily on the seam of Chris Old, Graham Stevenson, Simon Dennis and Peter Whiteley. The only spin came from Phil Carrick, and on this true pitch, Yorkshire needed something more varied than that, particularly with Turner playing with what one source called unerring judgement.

It was an innings in the mould of his more recent centuries, with 86 of the runs coming in the pre-lunch session on the Monday morning. In the final 44 minutes of Saturday's play, Turner and Mark Scott scored an untroubled 27 together, Turner 20 of them, and he got another 32 on the Sunday when Worcestershire lost easily to Yorkshire. Geoff Boycott, 91 not out in the limited-over game, left all his runs behind there: he got only 8 and 3 in the championship match! When that game resumed, Turner and Scott went quickly to the 50, in only another 22 minutes, but Scott was out a run later. But that success, at 11.52 am was the last for Yorkshire until Turner wearily conceded his wicket at 4.05 pm with Worcestershire then assured of full batting points. There is a nice evenness to the figures of the Turner innings. His first 50 (in 74 balls, 94 minutes) included eight fours;

there were another eight in the second 50 (a further 80 balls and 80 minutes); yet another eight in the third 50, which took 48 minutes and 55 balls.

His 279-minute innings, in which he faced 258 balls, included 26 fours all told, and there was just one chance, a sharp caught-and-bowled to Stevenson at 162, and with that, on this fine afternoon, Turner removed his sweater for the first time. But — and not surprisingly with the battery of seamers employed by Yorkshire — he retained his helmet throughout.

Scott apart, Turner batted only with Phillip Neale in this innings and they eventually amassed 231, in 240 minutes and 70 overs, for the second wicket. It was just 43 short of the county record for the wicket, established by H.H.I. 'Doc' Gibbons and the Nawab of Pataudi, firstly against Kent in 1933, then the following year against Glamorgan. It was Neale's tenth century. In what was left of the Monday, and all Tuesday, Worcestershire scored a fine fourth win of the season, achieved when Norman Gifford hit the penultimate ball for four.

93

161 for Worcestershire v Northamptonshire, Stourbridge, 29 July 1981

Worcestershire 376/5 decl (G. M. Turner 161, P.A . Neale 125, M. S. Scott 43) and 317/6 decl (Turner 101, D. N. Patel 87, Neale 38) drew with **Northamptonshire** 359/6 decl (A. J. Lamb 86, Kapil Dev 79, G. Cook 52, G. Sharp 44*, W. Larkins 43; N. Gifford 3/129) and 199/8 (T. J. Yardley 65*, Larkins 58; Patel 3/34).

First innings: c A. J. Lamb b T. M. Lamb 161
Second innings: c Sharp b N. A. Mallender 101

It was a pretty big day in England, not because we were back at Stourbridge for the first time in at least 15 years, but because it was Royal Wedding Day, with all those capital letters. So we had a big crowd there, a holiday crowd of 3000, and as I'd given up tossing by then, after only winning two in 13 tries, and with a couple of the marquees having television sets, I was able to watch the Prince Charles-Lady Di wedding right up to 10.45 am. David Humphries had done my job right, too, because as a general rule, when one plays on a ground not used for first-class cricket, one is doubtful of its lasting qualities and bats first. I must say, though, that this wicket looked reasonable, apart from a couple of doubtful patches where it was very bare,and it lasted pretty well.

Mind you, it started pretty well, too, and I was 120-odd by lunch. I was particularly severe on Jim Griffiths in the early stages but after I reached my 100, my last 20 or so to lunch were much slower. I'd run out of steam — one tends to, if one has played a full range of shots. You can get a bit spent, mentally as well; it doesn't leave you anything. After lunch, there were another 40, and I admit I had set my sights on a 200. But poor Phil Neale had one of those days when he could't get the ball off the square for long periods, and it was one of those days, too, when he couldn't return the strike. Not his fault, but I was running hot, then went off the boil. I was that hot, if you like, that in the first few overs, I picked up a lot up and over square-leg and mid-wicket — all airy stuff, but none of it to hand. Because of the day, naturally, a bit was made of it being a Regal innings — I suppose it should have the capital? — and it was certainly one of my quickest.

It was surely that, and it all contributed to a memorable day for Stourbridge, which was actually witnessing its first county championship game since 1962. Turner raced to his 50 in 49 minutes, from 47 balls, with eight sparkling fours on this glorious day. The second 50 took another 49 minutes, but 48 balls this time and nine fours. With that aforementioned self-induced and partly unavoided period, his 150 took 159 minutes, from 154 balls; the 161 lasted 190 minutes, 179 balls, and included 28 fours. That avoided running too much, for Turner had missed the previous match against the touring Australians, because of an ankle injury!

It was really small wonder that Northants used six bowlers before lunch — Kapil Dev, Griffiths, Tim Lamb — the Rt Hon Tim Lamb — Robin Boyd-Moss, Neil Mallender, a Yorkshireman, and Richard 'Chippie' Williams, an off-spinner, to provide relief from the seam of the other five. Peter Willey was at the test. Turner and Scott scored 198 for the first wicket in just 152 minutes, and if Scott was something even more than the junior partner, it was a continuation of a nice shaping-up as Alan Ormrod's stand-in. After five years on the MCC ground staff, he was called to Worcester in June and this was his eighth 50 partnership with Turner — a grounding as good as any he could have got at Lord's. Then Turner added 44 with Neale before being caught at mid-on from his first ill-timed shot.

It was an innings fit for a Prince — and Princess.

94

101 for Worcestershire v
Northamptonshire, Stourbridge,
30, 31 July 1981

Scoreboard as for Century No. 93.

Though less forceful than in that bucolic first innings century, Turner went assuredly, effortlessly, to his second century of the match, the fifth time he had accomplished the feat, and thus only Wally Hammond and Jack Hobbs still stood ahead of him in that particular chapter of cricket records. But where boundaries abounded in the first innings, this time he struck a Northamptonshire team conscious of the need to not allow Worcestershire to score too quickly, and to have too much time in which to force a win. So the field was set deep soon after the start of the innings, hence the detail peculiarities which had Turner striking three fours and a six in his first 25 runs; his next four took him to 51. Then there were three more fours between 51 and 75, while in his final 26 runs, there were three twos and a quite striking 20 singles. There were other factors, of course, one of them going by the name of Dipak Patel, who came in at 132 for two, when Turner was 71. He set after the bowling from the start, going to 39 with eight fours; reaching his 50 in 56 minutes or 53 balls; and his 87 (with 12 boundaries) in 87 balls. Hence, Turner was quite content to push the singles and to give Patel the strike.

Not to say, naturally, that Turner was a sluggard himself. He reached his 50 from only 54 balls — but such was the Northants' bowling rate (16 overs an hour for those two hours and a bit on the second evening) that he took 105 minutes. And despite all those singles, or perhaps because of them, his second 50 took only 93 minutes, but this time 71 balls. Two balls after reaching three figures, Turner was caught at the wicket by George Sharp, the same man who had been the first to shake his hand, more that eight years earlier, when he passed 1000 runs on May 31.

Turner and Mark Scott scored 37 in 39 minutes for the first wicket; Turner and Phil Neale 95 in 88 minutes for the second wicket, Neale falling first thing on the third morning. Then there was that resounding partnership of 99 in which Patel was the principal: it took only 20 overs, or 63 minutes.

Worcestershire was able to declare at lunch, and while it got close to victory, it was thwarted in the end by a Worcestershire old boy, Jim Yardley. Northants, in the second innings, used much the same attack as in the first.

95

111 for Worcestershire v Gloucestershire, New Road, 24, 25 August 1981

Worcestershire 251 (M. S. Scott 54, G. M. Turner 47, Younis Ahmed 42, J. D. Inchmore 37; D. A. Graveney 5/57, J. Childs 4/81) and 277/6 decl (Turner 111, P. A. Neale 66*) lost to **Gloucestershire** 250/8 decl (Zaheer Abbas 76, A. J. Hignell 41; J. Cumbes 3/55, A. P. Pridgeon 3/54) and 279/3 (Zaheer 103*, Sadiq Mohammed 61, Hignell 54*, B. C. Broad 41).

First innings: st A. W. Stovold b Childs 47
Second innings: c M. Stovold b Graveney 111

Under normal circumstances, this could have been considered a match-winning innings, one which enabled Worcestershire to declare just after lunch on the third day, leaving the home side plenty of time to bowl out Gloucestershire. The abnormal circumstance, however, was the remarkable Zaheer Abbas, the man then most closely threatening Turner in the small matter of being first — or nineteenth — to 100 centuries, and the man then just as prolific in scoring a pair of centuries in a match. Gloucestershire needed 279 in 130 minutes and the final 20 overs; the runs were made in ease, but without Turner guiding the Worcestershire fortunes on the field. He was called away to a contractural meeting with his cricket committee; surely such cricketing matters could have been left until the cricket was over for the day?

But he had been splendidly brisk in his batting effort for his team. In the 16 overs, 54 minutes to stumps on the second day, Turner and Mark Scott scored 58 together, Turner 46 of them, and he reached his half-century five minutes into the final day. It included six fours and required just 56 balls. The opening stand reached 91 in 82 minutes (24 overs) before Scott was caught at the wicket by Andy Stovold; Turner himself left 71 minutes later, at 172 for two, in the forty-sixth over, when the wicket-keeper's brother, Martin, scooped him up in the covers off the left-arm spin of David Graveney.

He had reached his 100 in 143 minutes, from 123 balls, with 11 fours. All told, there were to be 13 boundaries in the 134 balls faced by Turner before he fell at one of cricket's Devil numbers, or 'Nelson'. Then came Zaheer.

96
130* for Worcestershire v Glamorgan, Swansea, 28 August 1981

Glamorgan 351/7 decl (J. A. Hopkins 134, Javed Miandad 59, A. Jones 42, R. C. Ontong 34) and 160 (Hopkins 61; N. Gifford 6/67, D. N. Patel 4/48) lost to **Worcestershire** 237 (E. J. O. Hemsley 45, A. P. Pridgeon 34; B. J. Lloyd 4/33, Ontong 3/67) and 275/5 (G. M. Turner 130*, Younis Ahmed 46, Patel 43; Lloyd 3/97).

First innings: lbw b S. A. B. Daniels 23
Second innings: not out 130

When we went to Swansea, I was in good nick, as I had just got that 100 against Gloucestershire. But straight after that, there had been that 'retainers' meeting during the last part of the game at Worcester, and I had not been at all satisfied with it. It disturbed me, and I found it impossible to concentrate and get the best out of myself in the first innings, when I scored 20-odd. By the time of the second innings, however, I'd settled myself down and was able to concentrate fully on a very difficult job.

The wicket, by then, took considerable turn and gave a lot of bounce — quite frankly, it was a very good wicket on which to bowl. The Glamorgan attack was fairly well based on spin, too — they used Barry Lloyd, an off-spinner, quite extensively; Malcolm Nash, usually a left-arm medium, also tried spin because it was taking so much; Javed Miandad and his leg-breaks were used to try and break the partnership between myself and Younis which won the game; they had the off-breaks of Rodney Ontong; and the left-arm spin of a youngster from Essex, Neil Perry. He was so demoralised at being whacked around — one for 57 off 13 overs — on such a good bowling pitch, that I believed he asked to be left out of the next game, against Essex.

I had my own problems, too. One was Younis, who had

had to be stood down after two reports to Lord's earlier in the season. He returned after the Northants game, and in 11 innings since that time had two half-centuries. So he was pretty keen for runs and when he was nearing his 50, he charged Miandad, made it a full-toss, and smashed the ball straight to cover. He was partially committed and wanted the run; I said no, but he kept insisting. Then there was a misfield, which is not always the best time to think again, he kept coming, and was run out. To say he was highly pissed off is to be kind to the language he used to me!

It was a pity, as was his language, because he was in good touch at a time we needed a good partnership. Mark Scott and Phil Neale were out early, with the spinners on quickly, and I had had an early sort-of-life. I had one go at my flat-bat shot, the square-slash off the front foot, and I got a top edge which ballooned wide of square-cover. That was enough for me. From that point on, I decided the shot was not really on, as the ball was popping a little bit. It is an unusual thing for me to give away that shot because, given width outside the off-stump and particularly against left-arm spinners, I play it a lot. So that was the main discipline I imposed in an innings in which I played in a controlled manner through-out — positively, but relatively restrained as time was not a factor with us winning having just gone into the last hour. We did lose a couple more wickets, but Patel only after we were within 20-odd of the win, and Ted Hemsley just a few short.

Restrained or not, Turner certainly set the innings alight with his first 50 coming from just 55 balls, in 67 minutes, and with eight fours. But Scott and Neale had gone by then — for when Worcestershire was 56 for two, Turner was 40 — and the time of consolidation and no more wickets lost with Younis meant Turner's second 50 took 74 balls, or 85 minutes, though there were another seven fours and a six. There were another five fours before he finished his 200-minute innings, in which he faced 172 balls. Turner and Younis put on 115 for the third wicket in 70 minutes; Turner and Patel 83 for the fourth wicket in 55 minutes.

97

147* for Worcestershire v Warwickshire, New Road, 31 August 1981

Warwickshire 300/6 decl (D. L. Amiss 145, A. I. Kallicharan 82*; J. Cumbes 3/96) and 297/4 decl (T. A. Lloyd 120, G. W. Humpage 111) lost to **Worcestershire** 251/2 decl (G. M. Turner 147*, P. A. Neale 48) and 347/4 (Turner 139, D. N. Patel 138, E. J. O. Hemsley 38*).

First innings: not out 147
Second innings: c C. Lethbridge b V. Hogg 139

With rain reducing the time available on the first day, and the Worcestershire innings not commencing until the start of play, noon, on the second day, speed was the essence. Turner, clearly,was in the right form for a hurried innings, and he duly completed his third century in as many matches. Once again, too, there was an admirably sound contribution from Mark Scott — nothing sizeable about his 21, but it played its part in an opening partnership of 98 in 93 minutes, by which time Turner was 73. There were eight sparkling fours in the 64-minute half-century, scored from only 48 balls, with Turner taking a heavy toll from Gladstone Small, Willie Hogg and Colin Lethbridge, and not much less from Anton Ferreira and Simon Sutcliffe, the latter playing his first county championship match after starting off with Oxford University.

The second 50, as often proves the case, took a little more time: 87 minutes, and 61 balls more than the first with only another three fours. But it was still a remarkably brisk innings, the 147 coming from only 158 balls in the 225 minutes which occupied the Worcestershire innings before Turner declared. All told, he struck 15 fours, though there were long periods when a deep-set field could only be effectively countered by the taking of singles. So he went from 88 to 100 with a picket-fence look of a dozen singles. In this time, Turner was sharing a partnership of 101, in 81 minutes, with Phil Neale; and finally, there was 52 unbeaten with Dipak Patel in 49 minutes.

This match at New Road, the last of the 1981 season, was memorable in many ways. It gave Turner his tenth and eleventh centuries against Warwickshire, and two centuries in a match for the sixth time, he passed F.L. Bowley's record of 2188 runs against Warwickshire; and he became Worcestershire's second highest scorer (behind Don Kenyon) of all time.

98

139 for Worcestershire v Warwickshire, New Road, 1 September 1981

Scoreboard as for Century No. 97.

I'd fed them quite a lot of runs to encourage Dennis Amiss, captain in the absence of Bob Willis, to declare and that wasn't easy in itself. It seemed to me that with the wicket pretty good, they didn't feel they had much of a chance, so I had to make sure they got a suitable total so they would feel they had time to bowl us out. If it had been us, we would have declared at lunch and we expected them to do so, with their lead close to 300. Instead, they batted on for 20 minutes and left us three and a half hours to get more than 340. That really was a token declaration, but we needed the points and had nothing to lose, so we gave it a go. As it turned out, those winning points took us from second-to-last to eleventh equal.

The crucial partnership was with Dipak Patel, who had had the Young England tour of New Zealand — he scored easily his best 100, in only 91 minutes with three sixes. We even got to the strange situation of needing 120-odd in the last hour, with six wickets in hand, and at that point, the game was won. I got out after about five of those overs, but we still won with four overs to spare. We'd had a tough season, and to be able to end on that note after a very fine run-chase, particularly in view of one of our up-and-coming players having such a leading part, heartened our supporters and, certainly, our committee. The first group was pretty upset with the second with the announcement at much the same time that five players — Jimmy Cumbes among them — had been released, or sacked, but this result made the end-of-season function in the marquee something worth remembering.

Once again, Warwickshire relied on the seam of Gladstone Small, a big, black Brummy, Willie Hogg, Anton Ferreira, a

South African all-rounder, and Lethbridge, and the off-spin of Sutcliffe — a steady attack, rather than a ferocious one. I started off very quickly, then when Patel joined me and struck it so well, there was no need for me to take the same number of calculated risks. So from then on, I tended to just push it around, and make sure it all happened. I probably got to 50 pretty quickly, which got us on attack, and I blazed away on both sides of the wicket.

Also, it was a hot day, and we were running our backsides off. It was nearly killing me, with my helmet on, and for the first time all season, I took it off. It was almost preferable to get one in the gob than put up with the heat. And then I remember the cheeky young bugger coming up and saying: 'Are you all right?'

'The cheeky young bugger' and his captain were a startling double force for Amiss and his bowlers to try and combat, and their rates of scoring were remarkably similiar. Turner's 50 came up in 62 minutes, from 44 balls with eight fours; Patel's took only 51 minutes, but 49 balls, with two sixes — they were his first boundaries and took him to 13, then 20 — and five fours. The Turner 100 took 108 minutes, 95 balls, with 15 fours; that of Patel a minute less, four balls less, but he struck only one six, to go with all the twos and singles, between 50 and 100. Turner batted 170 minutes and faced 131 balls for his 139. Patel was there 152 minutes for his 138 and faced 133 balls. Turner hit 17 fours; Patel three sixes and nine fours, with that long, boundary-barren period from 59 to 100. Both hit 34 singles.

So much for all the similarities in that magnificent partnership, which came after Scott had fallen at 63 and Neale two runs later, and Turner already 47 by then. Worcestershire was 229 for two at the start of the final 20 overs; Turner was out at 265, then Patel and Ted Hemsley added 69 in 41 minutes. The rest of the runs were a giggle and there were still 25 balls spare when it all finished. This incredible Tuesday realised 587 runs for the loss of only six wickets, and was virtually the season's end for Worcestershire; only the rain-ruined Kent match at Canterbury remained.

There were just the records to wrap up the season which finished so startlingly. In the course of his century, in the thirties, applause from the Ladies' Stand brought home the information that he had passed Fred Bowley's total of 2183 against Warwickshire, accomplished between 1900 and 1922. It also took Turner to 2000 in the season, for the fourth time, and the pair of centuries in this match, as well as bringing him 10 against Warwickshire, also left only Walter Hammond ahead of Turner in the matter of scoring two centuries in a match. It was the sixth time Turner had done so. He also went past 21,000 runs for Worcestershire, a figure exceeded only by Don Kenyon, far distant still at 34,490.

The Century of Centuries, which must have seemed two seasons distant towards the end of July, were beckoning in 1982.

99

239* for Worcestershire v Oxford University, The Parks, 28 April 1982

Worcestershire 401/2 decl (G. M. Turner 239*, Younis Ahmed 70*, J. A. Ormrod 66) drew with **Oxford University** 211 (G. D. R. Toogood 83, R. S. Cowan 76; A. P. Pridgeon 3/51, S. P. Perryman 3/62) and 202/3 (R. G. P. Ellis 92, R. P. Moulding 67).

First innings: not out 239

In the lead-up games to this first first-class match of the season, I'd played pretty well considering I'd had no cricket for about seven months — or perhaps because of it — apart from the odd picnic game in Central Otago. I'd got several good scores, too, and in the last practice game before this, I made 108 from 79 balls at Taunton, against Somerset. So I had the right sort of background to score a century in my first match of the season for the third successive season, and two of the three were double-centuries with that 228 not out in 1980 against Gloucestershire. In fact all three — the 1981 ton was off Sussex — were in my first innings of the season at first-class level, too.

Unlike the start of 1981, though, the weather had been extremely dry. There had been literally no rain for three weeks, so none of those warm-up games were affected by stoppages. And not only were they dry, but they were pleasant temperatures too, and playing cricket was definitely very enjoyable. No shortage of people had their minds on the 100 centuries, and it had been put to me, or asked of me, whether I would seriously try for the two hundreds needed, against Oxford University or whether I would deliberately get out in the nineties.

Well, I've never been one for pomp or ceremony at the best of times, and I was hardly going to be able to do a Boycott. I

242

suppose it is rather nice to get the 100 hundreds in good fashion, under the right conditions and in the right place. No-one could have wished or achieved that more than Boycott, who got his at Headingley, before his home crowd, in a test match, and against the old rivals, Australia. Obviously for me, there was going to be no such chance of that; and equally obviously, to many people, to achieve such a . . . milestone, I guess . . . against a University side would be considered to lack occasion. The 100 hundreds are a culmination of events over a period of time, that which your career has spanned, and THAT day should not be so significant. Nevertheless, I suppose it is rather nice to get 100 hundreds in good fashion.

Having said all that, I insist that a century should be taken when it's there because hundreds don't come at one's will. My view, too, was that I could break a leg at any time and a century was not the sort of thing that one should play around with.

So wrote Turner immediately after this match. Little did he realise that, less than three months later, an appendix operation and not a broken leg, would bring down the curtain on his English and county career.

For the time being, however, a century was almost inevitable for Turner in this match, just as a second was equally surely averted by Worcestershire's new captain, Phillip Neale, choosing to enforce the follow-on. A. S. R. Winslaw, at the game for the *Daily Telegraph*, considered Turner made 239 not out 'with an almost expectant degree of ease'. Alan Gibson, of *The Times,* and who always seemed to write something charming when he reported a Turner century, spoke of an 'old master'. There was no pregnant pause in Turner's batting, nor anything elderly and stodgy. His first runs and boundary came with an on-drive from the third ball of the innings, and there were seven of them in his first 50, 10 of them in the two hours before lunch, when Turner was 75, Alan Ormrod 55, and Worcestershire 135 for none from 39 overs.

Straight after Ormrod was out at 169, scored in 144 minutes and in the 47th over, Turner struck his fourteenth four to go to his century, and a remarkable partnership of 44 with Neale followed. It took only 32 minutes, and in that time, Turner had 14 scoring strokes, eight of them fours, while Neale had just one — a single! Turner, mind you, had by far the greater share of the bowling and he was quite content with that century, swinging away with cheerful abandon. Then the 200 entered his mind, and he settled down to pursue it, not with any slackening of effort, for in the 188 partnership, unbeaten, with Younis Ahmed, Turner scored 101 to the 70 of his attacking partner. Interestingly, where each of Turner's first three 50s contained seven fours, there were only five more between 150 and 200. That particular milestone behind him, as well as taking his tally of fours to 29, he struck a huge six on to the pavilion roof, demolishing a tile — and, nearly, the press box — and sending his colleagues scurrying for cover.

Neale called it a day when Turner had batted two minutes over five hours, and the unbroken third wicket partnership had lasted 124 minutes, and poor Oxford was 30 for three in the 48 minutes to stumps. But the university lads had earned plaudits for their fine fielding, sometimes brilliant, and their positive attitude to the game, even with undergoing severe punishment. They still produced an average of 19 runs an over. Later, while they could not avoid the follow-on — and the weather turned cooler and damper — they comfortably saved the game.

The stage was set for the Century of Centuries.

100
311* for Worcestershire v Warwickshire, New Road, 29 May 1982

Worcestershire 501/1 decl (G. M. Turner 311*, D. N. Patel 88*, J. A. Ormrod 79) and 167/6 decl (Ormrod 43, Turner 32) drew with **Warwickshire** 380/9 decl (A. I. Kallicharan 235, D. L. Amiss 64, K. D. Smith 31; R. K. Illingworth 4/85) and 197/5 (Smith 62*, Asif Din 39, Kallicharan 35).

First innings: not out 311
Second innings: c and b G. C. Small 32

Between Oxford and this 311, I'd had six digs and only got to double-figures once, a 27 against Derbyshire. One of the cricket magazines noted that after I reached the hundredth, and the inference made was that, historically speaking, those who got 100 hundreds had a lean patch beforehand, which suggested that perhaps the player in question was over-cautious or over-concerned — in other words, psychologically it was affecting his performance.

I don't think it did affect mine, and I want to make that quite clear, a little bit the reverse, if anything. We had played on some bad wickets, very bad wickets, indeed, particularly a little bit earlier in the season, in the first two games. This was especially so against Derbyshire, when the pitch was reported as unfit. It was very, very dry, and the ball went through the top — I think the top score of the match was by John Wright. He got 60, but he was hit four times, once on the head, once over the heart, once on the upper arm, trying to drive or hit a half-volley through mid-wicket. Despite these low scores, I was in good nick early in the season, and I decided I would keep playing in the aggressive manner. I didn't want to regress, to go back to the earlier days when I did graft out runs. That would have ensured getting the hundredth 100, but I wanted to get it well when I did get it, and of course it took a bit of soul-searching, in a sense, to

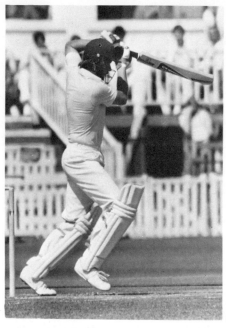

The early flourish, as Turner races towards his first 50.

carry on playing with full conviction when I was in a trough of low scores. There was obviously a tendency to say, 'bugger it, I'm going to make sure I get it', and graft.

But that didn't become the case, and eventually we got a flat pitch at Worcester. I have to qualify that, though, because what happened if we were going to get reasonable pitches at Worcester, we were going to have to dampen them right down, and the hose was going on earlier in the week. So while it rolled out flat, it was very crusty, and while there was not a lot of pace or bounce in it — in fact, very little; it certainly didn't help the seamers — the spinners got turn on it from the first day, from the first morning.

The Warwickshire attack, of course, was more suited to a seamer's wicket. The only spinners they had were a young guy, Simon Sutcliffe, an offy from Oxford University who had bowled against us the previous season. He's a tidy player, bowled a lot of overs in this innings and was fairly accurate and economical. He struggled on it, though, because what happened was that we got off to such a flying

246

start that they couldn't really afford, when he came on, to put people round the bat. So in the matter of us getting out, or him getting us out, he didn't really have much of a show unless we hung ourselves by getting caught in the inner ring, or the outer ring, of fieldsmen. Then they had Asif Din, who bowled leg-breaks and googlies. He bowled a few overs and the statistics show that he was reasonably economical and was under-bowled somewhat. 'Kalli' bowled a few overs, too, so they did have cover in the spin department, but not of the highest quality.

The hundredth century is seen as of more significance than any of the others, though I can't agree entirely. Still, it became a matter of some interest that I should get it against Warwickshire — my original 'county', if you like, though I don't see that as significant. More, it was to get the runs at Worcester, on a Saturday when there was a goodish crowd and the day was set fine, and it was at the county ground of the team for which I had scored the majority of my centuries. It was, too, the ground on which I had scored most centuries, though I do like to make the point always that I have scored more centuries for Worcestershire away from New Road, than at it. But here it was, as it happened, that I was scoring the runs in front of those supporters and in front of Billy Ibadulla, whose winters away from New Zealand now are spent as a first-class umpire in England. He lives in one of those houses on the ground at Edgbaston and just happened to have three days off, so he was able to come down with the Warwickshire lads — so for it all to work out on that day was magic all-round.

That was the setting for the innings, and I guess I was set very early, because I started very aggressively and hit a couple of sixes early on. The second of them was a hook off Gladstone Small: he bounced me, and I played it rather later than I intended. I followed it round a little, and while I hit it well, I did have a slight flutter because Jim Cumbes was down at deep fine leg, rather finer than the run-chart of the innings shows, I fancy. Of course, he used to play for Worcestershire and was a soccer goal-keeper, a very tall guy at 6 foot-2 and at one stage, I thought he was catching it, but it sailed over his

247

head for six.

Within that first hour, I got 68 or 70, then Willis emptied me out at mid-off on 77. He's not the greatest of movers, and I felt it was always doing him because he was standing a little bit closer than most, in an orthodox position to stop the singles. I went to pick one up over mid-wicket from Chris Lethbridge and I got a thick outside middle, more than an outside edge. It spooned over Willis's head; he ran back and got a finger-tip, or half a hand, to it, and wasn't able to hold it. Obviously, I was willing it to drop clear, but as it was

The Century of Centuries, and Billy Ibadulla plays drinks waiter. Gin and tonic, double, twice, sir. Ice, no lemon... and well done, sir. Dennis Amiss finds it all very amusing.

going over his head, I thought I had a fair chance of it doing him.

The only other flutter, really, in those early stages — and they started when I whacked Willis's first ball for four over mid-wicket — was when Jim Cumbes bowled to me. He didn't have a slip in, and where first slip would have been, I did nick one. But, of course, you can't have it all ways, and he had all his fieldsmen back in the run-saving positions, trying to strangle me. So obviously I didn't feel too bad about that, though the Octopus (he's all long arms and legs, tentacles I

The first 100 well out of the way, Turner nears his 200, and the crash helmet has been replaced by a floppy.

Now for the 300, and Geoff Humpage can only watch — again.

Turner returns to the pavilion, unbeaten on 311, as Worcestershire declare their first innings at 501 for one wicket.

call them) threw up his arms in despair.

That 70-odd in the first hour started me off pretty well, and at New Road, we have a 2¼-hour session, starting at 11am and lunch at 1.15. I think I eventually got to my 100 at about five minutes to one, but I was in the latter nineties — 98 to 100, say — for about five overs, before I got the three which took me to 102. In the context of the limited time it took me to score the century, that was quite a long time but, unbeknown to me, it did give Billy Ibadulla time to find the appropriate white waiter's coat to put on, and to make his appearance at the wicket with the two double gin and tonics more authentic. They were large ones, without lemon of course, and my only concern, I suppose, was that the ice would have melted by the time he came out. It was a nice touch, as well as coming as quite a surprise, so play was held up for quite a time, seven or eight minutes, I suppose. They gave the opposition about that much time towards their bowling rate, which is so crucial in England these days with fines for slow over-rates.

251

Turner acknowledges the milestones: left, *Dennis Amiss is first on the scene when the 100 is reached;* centre, *200 under his belt;* right, *Dipak Patel says 'well done' for the 300.*

From then, until lunch, 20-odd minutes, I felt I was a little vulnerable. I tried to fight against that, because there is bound to be a certain vulnerability when one gets to a career mark, or whatever one calls it, of that nature. I played and missed once or twice and made a few mistakes without giving a chance, but I was happy when lunch came around as I was able to collect my thoughts a little bit over the lunch

period.

I remember quite vividly that Dennis Amiss mentioned to me after about the first hour: 'Oh, you could get 300 here today.' Obviously, he wasn't too serious, perhaps, because 300 in a day is not done too often. But he did mention it to me, and it went through my mind that it was a real possibility, if one played well enough, and it had been on one

Now what time did those milestones arrive? Turner was the No. 1 batsman of course; Alan Ormrod No. 2, and Dipak Patel No. 3.

century back, as I mentioned earlier.

So it didn't seem out of the question, even at lunch when I was 128 not out, was it? — something like that. Between lunch and tea, I got much the same number, and after tea, we pulled out, leaving them about 40 minutes batting. We discussed it at tea, and obviously Phil Neale wasn't going to pull out before I got my 300. I think I was 254 at tea, so obviously if I was going to get 300, I was going to get it easily before the close. What we were not aware of — I wasn't, certainly, and nor was the skipper, Phillip Neale — was that there was a record going for the highest score in a day. Accordingly, when I got the 300, I expected him to pull out then, but they'd just taken another new ball and we'd hammered that for the brief time it was bowled to us. Then when he didn't pull out straight away, I thought he must have been going to play for Dipak Patel's 100, because Dipak was in the

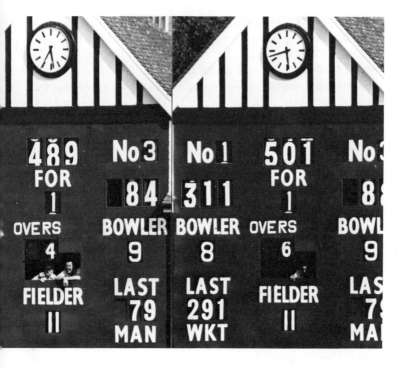

eighties. If we'd stayed, I'd have looked to give him the strike to get his 100, and totally ignored my own score from the point of view of getting to that landmark, that 340-odd. However, if someone had told us about it, I suppose we probably would have stayed out there for that, but in a sense, I was that stuffed, anyway, that he was almost rescuing me from a further hammering of my body!

Although I have batted for a lot longer, like in the West Indies, for nine and a half, and 11 hours or whatever, and that from the endurance view they were a lot tougher, this one was difficult in another sense. Such a high tempo had to be maintained throughout the day to get up to that sort of total that I had taken my helmet off by mid-afternoon. Although there was a lack of bounce in the wicket, you can get a top edge sweeping a spinner, or whatever, and I've become a great believer in leaving the helmet on whenever *possible. But I weighed it up, and I felt I was probably wiser, from a stamina view, to make the sacrifice and take the risk: getting hit or keeping fresh. So I took on a floppy hat, which is very unusual for me. I think there was only two innings in which I have done that — the one at Oxford, and this one. It seemed to work, and on a very fine, warm day like this, it helped keep me alive, especially with all the running between the wickets we had to do.*

To sit back now and analyse that innings, I feel it was a good one, from the point of view that I was able to play a wide range of shots — I had to, getting 300 in that period of time. I only actually hit two over the edge, sixes, but I played pick-ups, I played drives, and I played the thing I've developed and got a little bit known for in England. That is the 'chipping' of the spinner, particularly chipping him over the inner ring, saving the single, yet short of the boundary fielder, a shot which can often give you two runs. It's a valuable shot if they have a cordon of leg-side fielders, as Simon Sutcliffe had: he bowled to a 6-3 on-side field, and bowled tightly enough that one was hardly able to hit him successfully through the off-side field, he didn't give the room. It was taking a lot of chance to get outside leg-stump to do that with the ball turning back in anyway, and so I chose to chip him over the ring. Eventually, they had a long-on, a deep mid-wicket, obviously a man on the sweep as well. Then they introduced this other fellow in a halfway house . . . no, not a halfway house . . . halfway to the boundary, between the inner ring and the outer ring to stop my chipping there. So that meant there were a tremendous amount of singles there, and from the run-chart, it can be seen that I got a helluva lot of runs down to deep mid-on, off the off-spinner, just collecting. It meant, too, that I became reliant on the batsman at the other end in the latter half of the innings. When Ormrod got out, it was Dipak Patel, and he was able to keep the strike changing so I didn't become strangled. It's very easy to get a run off the first ball of an over, and then not see the ball for the next five. And if you're only seeing one ball out of six, it's bound to 'strangle' one. But Dip was able to keep it ticking over to the extent that I saw the strike often enough to pick up three singles in an over, perhaps, and therefore to keep my tempo going against the spinner without having to commit suicide or to take stupid risks. With the defensive nature of their field, it would have been taking too many chances to try and clear the edge, so my momentum was maintained by the other method.

I also improvised. I got outside leg stump and hit the seamers through the off-side, then went the other way and picked them up, so I felt I gave a full range of shots in that innings. In a way, one was able, in this innings, to enjoy the satisfaction of being able to produce what one had learnt, really, in the previous 15 years. It was also pleasing, from my point of view, to overcome the danger of getting to a record like that, then finding it very easy to give it away and to get on with the celebrations side of it. From the professional point of view, I was happy to press on, to force myself to bat on and on, and of course to get a big score. Anyone who gets them will tell you that it is necessary sometimes to hurt yourself to do that, to be able to push yourself to the limit, to keep willing yourself to get more and more and more, and to be hungry for them until the declaration, or whatever, comes.

Then it was over, and the first reaction was that I had to get on the rub-down table and get my 'housemaid's knee' — that was what was diagnosed — treated. I had been getting some soreness with the boot I was wearing on my left foot, and without realising it, I was probably trying to favour it, and was putting more pressure on my right leg. When I came off, I found I had a bit of a puffy knee, which I'd never had before; I've never had problems that way. Apparently it means that the tendon below the patella becomes very sore as the day wears on and it was something I had to live with in this particular season.

Obviously, too, the committee put on drinks straight away and there was a bit of champagne flying round the dressing room. They put on a do in the committee room, too, to which both sides were invited, so by the time I'd had my treatment, done the interviews and what-not, I ended up there in my whites. Needless to say, that evening one had

257

more than one normally would, and I went straight from the
ground with a few friends to a wine bar and stayed till
closing time. I'm very pleased they closed at 11 o'clock,
otherwise I might have still been there. As it was, I was rather
later than usual for my meal!

That was about the only occasion for which Turner was late
on this momentous day, just three days after his thirty-fifth
birthday. The bare details of his various milestones, always
bearing in mind that the two sixes he struck in the innings
both came in the first 50 runs, were:

  50: 34 minutes, 32 balls, seven fours.
  100: 114 minutes, 123 balls, 13 fours.
  150: 147 minutes, 176 balls, 22 fours.
  200: 204 minutes, 216 balls, 28 fours.
  250: 261 minutes, 260 balls, 34 fours.
  300: 336 minutes, 329 balls, 38 fours.
  311: 342 minutes, 333 balls, 39 fours.

At lunch, those 135 minutes less the seven or eight drink-
ing time for Turner, Worcestershire was 181 for none from 44
overs, Turner 128, a score exceeded by only nine batsmen in
the morning session of the first day of a first-class match. It
was the fifth occasion he had scored a century before lunch
and every one of them was on the first day of the game.

Alan Ormrod reached his own 50 in 159 minutes, with two
fours, and Turner reached his 200 just after his opening
partner was out at 291, in 198 minutes, and in the 64th over.
That was a record opening partnership for Worcestershire
batsmen against Warwickshire, exceeding the 259 by Turner
and Ron Headley in the latter's Benefit match in 1972; and 18
short of the all-time Worcestershire record first wicket partnership, by Fred Bowley and H. K. Foster, against Derbyshire at Derby in 1901.

Five minutes after the tea interval, when he was 254,
Turner went to 260, bettering his personal record of 259,
twice, and in successive innings, in the West Indies in 1972. A
quarter-hour later, Turner went to 277, beating the Worcestershire record score, by Bowley again against Hampshire at
Dudley in 1914. Then only the target of 300 remained —
no-one who mattered knowing that the record score in a day

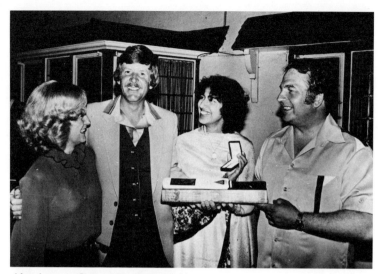

After the event, Duncan Fearnley (with his wife, Mary, at left) presents a mounted miniature bat to Glenn, and a necklace, complete with gold bat, to Sukhi.

was Charlie Macartney's 345 against Nottinghamshire in 1921 — and when that arrived, it was for the first time in England since John Edrich did so in a test against New Zealand in 1965; the first in a county championship match since Raman Subba Row's neat 300 for Northamptonshire against Surrey in 1958. And it was the first example of 300 runs in a day's play since Jack Robertson did so against Worcestershire, for Middlesex, at New Road in 1949. Turner's 311 is a total exceeded in a single day by 10 batsmen — one of them a New Zealander, Roger Blunt — but never by such giants of batting as Bradman, Jessop, Compton or Grace, for example. The highest score by a Worcestershire batsman in first-class cricket, incidentally, was the 287 R. E. Foster scored on his test debut, in Sydney, in 1903.

Turner had 154 scoring strokes in his first triple century: in round figures, that means he averaged a run a ball, he averaged a scoring shot every second ball, and he clearly dominated the partnerships with Ormrod (79 of 291) and Dipak Patel (88* of 210*), though not having a dominant

At New Road, Worcester   versus WARWICKSHIRE   SCHWEPPES CHAMPIONSHIP   Saturday 29th May 1982

311 not out in 342 minutes from 333 balls received.   Striking rate 5.57 runs per over.   154 scoring strokes.   Weather - sunny & fine.

128 before Lunch, and 126 between Lunch and Tea.   Highest Score of career, Fifth century scored before lunch.

			O M R W
1st 50 in 34 mins from 32 balls	Willis, Small & Lethbridge Bowling	Runs scored from Willis 50	Willis 12 0 76 0
2nd 50 in 114 mins from 123 balls	Willis Small Cumbes Sutcliffe "	Runs scored from Small 44	Small 7 0 54 0
3rd 50 in 147 mins from 176 balls	Din Sutcliffe Lloyd Lethbridge "	Runs scored from Cumbes 44	Cumbes 9 0 58 0
4th 50 in 204 mins from 216 balls	Din Sutcliffe Kallicharran "	Runs scored from Lethbridge 63	Lethbridge 20 1 94 1
5th 50 in 261 mins from 260 balls	Willis Small Lethbridge (New ball)	Runs scored from Sutcliffe 64	Sutcliffe 40 5 127 0
6th 50 in 336 mins from 329 balls	" " "	Runs scored from Din 21	Din 10 1 29 0
Shared in stand of 291 with Ormrod & 210* with Patel		Runs scored from Lloyd 15	Lloyd 7 1 22 0
		Runs scored from Kallicharran 10	Kallicharran 7 0 18 0
			Extras 23

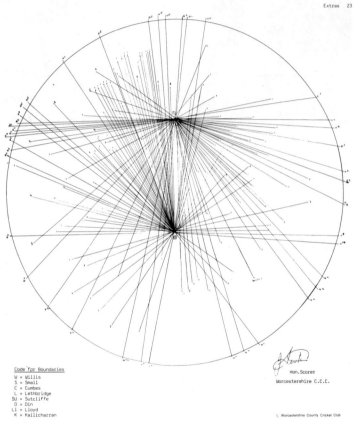

Code for Boundaries
W = Willis
S = Small
C = Cumbes
L = Lethbridge
SU = Sutcliffe
D = Din
Ll = Lloyd
K = Kallicharran

Hon. Scorer
Worcestershire C.C.C.

© Worcestershire County Cricket Club

WORCESTERSHIRE COUNTY CRICKET CLUB

Schweppes *Championship*

WORCESTERSHIRE v WARWICKSHIRE

AT New Road, Worcester. ON 29th, 31st May, 1st June.

WORCESTERSHIRE

		1st Innings		2nd Innings	
1.	G.M.Turner	Not Out	311	c and b Small	32
2.	J.A.Ormrod	c Cumbes b Lethbridge	79	c Humpage b Lethbridge	43
3.	D.N.Patel	Not Out	88	b Lethbridge	22
4.	Younis Ahmed			c Willis b Sutcliffe	10
* 5.	P.A.Neale			Not Out	17
6.	E.J.O.Hemsley				
+ 7.	D.J.Humphries			c and b Kallicharran	5
8.	R.K.Illingworth				
9.	A.P.Pridgeon			b Sutcliffe	12
10.	N.Gifford			Not Out	14
11.	S.P.Perryman				
	Extras 1b 19lb wd 3nb		23	2b 4 lb wd 6 nb	12
		TOTAL 501 - 1 dec.		TOTAL 167-6dec.	

Runs at fall	1- 291	2-	3-	4-	5-	6-	7-	8-	9-
of wicket	1- 50	2-103	3-106	4-124	5-129	6-	7-	8-	9-

Bowling analysis:	O	M	R	W	Nb	Wd	O	M	R	W	Nb	Wd
Willis	12	0	76	0	2		5	1	17	0		
Small	7	0	54	0			8	3	33	1	6	
Cumbes	9	0	58	0								
Lethbridge	20	1	94	1	1		11	5	26	2		
Sutcliffe	40	5	127	0			16	3	60	2		
Asif Din	10	1	29	0								
Lloyd	7	1	22	0								
Kallicharran	7	0	18	0			7	1	19	1		

WARWICKSHIRE

		1st Innings		2nd Innings	
1.	D.L.Amiss	Run Out	64	c Humphries b Gifford	21
2.	T.A.Lloyd	c Ormrod b Perryman	0	c Turner b Gifford	3
3.	A.I.Kallicharran	c Perryman b Patel	235	b Patel	35
+ 4.	G.W.Humpage	c Patel b Illingworth	15	c Patel b Illingworth	23
5.	K.D.Smith	c Pridgeon b Gifford	31	Not Out	62
6.	Asif Din	c Humphries b Illingworth	12	c Turner b Illingworth	39
7.	C.Lethbridge	c Neale b Illingworth	0	Not Out	2
8.	G.C.Small	c Gifford b Patel	0		
* 9.	R.G.D.Willis	c Humphries b Illingworth	7		
10.	S.P.Sutcliffe	Not Out	1		
11.	J.Cumbes	Not Out	4		
	Extras 2 b 8 lb wd 1 nb		11	1b 9 lb wd 2 nb	12
		TOTAL 380 -9 dec		TOTAL 197 - 5	

Runs at fall	1- 4	2- 168	3- 217	4- 283	5-326	6- 346	7- 347	8- 364	9- 372
of wicket	1- 34	2- 35	3- 81	4- 101	5-188	6-	7-	8-	9-

Bowling analysis:	O	M	R	W	Nb	Wd	O	M	R	W	Nb	Wd
Pridgeon	15	2	54	1	1		7	2	15	0	2	
Perryman	10	2	20	0			4	1	9	0		
Gifford	41	11	100	1			20	1	59	2		
Patel	40	8	110	2			13	3	60	1		
Illingworth	37	9	85	4			19	7	42	2		

Worcestershire **won the toss and elected to** bat. Match Result: Drawn.

share of the bowling: he faced 333 of the 678 balls. He also dominated the scoring from each of the bowlers, who between them had only eight maidens in the innings, Sutcliffe five of them, Lethbridge, Din and Alan Lloyd one each. Of the 76 runs conceded by Willis, Turner scored 50; 44 of Small's 54; 44 of Cumbes's 58; 63 of Lethbridge's 94; just 64 of the 127 taken from Sutcliffe; 21 of the 29 off Din; 15 of the 22 from Lloyd; and 10 of the 18 scored from Kallicharan's bowling. There were 23 extras in the innings.

The bat which scored the hundredth century is not destined for the Long Room: it went back to its maker, Duncan Fearnley, the man who faded out of county cricket because of the emergence of Turner as an opener — at a price, of course! Fearnley himself nearly lost the bat within a matter of days. He took it with him to New Zealand, where he set up a business with John Morrison, the Wellington captain and a test cricketer, and it disappeared somewhere along the line, eventually turning up in Customs, at Auckland Airport. Fearnley went big into the occasion of the most valuable of his 'stable'. He had manufactured 100 numbered commemorative ties; 100 commemorative bats, illustrated!; and a limited edition porcelain plate.

Following On: Nos 101, 102, 103

Being, for the record, the centuries scored — all in very quick time — by Glenn Turner after the completion of his hundredth century. They complete the full first-class century list of Glenn Turner from his first, in 1968, to his fifth and final century of his final, 1982, season in English county cricket.

101
115 for Worcestershire v Lancashire, New Road, 29 June 1982

Worcestershire 264/7 decl (G. M. Turner 115, D. N. Patel 34, Younis Ahmed 32, P. A. Neale 31; L. McFarlane 4/64, J. A. Simmons 3/71) beat **Lancashire** 175 (D. P. Hughes 39, A. Kennedy 38; Patel 7/46, R. K. Illingworth 3/17) in a match reduced by rain to one day.

First innings: c B. W. Reidy b McFarlane 115

With the strain — such as it was to which he would admit — behind him, Turner was clearly of a mood to entertain the crowds, his team-mates and (mostly) himself in his final season, and there were some bowlers waiting to suffer.

Firstly, there were those of Lancashire, who were much overdue to be at the hands of another Turner century, and the Worcester crowds had not seen one, either. They had to wait in this game, too, for rain prevented play on either of the first two days, and things were not promising on the third. When play did become possible, the Lancashire players probably preferred it was not, for Turner tore into them on the way to his fastest century. It took only 81 minutes, from 80 balls, and included 18 fours. His opening partnership of 104 with Ormrod (23) took only 54 minutes, and only Paul Todd, of Nottinghamshire, in 1982 scored a faster century — 75 minutes — than this one of Turner's. He was out half an hour before lunch, caught at cover from a mistimed drive, and the other bowlers to suffer, apart from the two responsible for his dismissal, were Colin Croft, he of the Fred Goodall shoulder-charge, Jack Simmons and Ian Folley. With Dipak Patel and Richard Illingworth spinning out Lancashire, Worcestershire enjoyed one of its rare moments of victory in 1982.

102
112 for Worcestershire v Yorkshire, Sheffield, 8 July 1982

Worcestershire 267 (G. M. Turner 112, A. Warner 43, P. A. Neale 30; P. Carrick 6/90) and 362/9 decl (Turner 70, J. D. Inchmore 58, D. N. Patel 53, E. J. O. Hemsley 49, D. J. Humphries 30; Carrick 3/107) drew with **Yorkshire** 424 (G. Boycott 159, Carrick 93, C. W. J. Athey 44, R. Illingworth 30; Patel 4/142, Warner 3/98).

First innings: c Boycott b Carrick 112
Second innings: c C. M. Old c Carrick 70

Sheffield these days meant Abbeydale Park, not the Bramall Lane test venue of old, but there was one distant throwback to the past in the shape of Raymond Illingworth. Becoming Yorkshire's cricket manager well after the finish of his playing days for Leicestershire, which in turn came well after the finish of his playing days for Yorkshire, Illingworth was resurrected in a time of desperate need. From the time of his appointment, the other principal of the recent Yorkshire 'troubles', Geoffrey Boycott, started scoring centuries again — in this game, indeed, he equalled Len Hutton's total, the record for a Yorkshireman, of 129.

Not that the county scene's other century-prolific opener was a sleeping partner, for Turner continued a remarkable recent run against Yorkshire, scoring a century off the bowling of the White Rose for the fourth successive season. One observer reckoned the pitch was typical of the ground: light brown in the midst of a lush, green surround. But Turner batted as though it mattered not if the ball was seaming, and went after virtually everything on the front foot, except when the ball was too short; hit most in the middle; and many of his 14 fours were hit over mid-wicket. He was out when he mis-hit one the other way, towards cover, but before that, he had made 44 of the 61 for the first wicket with Mark Scott, who got 13.

103
118 for Worcestershire v Kent, Hereford, 21, 22 July 1982

Kent 321/7 decl (M. R. Benson 107, D. G. Aslett 75, L. Potter 39, C. S. Cowdrey 38; D. N. Patel 3/81) and 287/6 decl (Benson 80, A. P. E. Knott 56*, Potter 44, N. M. Taylor 38; Patel 3/101) drew with **Worcestershire** 321 (G. M. Turner 118, D. J. Humphries 60*, Patel 56; G. Dilley 7/87) and 122 (Turner 66, P. A. Neale 32).

First innings: c Cowdrey b K. B. S. Jarvis 118
Second innings: c G. W. Johnson b Jarvis 66

Kent scored extremely well in this second county championship game to be played in the middle of the racetrack at Hereford, and no doubt looked forward to a wicket or two in the 45 minutes at the end of the day. Both Graham Dilley and Keith Jarvis were test bowlers, after all. But when they wandered off shaking their heads those three-quarters of an hour later, Worcestershire was 69 without loss, Mark Scott on 4. Turner was 60 by then, reaching 53 with his tenth four, from a score of 61, in only 31 minutes, fierce, dynamic driving and pulling, and just the occasional lucky shot, giving the Kent openers an unhappy evening.

But when Scott, then Phillip Neale, were out early next morning, it was a more circumspect Turner who gave the bowlers seemingly no chance, certainly not before he had reached his century, his first at Hereford, his last in the county championship. There were two hard chances, but only after Turner again sought to force the pace after his century, and at third time of asking, yet again from a fierce drive, Chris Cowdrey caught him above his head at mid-off. Appropriate, perhaps, that the son — and eventual successor as Kent captain — of another 100 centuries-maker should signal the end of Turner's 67th county championship century.

Memorabilia

While these bits and pieces do not purport to list all high-lights of records of Glenn Turner's career, they include all those of major significance.

1964: Made his debut on Christmas Day, just having completed his final year at Otago Boys' High School, going in at No. 6 for Otago and facing Canterbury's fearsome Dick Motz. He scored 10 and 13, an inauspicious start and curiously, by the end of his 1982 English season, had still not scored a century against Canterbury.

1967: Made his debut in England, for MCC against Oxford University; also made his debut for Worcestershire, v Pakistan, and took his best bowling figures, three for 18, the victims including Hanif Mohammed.

1968: County championship debut for Worcestershire, against Gloucestershire at New Road; scored his first century, 106 against Middlesex, also at New Road; and passed 1000 runs in the season, a feat he was to repeat every season until 1982.

1969: Made his first international (not test) century, for South Island against West Indies at Carisbrook, Dunedin; and made his test debut (and first test duck, in his first innings!) against West Indies.

Made his first century for New Zealand (124 v Middlesex), his first test century (against Pakistan at Dacca), and batted through the innings of a test, the youngest to do so, at 22 years 63 days.

1970: Made a 'pair', his only pair of ducks, for New Zealand against Victoria; then returned to England and made a Worcestershire record of 10 centuries in the season. Also scored 2000 runs in the season for the first time.

1972: Scored his first double-century (202 at Montego Bay), then 223* at Kingston in the next innings to become the first New Zealander to score centuries in successive innings. The latter score was the highest score for a player carrying his bat through a test innings, the record-equalling second time Turner had carried his bat in a test.

Went on to score four double-centuries in the West

266

Indies, equalling Patsy Hendren's record, twice scoring 259, once in the test at Guyana (New Zealand's highest test score) in 704 minutes, the sixth longest innings in first-class cricket, and the first in test cricket to be spread over three different days. His partnership of 387 for the first wicket with Terry Jarvis is the second highest for the first wicket in all test cricket, and New Zealand's highest for any wicket.

In the seventh match of that tour, against Trinidad, Turner batted at No. 11 for the first time in his career — he had an injured knee, and scored eight not out.

In the ninth match, against Barbados, he captained New Zealand for the first time, and won the toss.

1973: Reached 1000 runs for the English season on May 31, during New Zealand's tour match against Northamptonshire, the seventh player to do so by the end of May. The others included four other century-of-century-makers: W. G. Grace, Tom Hayward, Wally Hammond and Don Bradman (twice), plus Charlie Hallows and Bill Edrich. That season, he scored most runs (2416 — the only batsman to pass 2000 that season) at the best average (67.1), with the most centuries (nine), five of those on New Zealand's 'short' tour also constituting a record.

He also married, between the end of New Zealand's tour and returning to county cricket, the then Sukhinder Kaur Gill.

1974: Became the first New Zealander to score centuries in both innings of the same test, against Australia at Lancaster Park, Christchurch.

Later the same year, made a century in each innings for Otago against Northern Districts in the first first-class match on the Harry Barker Reserve, Gisborne.

1975: A week and a half after scoring two centuries against Northern Districts (see above), repeated the feat for Otago against Central Districts, the fourth time he had scored a century in each innings of a first-class match. Had the leading aggregate in the first Prudential Cup competition.

1976: Completed a record aggregate of 1244 runs in the 1975-76 New Zealand season.

1977: In carrying his bat for 141 of Worcestershire's innings of 169 against Glamorgan at Swansea, set a world record of 83.4% of the score.

1978: Benefit season.

1979: With his 75th century, against Lancashire at Southport, completed centuries against every county, as well as both Oxford and Cambridge Universities, MCC, four of New Zealand's five test-playing opponents, and four of the six New Zealand associations.

Had the leading average in the Prudential Cup competition.

1980: Appointed captain of Worcestershire for the next season.

1981: Progressed to 98 first-class centuries, including centuries in both innings of the matches against Warwickshire and Northamptonshire. The latter innings, at Stourbridge, meant Turner had then scored 'home' and 'away' centuries against all the counties except Kent and Lancashire and, perhaps obviously, Worcestershire. The matter of Lancashire was rectified the next season, after he had reached his hundredth century. The 'home' and 'away' series of centuries have also been scored against Cambridge University, Oxford University (with his 99th century), India, Pakistan, West Indies, Wellington, Auckland, Northern Districts and Central Districts.

1982: Glenn Turner scored his 100th century, and his first triple century, with a score of 311* against Warwickshire, the 19th player and third youngest (35 years 3 days) to do so, only Wally Hammond (32) and Dennis Compton (34) being younger.

He reached 400 catches in first-class cricket.

He passed 6000 runs in the John Player Sunday League, his total being some 1000 runs greater than that of the next player, a club-mate, Younis Ahmed. Yet he only reached one first-class milestone in English seasons. He reached 10,000 runs in the West Indies early in 1972; passed 20,000 in the 1975-76 New Zealand season; but passed 30,000 in England in 1980.

Favourite Grounds, Favourite Opponents

Of Glenn Turner's first 100 centuries, 69 were scored for Worcestershire, 35 at 'home' (33 at New Road, two at Stourbridge) and 34 'away'. After passing the century of centuries, he scored another three centuries, two at 'home' (one each at New Road and Hereford) and the other 'away' (at Sheffield).

With Turner also scoring a century at New Road for New Zealand against Worcestershire, 34 of his 100 centuries have been scored on that ground. Eight have been scored at Carisbrook, Dunedin; five at Edgbaston, Birmingham; and three each at Northampton, Swansea and Lancaster Park, Christchurch.

Glenn Turner has scored two centuries at each of Chelmsford, Stourbridge, Fenner's, Bristol, Leicester, Trent Bridge, Lord's, Bourda Oval (Guyana), the Basin Reserve (Wellington) and the Harry Barker Reserve (Gisborne).

The remainder of the 40 different grounds on which he scored his 100 centuries were Leyton, Colchester, Portsmouth, Southampton, Cheltenham, Bath, Wellingborough School Ground, Kingston, The Oval, Eastbourne, Chesterfield, Bradford, Cardiff, Hove, Guildford, Southport, The Parks, Dacca, Montego Bay, Launceston, Kanpur, Eden Park (Auckland), Molyneux Park (Alexandra) and Napier. That list of grounds was extended after Turner reached 100 centuries, with Hereford and Sheffield.

He has scored 11 centuries against Warwickshire, six at New Road, five at Edgbaston; seven against Essex; six each against Gloucestershire and Northamptonshire; five against Nottinghamshire, Glamorgan and (after his 100th) Yorkshire; four against Wellington; three each against Middlesex, Hampshire, Leicestershire, Somerset, Sussex, Surrey, Cambridge University, West Indies (two in tests), India (two in tests), Auckland, Northern Districts, Central Districts and (after his 100th century), Kent. He has scored two centuries each against Derbyshire, Oxford University, Australia and (again, after his 100th) Lancashire. His other centuries have been scored against Derrick Robins' XI, Pakistan, MCC, Tasmania, Worcestershire, Guyana and the President of the West Indies Board of Control's XI.

Glenn Turner's First-Class Career

	Matches	Inn.	N.O.	H. S.	Agg.	Ave.	50	100	Catches
1964-65 (NZ)	6	10	1	28	126	14.0	0	0	5
1965-66 (NZ)	6	11	4	95	330	47.1	3	0	0
1966-67 (NZ)	6	11	1	64	224	22.4	1	0	6
1967 (UK)	2	3	1	14	23	11.5	0	0	0
1968 (UK)	25	44	3	106*	1182	28.8	8	1	17
1968-69 (NZ)	10	16	1	167	708	47.2	3	2	9
1969 (UK)	11	19	4	66*	502	33.4	3	0	14
(NZ in UK)	12	22	3	124	644	33.9	4	1	14
(NZ in Ind & Pak)	7	13	1	110	458	41.6	4	1	11
1969-70 (NZ in Aus)	3	6	0	99	205	34.2	2	0	6
(NZ)	5	9	1	57	160	20.0	1	0	4
1970 (UK)	25	46	7	154*	2379	61.0	9	10	25
1970-71 (NZ)	8	16	1	76	517	34.5	4	0	12
(v WA)	1	1	0	8	8	8.0	0	0	0
1971 (UK)	19	31	4	179	1126	41.7	6	2	21
1971-72 (NZ)	5	10	3	101*	424	60.6	2	1	7
(NZ in WI)	12	17	2	259	1284	85.6	3	4	14
1972 (UK)	21	38	4	170	1764	51.9	6	7	13
(Rhod.)	2	3	0	91	143	47.7	1	0	1
1972-73 (NZ)	8	14	1	132	644	49.5	1	2	7
1973 (NZ in UK)	17	28	6	153*	1380	62.7	6	5	14
(UK)	9	16	2	140	1036	74.0	6	4	6
1973-74 (NZ in Aus)	6	10	1	106*	265	29.4	0	1	3
(NZ)	4	7	1	110*	449	74.8	2	2	2
1974 (UK)	20	31	9	202*	1332	60.5	5	3	13
(Rhod)	1	2	0	27	36	18.0	0	0	0
1974-75 (NZ)	8	15	1	186*	838	59.9	2	4	2
1975 (UK)	17	29	5	214*	1362	56.8	8	3	11
(Rhod)	2	4	1	74	162	54.0	1	0	3
1975-76 (NZ)	11	20	4	177*	1244	77.8	5	5	15
(SA)	3	6	0	66	157	26.2	1	0	0
1976 (UK)	20	37	2	169	1752	50.1	10	4	27
1976-77 (Pak & Ind)	7	13	0	113	423	32.5	2	1	10
(NZ)	9	16	2	177*	750	53.6	5	1	11
1977 (UK)	22	38	5	153	1380	41.8	6	3	16
1978 (UK)	22	38	7	202*	1711	55.2	4	6	20
1979 (UK)	18	31	2	150	1669	57.6	5	8	10
1979-80 (NZ)	7	13	0	136	327	25.2	1	1	10
1980 (UK)	22	35	4	228	1817	58.6	7	7	14
1981 (UK)	24	42	4	168	2101	55.3	5	9	21
1982 (UK)	9	16	3	311*	1171	90.1	3	5	7
TOTAL	452	787	101	311*	34213	49.9	145	103	401

Glenn Turner's analyses in limited-over cricket in England:

John Player Sunday League	Inn	N.O.	H.S.	Agg.	Ave.	50	100	Catches
1969	6	0	52	113	18.8	1	0	1
1970	15	0	66	411	27.4	3	0	13
1971	11	1	43	308	30.8	0	0	7
1972	15	1	121	642	45.8	3	2	2
1973	8	1	129*	358	51.1	3	1	3
1974	9	0	88	298	33.1	3	0	1
1975	14	2	97*	549	45.8	4	0	7
1976	16	1	96	667	44.5	6	0	9
1977	13	2	79*	447	40.6	4	0	2
1978	15	1	89	539	38.5	4	0	3
1979	13	1	85	628	52.2	7	0	14
1980	14	0	147	451	32.2	2	1	6
1981	16	0	69	494	30.9	3	0	5
1982	8	0	73	222	27.7	2	0	2
Total	173	10	147	6127	37.6	45	4	75
Gillette Cup 1969-80	20	2	117*	752	41.8	1	4	7
NatWest Trophy	1	0	59	59	59.0	1	0	0
Fenner Trophy 1981	1	0	20	20	20.0	0	0	0

Glenn Turner's record for Worcestershire 1967-1982:

	M	I	No	HS	Runs	Ave	50	100
Derbyshire	16	27	4	182*	1102	47.91	6	2
Essex	19	36	5	168	1736	56.00	7	7
Glamorgan	23	41	7	154	1799	52.91	8	5
Gloucestershire	23	40	4	228*	1757	48.81	6	6
Hampshire	11	21	2	155*	931	49.00	4	3
Kent	13	23	2	138	997	47.48	5	3
Lancashire	17	28	1	115	1091	40.41	6	2
Leicestershire	13	23	3	120	904	45.20	5	3
Middlesex	12	19	3	106*	717	44.81	4	2
Northamptonshire	10	17	2	161	888	59.20	2	5
Nottinghamshire	19	37	6	169	1609	51.90	10	5
Surrey	14	25	3	150	1131	51.41	6	2
Somerset	20	35	5	135*	1181	39.37	6	3
Sussex	16	27	3	150	987	41.13	5	3
Warwickshire	23	41	8	311*	2636	79.88	7	11
Yorkshire	15	24	1	168	1270	55.22	3	5
Oxford University	6	6	2	239*	568	142.00	—	2
Cambridge University	4	5	2	202*	345	115.00	—	2
Pakistanis	3	4	0	179	269	67.25	1	1
West Indians	3	6	1	49	147	29.40	—	—
Australians	1	2	1	69	88	88.00	1	—
Indians	1	2	0	23	32	16.00	—	—
Sri Lankans	1	2	0	45	58	29.00	—	—
MCC	1	2	0	55	55	27.50	1	—
TOTALS	284	493	65	311*	22,298	52.10	93	72

Index

The numbers which follow entries in the index refer to the number century scored by Glenn Turner. Some of those entries may also appear elsewhere, and they are key-noted as follows:—

Acknowledgements, A; Glenn Turner's chapter, T; Ray Cairn's chapter, C; Following On, the second hundred chapter, S. An entry such as 65-72 indicates that the subject is referred to from Centuries 65 to 72 inclusive.

Bracewell, D. W. 64
Bracewell, J. G. 82
Bradford, Century at 85
Bradman, D. G. 100
Brain, B. M. 14, 33, 38-40, 44, 45, 51, 73, 83
Breakwell, D. 12
Brearley, J. M. 4, 84
Brettell, D. N. 52
Bristol, Centuries at 8, 27
Brittenden, R. T. C
Broad, B. C. 83, 95
Brown, A. S. 8, 27, 46
Brown, D. J. 10, 15, 24-26
Budd, W. L. 71
Burgess, G. I. 11, 60, 67
Burgess, M. G. 4, 5, 19-22, 32, 35, 55, 58, 63
Burtt, J. W. 3, 50
Butcher, A. R. 36
Butcher, R. O. 84
Buxton, I. R. 13

Cairns, B. L. 49, 50
Cambridge University, Centuries against, 23, 45
Campbell, K. O. 22, 47, 49, 56
Cantlay, C. P. T. 52
Cardiff, Century at 37
Carew, M. C. 3, 20
Carisbrook, Centuries at 2, 3, 31, 49, 50, 55-57
Carrick, P. 24, 85, 92, S
Carter, R. G. 9, 13-15, 17, 23, 24
Carter, R. M. 68
Cartwright, T. W. 11
Cass, G. R. 7, 8, 38, 44, 52
Castell, A. T. 7
Cederwall, B. W. 54
Central Districts, Centuries against 49, 50, 64
Centenary test 88
Centuries, against all counties 15, 34, 61, 75, S; before lunch 40, 70, 75, 86, 93, 100, S; each innings of a match 25-26, 42-43, 47-48, 49-50, 93-94, 97-98

Chatfield, E. J. 54
Chandrasekhar, B. S. 57, 58, 63
Chappell, G. S. 42, 43
Chappell, I. M. 43, 63
Chapple, M. E. 63
Charles, Prince, and Princess Diana 93
Chelmsford, Centuries at 39, 71
Cheltenham, Century at 46
Chesterfield, Century at 13
Childs, J. 95
Christ's College, Century against 66, C
Clarkson, A. 11
Clifford, C. C. 80, 86
Close, D. B. 14, 67
Colchester, Century at 88
Coles, M. 2, 54
Collinge, R. O. 31, 32, 36, 42, 43, 56, 58, 64
Collymore, R. C. 21
Compton, D. C. S. 100
Coney, J. V. 31, 41, 42, 43
Congdon, B. E. 3, 5, 19-22, 30-35, 42, 43, 58, 63
Connolly, A. N. 4
Cook, G. 62, 68, 93
Cook, N. G. B. 78
Cook, Peter 5
Cooper, N. H. C. 73
Cope, G. A. 14
Cordle, A. E. 37, 53, 66
Cottam, R. H. M. 34
Coverdale, S. P. 45
Cowan, R. S. 99
Cowdrey, C. S. 89, S
Cowdrey, M. C. 44, S
Cowley, N. G. 65, 69
Crapp, J. F. 71
Croft, C. 83, S
Crown Sports, 85
Crump, B. 12
Cumbes, J. 24, 25, 45, 66, 76-78, 95, 97, 98, 100
Cunis, R. S. 20, 30, C
Currie, E. 56
Curtis, T. S. 86

277

280

No	Score	For	Against	Venue	Date
1	106*	WORCESTERSHIRE	MIDDLESEX	WORCESTER	18 Aug 196
2	167	OTAGO	WELLINGTON	DUNEDIN N.Z.	1968-9
3	123	SOUTH ISLAND	WEST INDIES	DUNEDIN N.Z.	1968-9
4	124	NEW ZEALAND	MIDDLESEX	LORDS	1969
5	110	NEW ZEALAND	PAKISTAN	DACCA	1969
6	122	WORCESTERSHIRE	ESSEX	WORCESTER	1970
7	137	WORCESTERSHIRE	HAMPSHIRE	SOUTHAMPTON	1970
8	154*	WORCESTERSHIRE	GLOUCESTERSHIRE	BRISTOL	1970
9	112	WORCESTERSHIRE	LEICESTERSHIRE	WORCESTER	1970
10	106	WORCESTERSHIRE	WARWICKSHIRE	EDGBASTON	1970
11	118*	WORCESTERSHIRE	SOMERSET	WORCESTER	1970
12	110*	WORCESTERSHIRE	NORTHAMPTONSHIRE	WELLINGBOROUGH	1970
13	142*	WORCESTERSHIRE	DERBYSHIRE	CHESTERFIELD	1970
14	140	WORCESTERSHIRE	YORKSHIRE	WORCESTER	1970
15	133*	WORCESTERSHIRE	WARWICKSHIRE	WORCESTER	1970
16	179	WORCESTERSHIRE	PAKISTAN	WORCESTER	1971
17	101	WORCESTERSHIRE	ESSEX	WORCESTER	1971
18	101*	OTAGO	WELLINGTON	WELLINGTON N.Z.	1971-72
19	202	NEW ZEALAND	PRES W.I. B.C. XI	MONTEGO BAY W.I.	1971-72
20	223	NEW ZEALAND	WEST INDIES	KINGSTON JAMAICA	1971-2
21	259	NEW ZEALAND	GUYANA	GEORGETOWN	1971-2
22	259	NEW ZEALAND	WEST INDIES	GEORGETOWN	1971-2
23	111	WORCESTERSHIRE	CAMBRIDGE UNIV.	CAMBRIDGE	1972
24	156	WORCESTERSHIRE	WARWICKSHIRE	WORCESTER	1972
25	122	WORCESTERSHIRE	WARWICKSHIRE	EDGBASTON	1972
26	128*	WORCESTERSHIRE	WARWICKSHIRE	EDGBASTON	1972
27	170	WORCESTERSHIRE	GLOUCESTERSHIRE	BRISTOL	1972
28	154	WORCESTERSHIRE	ESSEX	LEYTON	1972
29	107	WORCESTERSHIRE	NOTTINGHAMSHIRE	TRENT BRIDGE	1972
30	132	OTAGO	AUCKLAND	AUCKLAND N.Z.	1972-3
31	131	OTAGO	WELLINGTON	DUNEDIN	1972-3
32	151*	NEW ZEALAND	DEREK ROBBINS XI	EASTBOURNE	1973
33	143	NEW ZEALAND	WORCESTERSHIRE	WORCESTER	1973
34	153*	NEW ZEALAND	M.C.C.	LORDS	-1973
35	111	NEW ZEALAND	NORTHAMPTONSHIRE	NORTHAMPTON	1973
36	121*	NEW ZEALAND	SURREY	THE OVAL	1973
37	109*	WORCESTERSHIRE	GLAMORGAN	CARDIFF	1973
38	110	WORCESTERSHIRE	LEICESTERSHIRE	LEICESTER	1973
39	106*	WORCESTERSHIRE	ESSEX	CHELMSFORD	1973
40	140	WORCESTERSHIRE	NOTTINGHAMSHIRE	WORCESTER	1973
41	106*	NEW ZEALAND	TASMANIA	LAUNCESTON	1973-4
42	101	NEW ZEALAND	AUSTRALIA	CHRISTCHURCH N.Z.	1973-4
43	110*	NEW ZEALAND	AUSTRALIA	CHRISTCHURCH N.Z.	1973-4
44	138*	WORCESTERSHIRE	KENT	WORCESTER	1974
45	202*	WORCESTERSHIRE	CAMBRIDGE UNIV.	CAMBRIDGE	1974
46	181	WORCESTERSHIRE	GLOUCESTERSHIRE	CHELTENHAM	1974
47	135	OTAGO	NORTHERN DIST.	GISBORNE N.Z.	1974-5
48	108	OTAGO	NORTHERN DIST.	GISBORNE N.Z.	1974-5
49	105	OTAGO	CENTRAL DIST.	DUNEDIN N.Z.	1974-5
50	186*	OTAGO	CENTRAL DIST.	DUNEDIN N.Z.	1974-5